DANCES WITH SHEEP

DANCES WITH SHEEP

Memoirs of a Vet Student

Steve Weddell

Book Guild Publishing
Sussex, England

920. WEDD

First published in Great Britain in 2006 by
The Book Guild Ltd
25 High Street
Lewes, East Sussex
BN7 2LU

Typesetting in Times by
Keyboard Services, Luton, Bedfordshire

Printed in Great Britain by
CPI Bath

A catalogue record for this book is available from the
British Library

ISBN 1 85776 999 6

For Rita

Contents

Part II – The Clinical Years

Acknowledgements

I wouldn't have got within even a sniff of vet school were it not for the considerable sacrifices of my parents, therefore I need to thank them for sticking by me as well as making sure I had the time and space to put this book together. None of this would have been possible without them. So many of those I encountered at vet school need, also, to be thanked. The following people came to my aid when the hour seemed at its most bleak and, for that, I remain eternally grateful: Dr Agnes Winter, Adam Hargreaves, Dr Richard Murray, Alex Dugdale and Emily Hellewell. There are others whose presence lit up vet school and the days would have been all the poorer without them. I hope the following feel I did the days we spent together justice: Sean Wensley, James Poff, Mark Neall, Fish, Claire McCabe, Anna Wain, Ellen Eaves, Andy McIntosh, Angela Dixon, Emma Breaden, Oli Hogkinson, Jo Knox, Vicky Wilkinson, Seamus O'Shea, Louise Cox, Matt Downey, Rachel Sekules, Steve Brogden, Rona Stewart, Becky Forster and Zoe Costigan. Finally I'd like to thank Liverpool's finest Redmen, Rob and Alan (killer Kenny) O'Hare as well as Ross Millar.

Steve Weddell, May 2005

Foreword

This is not a book for the faint-hearted. A tale strongly told of a young man who, in spite of the hazards of arthritis, decides to become a vet. The secret world of the learning vet is not often revealed; here we mentally visit every aspect of it, with descriptive sentences of places we would fear to tread and others which fill the heart with hope for the creatures so much in need of compassion.

Threaded through this book are the dreads of the job of a would-be animal doctor, sometimes harrowing, sometimes uplifting, sometimes humorous. A book which should have been written a long time ago.

Carla Lane,
September 2005

1

Prologue

Vet school! I'm actually at vet school you know! Yeah, studying Veterinary Science at Liverpool! All the possible permutations for relaying this basic truth floated deliciously through my mind as I pictured myself, chiselled and purposeful, against a backdrop of swooning nurses and grateful pet owners. For a man who'd spent a large chunk of his 30 years viewing himself through other people's eyes and choosing to interpret the results negatively, I seized on this opportunity to face my demons head-on before smothering them with the vocational virtuosity of this new path. So I'm almost shamed to admit that when, on 3rd April 1998, my UCAS letter arrived bearing the glad tidings, I was content to set aside any thoughts about actual physical involvement with the course and take pleasure purely from knowing I could now tell people, 'I'm a vet student' and then feed off the anticipated admiration.

This selective celebrating had its origins in a deep-rooted fear of mine; that I'd bitten off seriously more than I could chew with this course and that vet school would soon have me choking on my own inadequacies. I think it's fair to say there hasn't been a vet student born who has not spent long hours agonising over their ability to go the distance. I also think, sadly, that this gnawing, relentless fear is a prerequisite for actual completion of the course. However, beyond this insistent background hum, a deeper growl of fear could be heard. From the age of 21 I'd been plagued with recurring bouts of arthritis. This not only affected my mobility and could at times be very painful, but had also seriously restricted the amount of pre vet school animal experience I'd been able to gain. This meant there were times when vet school, for me, seemed like nothing more than a particularly long episode of Channel 4's

1

'Faking it'. *This year an average Joe has somehow wangled his way on to the Vet Science course. Let's see just how long it takes the members of his faculty to realise he has absolutely no business being there.*

Vet school means something completely different to each and every person who's had the privilege of entering its hallowed gates. The following is my personal account; everything you read in this tale actually took place, although the names have been changed to protect the innocent. Many animals were probably harmed in the making of this story...

PART ONE

*Selected Tales from the
Pre-clinical Years*

1

Endings and Beginnings

It wasn't the fact that my mortarboard was two sizes too small for me and perched precariously on my head like a fez, and it had nothing to do with the graduand to my left who'd been inadvertently treading on the hem of my gown for the best part of two and a half hours. It was something altogether different. Michelle, similarly attired, kept glancing across at me but I pretended not to notice her.

Graduation day is, by all accounts, one of the proudest of one's life. All around me fresh-faced graduands beamed, their radiant smiles effortlessly effusing quiet satisfaction. Up in the gods a parental constellation twinkled with reflected glory. I sat, dissatisfied and hunched, in the cheap seats below. Intermittent applause marked the shuffling progress of this funereal procession and I took little solace from the fact that each hollow handclap was bringing my moment that bit closer. The whole lower floor of the Philharmonic Hall was bedecked with a velveteen crush of gowned individuals clapping like Duracell monkeys. Eventually our row stood up and wordlessly trudged stageward. Not for the first time that day I silently cursed my rashness in opting to study a subject – Zoology – beginning with a letter so far down the alphabet. Those lucky sods finishing the likes of Applied Biology, Chemistry and Dentistry would be in the bar by now, a laminated degree in one hand, a pint in the other and an odd scar-like indentation tracking horizontally across their foreheads.

Despite the imminent receipt of my own degree I was struggling to muster a grain of enthusiasm, the empty feeling in the pit of my stomach accompanying me up the steps to the stage. To either side of me each soon-to-be-graduate had turned, feverishly scanning the heavens in the hope of catching a vindicatory eye or two. I stared straight ahead, unblinking. On cue I whispered the proper pronunciation of my name and, seconds later, stepped gingerly on to the red carpet and strode forward to receive my degree and unnecessarily firm handshake. Clambering down the stairs, Pavlovian applause still rippling metronomically through the hall, my mind flitted back to the note my mother had given me that morning. 'Well done my lovely son, now for the next one!!!!'

I slipped away from the university, part of the throbbing post-ceremonial throng, and was consumed with the daunting prospect of returning in around ten weeks to start the whole process all over again, but this time for two extra years. Don't get me wrong, the prospect of starting at vet school sent frissons of excitement charging through me and was enough to keep me awake at nights. But as my fellow Zoology graduates peeled off into the sunset it was hard not to feel a pang of regret as a palpable post-exam euphoria still glinted tantalisingly in the twilight. These same pathways and buildings, which bustled with the comfort of familiar faces, would all too soon become cloaked once again in anonymity.

It had been a ponderous and at times lonely progression through the three-year course. Impersonal early lectures containing upwards of two hundred students hadn't helped. Neither had a rushed search for accommodation which led to a dank fleapit in Aigburth. It would take until Easter of first year before Saturday nights came to represent anything more than copious solo wine drinking, Match of the Day and bed. Three years on also meant I was now thirty and not quite so sure of my ability to blend into another first year and make new friends. And so as summer gave way to autumn the white-hot excitement of starting vet school was tempered somewhat by the cool of my own personal misgivings.

Graduation day drew to a close and I could already feel the insistent dawn of a new era tugging at the sleeve of my hired gown. Michelle and I walked hand in hand past the zoology lecture theatre where our love had blossomed and been sustained through the often fraught final year. Standing silently in front of the Vet Building my heart felt as if it had burst, leaking corrosive fluid into my very soul. The zoology chapter was closing like that door in the opening sequence of *Raiders of the Lost Ark*. Michelle had got a job in a vet laboratory near home. Every time I thought of us post-zoology it cut me to my core. I decided I would rather end our relationship on a high, when it was still rich, than face its steady demise, constantly being haunted by the ghosts of our former selves and how happy we used to make each other.

2

Always Keen to Meet New People

I sat towards the back of the lecture theatre and surveyed the proceedings. A deafening cacophony rose like a jet powering down the runway. It seemed bizarre to think that these people had literally only just met each other, as all around the room were little explosions of sound and the recognisable air of people getting on famously. I couldn't get over just how confident everyone seemed; from acne-ridden, thick-necked guys in rugby tops with the collar turned up, to peach-complexioned, blonde pony-tails whose very demeanour screamed equine ownership. Even the science prize geeks, for whom such a gathering must have represented something of a social first, had an air of calm confidence, perhaps relishing the prospect of showcasing their talents on such a grand stage. I saw myself, tongue-tied and friendless, as the course meandered through the years. It occurred to me that I might already have missed the boat. The friend-ship could already have sailed. Everyone was fast making all the friends they were ever going to need and here I was, cut adrift, condemned to do the course all on my lonesome.

Every course has its dangerous loner. The student who always sits at the front of the class and laughs a little too eagerly at all the lecturers' half-assed attempts at humour. I'd always been mortally afraid of becoming that guy. There was no denying that I treasured my independence but not to the point of being a social outcast. During the lull in proceedings as we waited for the lecture theatre doors to swing open, I struck up a conversation with a lean, blond-haired guy called Sam. Although our commonality, at this point, hinged on a shared recollection of Formby Point Nature Reserve – his house backed on to it, I'd been there on a zoology field trip – it was a link I was grateful to seize upon. To have sat any longer unengaged in conversation as the room babbled all around me would've been grist to the gremlins in my head. As conversation with Sam progressed, encompassing shared interests in zoology, conservation, Liverpool FC and the fact that one of the girls in our year was the absolute spitting image of Cameron Diaz, the tight feeling in my chest lifted. The prospect of coping socially at vet school suddenly appeared far less of an ordeal.

As we'd been talking, a questionnaire had been fluttering its way back and across the rows, the premise being that 'they' wished to gauge the range of our knowledge. Starting as I meant to go on, I leant over, sneakily peeking at the answers of the person sitting next to me, whose name was Greg. While we were wrestling with this veterinary conundrum a short video on Teat Surgery in Cattle was shown. A collective hush fell over the audience as the desire to convey superiority gripped the masses. To this day I still give silent thanks that I chose not to copy some of Greg's more contentious answers. *Question 5: If you were doing a calving with a farmer and he suggested that the both of you strip down to your underwear as it was unbearably hot, would you (a) refuse, possibly creating a bad atmosphere, or (b) comply?* Answer: If he had big tits I'd comply.

Unbeknown to us the whole exercise was a ruse by the fourth year to discover which members of this new intake had a little bit too much to say for themselves. These findings would be filed away for later use.

Freshers' week kicked off on the Sunday evening in Dovedales on Penny Lane, stretching to the following Friday and initiation. This night was specifically designed to allow us to get to know our fourth-year tutors. I turned up at 8 o'clock on the dot with a deep sense of trepidation. I felt my heart sink as I was met by a wall of people – the pub was positively bursting at the seams. I managed to ascertain, after pressing my way through the swell of bodies, that my own tutor wouldn't be making the trip.

'She's been detained by … ahem … activity of the horizontal type' I was informed, with a hearty wink and an elbow in the ribs, by one of her mates.

'Lucky her…' I forced a tepid smile before fighting my way to the bar. I was struggling to feel any semblance of belonging in this thronging, boorish mass and felt badly in need of a drink to ease the pain of this social ordeal. I'd split up with Michelle in the early hours of the previous morning and all the frivolity and high spirits made the heaviness in my heart seem all the more acute, social contact smarting like salt on an open wound. I'd only forced myself out through a sense of duty to my tutor, but as she hadn't even had the decency to kick off her duvet I felt there was no point in me being there. The fact that her absence was due to a romantic interlude added injury to insult.

Unable to shake the image of Michelle from my mind, I turned and headed for the cool, welcoming rush of evening air. The vacuum within me would be filled in good time, but at that precise moment I felt utterly spiritless. The need to get to know my new year was compelling, but I didn't have the stomach for it. I left the glow of the pub and stepped out into the October chill, immediately feeling refreshed by the prospect of returning to my flat and quietly laying my time with Michelle to rest.

By the time Friday arrived, those members of the year who had decided they would attend initiation had been whipped into a frenzy by a week of wind-ups and dark tales. A small percentage of the year had opted to give the ceremony a body swerve, concluding that the threat of being doused with flour and eggs at any given moment was an idle one and that, as they hadn't attended any of the week's festivities, it was highly unlikely any of the fourth year had the remotest idea who they were anyway. For my part I genuinely wanted to experience initiation. The way I saw it, vet school was going to be a series of 'moments' and during the following five years I wanted first-hand experience of as many of these as possible. I didn't want to be happily immersed in the witty banter of sophisticated adults at a future party and when asked, 'So, what happened to *you* the night of initiation?' to have to say, 'Well, I watched a *Question of Sport*, *TOTP* and *Friends* – it was a really good one, though, the one where Joey puts all of Chandler's clothes on...'

The only problem was that I'd been suffering intermittent flare-ups of psoriasis since the age of eighteen and my back was covered with scaly patches. I'd heard a rumour that I'd been earmarked to spend much of the ceremony stripped to my boxers, relinquishing

10

clothes and dignity in equal amounts. The idea of this disturbed me, greatly. In the days leading up to Friday I could feel my patience being pushed to its limits. I spent ridiculous amounts of time attempting to track down the organisers to persuade them to spare me the humiliation of exposing my psoriatic back. As Friday loomed I could feel the bile rising to the back of my throat. Was this the reason I came to vet school? Was this what my parents were paying £13,000 a year for? Was this why I did a degree in zoology? In order to spend three non-productive days searching for someone I'd never met, begging them not to make me take my T-shirt off in front of upwards of a hundred total strangers? I desperately wanted to attend and be a part of the festivities, but not to be made to feel ashamed of my appearance. Having eventually been assured I'd get to keep my T-shirt on, I felt free to join the rest of my year in the pub as we prepared for the onslaught the best way we knew how.

At 6 pm we made our way into the common room in the Vet Faculty. On arrival we were met by this big American guy in a black suit and tie. I think he was trying to be Michael Madsen in *Reservoir Dogs*.

'Should've worn your ear muffs, eh?' I smirked, nudging the nonplussed guy standing next to me. 'You know ... in case Mr Blond here's brought his cut-throat razor.' I shrugged as he stared at me with a glazed expression, before he turned and vomited all over the floor.

The suggestion was that the whole year got into alphabetical order with Mr Blond screaming at us all the while and randomly singling people out for concerted abuse. Being a 'W' meant this task wasn't overly taxing and once in position, with Sam in front of me and Karen behind me, I made a deliberate point of avoiding eye contact with this burly, suited psychopath. Without warning the door to the common room was suddenly booted open by one of the initiating fourth years. She stood provocatively in the doorway, sporting a PVC cat-suit, not dissimilar to the one worn by Michelle Pfeiffer in *Batman Returns*, and cackled demonically, all the while cracking a bona fide whip for all she was worth.

'Right,' she intoned breathily, 'the following people have been very, very bad and need to come with me right now!'

On the 'right now' part she cracked her whip, smashing one of the room's light fittings. Showing admirable cool she remained in

11

character and read out a list of six names, the last of which happened to be mine. She then turned and wordlessly marched us down the corridor and into one of the changing rooms. Once inside, Catwoman slammed the door shut behind us and ordered that we strip to our boxers, before yelling 'You! Keep your T-shirt on!' in my direction. She then ordered that we all lie in a row and do press-ups. As we toiled and sweated on the tiled floor she stood over each of us in turn and demanded we kissed and licked her feet. If we failed to perform this act to her complete satisfaction, she whipped us.

After being 'softened up' for a while downstairs we were ushered back up towards the main lecture theatre where the whole pantomime was on the verge of starting. The walk took us past the common room where a disembodied yelp offered a brief insight into the carnage taking place inside. I shivered and quickened my gait. Despite the fact I was quaking with anxiety about what they were going to do to me, I was still relieved to be free from the sadistic clutches of Mr Blond. Outside the lecture theatre I slowly became aware that people inside were thumping on the desk tops. Catwoman poked her whiskery nose through the door and that seemed to be the trigger for the noise to rise in an ear-splitting crescendo. Before I could act upon instincts honed over a million years of evolution, I was grabbed roughly from behind and my arms were pinned to my sides. Another pair of hands crudely applied a blindfold. I spluttered in indignation, 'Watch my contac...' but was halted in my protestations by a well-aimed spoonful of a putrid concoction. Gagging on what was, if later years were anything to go by, almost certainly a mixture of dog food, baked beans, tuna and slurry, I dropped to my knees and crawled through a polythene tunnel and into the lecture theatre.

The desk thumping had reached feverish proportions by the time I emerged from the tunnel. Still blinded, I knelt quivering on more polythene as gelatinous goo was tipped over my head, matting my hair and making my T-shirt cling like a second skin. The stench was almost unbearable and I quickly ran my hand over my mouth, gagging and spluttering. The baying mass were now bellowing the mantra, 'We want freshers' inordinately loudly and had to hushed by the compere who, I later discovered, was dressed as The Devil, right down to the red body paint, horns and pointy tail.

'Kneel, you disgusting animals' was his opening salvo, which he followed up with 'We're going to make you play *guess the vegetable.*' That doesn't sound too bad, I thought to myself. I nudged the guy next to me. 'I say, that doesn't sound too bad does it?' I did this mainly to check we were still all together as a unit and I hadn't been singled out to face this baying mob alone. The same thought must have occurred to Neil, as all he could muster was a barely audible 'Don't leave me...'

Beelzebub reiterated his request for quiet before poking me in the ribs with a sharpened implement, possibly some kind of trident. 'You're going first you worm! Come on number one; tell us your name and where you're from.'

'Hi Cilla, my name's Steve and I'm from Edinburgh,' I grinned, momentarily forgetting where I was. Suddenly I became aware of someone hovering over me. I heard a female voice command, 'Get your gums round this, Jock' seconds before a pointed object smeared with whipped cream and more lovely dog food was rammed between my gritted teeth. I bit down hard, doing my best to ignore the sickly sensation of dog food smearing between my teeth, and spluttered the word 'carrot' to deafening jeers from the packed arena. The four victims to my left were subjected to much the same torture and before long we were being ushered into seats set aside in the first few rows. Our part in the ceremony had come to an end; all that remained was to sit, quietly dripping, and watch the spectacle as it unfolded before our eyes, the taste of dog food never very far from our lips.

As initiation wore on, the punishments meted out became more and more stringent. Students were emerging bleary-eyed from the tunnel in varying states of undress. One guy, Danny, was wearing a tutu and had been sellotaped to a girl he'd enjoyed a brief liaison with at some point during the week. Greg, the Questionnaire King, now sported a completely shaved head and appeared to be wearing nothing other than a couple of Tesco's bags strategically taped to reveal his shame. Another group were handcuffed and forced to guddle for raw eggs in a tray of cow entrails. And then they had to eat the eggs. By the end I felt a minuscule tinge of regret that my treatment had been so tame in comparison. That feeling vanished, though, as soon as I caught sight of Vincent, his hands taped behind his back, as he slipped on the now treacherous polythene, smacking his head sonorously on the podium. I was immediately immensely grateful for the low profile I'd kept, even though it had been as much by accident as design. There was absolutely no doubt in my mind that this goo-soaked, manure-infested extravaganza served its purpose. Being stripped of clothes, abused, doused in foul-smelling swill and forced to eat dog food was a killer ice-breaker, and the adversity pulled us together.

The week had begun with me seriously doubting my ability to fit in, deeply concerned that I wouldn't make any friends. It was drawing to a close now and I felt like a valued, if still somewhat quiet, member of a massive extended family. I stood at the bus stop, distractedly tugging at my brittle hair, caked as it was in solidified animal waste. Vincent, minus his smashed glasses, dug me in the ribs. 'Ten o'clock, Baa Bar's?'

'All right, cheers mate, very possibly…' I responded, but without very much conviction. The day's exertions had left me physically and emotionally drained and I doubted if there was anything left in the tank for socialising. That morning I had been so nervous about what the day would hold that I'd barely eaten. Now all I wanted to do was clog the shower with the remnants of initiation and fill my complaining stomach with food, content in the knowledge that I'd taken my first faltering steps in a bigger world.

3

Academia, Nuts

Nothing in life quite prepares you for your first lecture at vet school. There's a wonderful sense of having made it, of finally getting the chance to put a well-heeled shoe to the slip road of the vet highway. Then the lecturer opens his mouth. You could have cut the sense of anticlimax with a hoofing knife, as Mr Williams talked for 50 minutes on the subject of fences and hedges. The enthusiasm visibly drained all around me, minute after inexorable minute. As I sat, third row centre, hurriedly scribbling down notes on everything from the merits of privet hedges to the optimum number of bars on a gate (four, but five is still OK), it was an effort to keep my mind fixed on the bigger picture.

Animal husbandry progressed, swiftly moving through the gears. The disappointment of such an uninspiring start became displaced by stoical tolerance as monotonous lectures stacked up nose to tail, all day every day. Topics came and topics went. The kidney. Tick. The fore limb of the dog and the hind limb of the dog. Tick. And tick. Irrespective of the subject matter, a routine was established. A flustered individual would enter brandishing a sheaf of papers. Beginning with the inevitable 'We've a lot to get through today, so...' he or she would pause for a few seconds as the room emitted a collective sigh, before launching headlong into an unremitting fifty-minute monologue, pausing only to draw breath or discourage questions. We would sit, crammed together like one hundred and nine cloned embryos in a test tube, genetically programmed to transcribe each and every syllable regardless of its relevance to anything whatsoever. A blur of scrawl on ten to twelve sides of lined A4, followed by the obligatory ten-minute wait for feeling to return to my right hand, punctuated by the yells of people all around me, flapping their notes and imploring desperately, 'Did you get that bit about…?' This was how the early information needed to make us vets was pumped into us. At times lecture theatre B seemed more like a pig-fattening unit, a place in which we were force-fed facts, propelling us bloated to the next level.

Practical dissection classes offered a brief respite. In groups of six to eight we'd be invited into the freezer to choose a brick-hard dog to drag out and spend a succession of Wednesday and Friday mornings dismantling. This was aided loosely by a dissection guide, and I often felt like a hapless motorist lost by the roadside, scratching my head and peering without comprehension at an AA roadmap. Lost somewhere in the midst of the canine ante brachium, searching in vein for the radial nerve, invariably our requests for directions would result in Teddy coming to our aid.

Teddy was not a vet, and it often seemed as if all that separated him from us was that his notes were laminated and slightly more detailed than ours. His lot in life consisted of switching the fans on and off during dissection class and being treated with utter contempt by the first year during his series of bumbling lectures. In much the same way as the bitch confers immunity to her young during those vital first few hours of life, so first years emerge blinking into the daylight of the course with an inherent lack of respect for Teddy. The man didn't stand a chance.

One particular lecture on birth defects saw Teddy linger, for what was deemed an inappropriate length of time, on the teratogenic and carcinogenic effects of smoking on neonates. After ten minutes of restless and widespread whispering, querying the relevance of a specifically *human* condition to prospective vets, a hand was tentatively raised: 'Sorry, can I just ask, is this important in those cases where farmers smoke too much around pregnant heifers and they breathe in?'

On another occasion, during dissection class, a group of students filled part of a latex glove with water and placed it surreptitiously within the layers of tissue of their dog's hind limb. They then summoned Teddy over. He gawped in turn at this mysterious structure and at his laminated notes, his eyes magnified ridiculously beneath his thick glasses. Many minutes passed during which Teddy wondered aloud what this seemingly uncharted anomaly could possibly be. After contradicting himself repeatedly, he eventually surmised that it was in all probability some sort of tissue cyst.

16

Chris, whose idea the prank had been, then blurted out, 'Don't be silly Teddy, look, it's just a piece of glove!' And popped it with his scalpel.

The pace being set remained unforgiving and we barely drew breath as Christmas approached. A timetable already groaning under the weight of lectures and practicals was further stretched with animal handling classes out at Leahurst. The logic behind these sessions was extremely sound: individuals who lacked genuine hands-on experience had the opportunity to attain a level of expertise more in keeping with the assorted farm hands, stable girls and Saturday morning local vet practice tea boys who made up so much of our course. As someone whose profile fitted none of the above and who'd spent most of his teenage Saturdays following Heart of Midlothian FC, I found these sessions most welcome and couldn't start soon enough.

The thought of excursions to the large animal hospital at Leahurst was one that excited me greatly. Once we'd been loaded up with three years' worth of lectures, we'd relocate there and be given the opportunity to put all that learning into practice. The clinical years four and five lay far enough beyond the horizon for me still to feel excited at their prospect without any sense of trepidation. The thing was, I'd never actually been to Leahurst. A trip had been made available on the day of my interview but I was entering the final straits of my zoology degree and had a date that afternoon with an electron microscope and a south Atlantic fish tapeworm. It was therefore with mounting excitement that I sat on the coach heading over the water for our first class. I could feel the hairs rising on the back of my neck and my heart was palpitating like a snare drum as we juddered over the cattle grid and up the drive to the main entrance.

My first class was the self-explanatory 'Horse I' and consisted of tuition on how to place a head collar on a horse properly, how to tether it deploying a slip knot and finally how to perform a brief clinical examination. Just how banal and pointless this was to some members of the group was scrawled, unflatteringly, all over their faces. For me, were I to compile a table of my equine experiences, this session would probably be entering the charts at number one. Observe: June 1975; fed horse polo mint. September

1977; dragged kicking and screaming from back of pony 10 seconds into a subsequently aborted afternoon's pony trekking. Now, after an ungainly start in which no matter how I orientated my head collar, I just couldn't get my head around it and it around my pony's head, things slowly came together. It helped that the Leahurst staff had hand-picked the most amenable, benign ponies imaginable.

With the session at an end I made my way back to the common room, chatting with Sam. I was feeling a mixture of emotions, mostly relief at having completed my first practical at vet school without mishap. This made me much more hopeful than I had been of late, when I considered how I might fare when it was my turn for clinical rotations. At my core, though, I also felt a slight, nervous twinge; it would be unrealistic to expect *stallions and pregnant mares* to stand so politely while I struggled to disentangle and buckle a head collar.

The Friday afternoon jaunts to Leahurst soon became an accepted part of our curriculum and I began to relish these outings into the countryside to escape the sterile lecture theatre. They seemed to remind us that we were training to be vets; it was very easy to lose sight of this fact as the hours in the lecture theatre built up. The chance to fill my city-infested lungs with country air and get some good old-fashioned dirt under my fingernails was truly invigorating. There were sessions teaching us how to drench a cow, and an afternoon in which we fed chocolate cake to pigs, chased them around for a while with boards and then weighed them. There were further equine handling classes where we learnt all about tail bandaging, hoof cleaning and lameness examinations.

Our classes stretched right up until the last Friday of term before Christmas. On this occasion the last remaining session was 'Sheep handling'. The main thrust of the exercise consisted of an informal clinical examination of a breeding ram. A major part of this exam related to an assessment of the ram's breeding capabilities. Vincent, with experience of animal handling during his access course at Lincoln, planted his legs either side of one particularly grizzled and battle-scarred ram, placed both arms under its shoulders and hoisted the big old boy back on to his haunches. The rest of us then formed an orderly queue and, under the supervision of Dr Helen Sutton, were shown how to carry out our assessment. First of all we gently compressed the ram's testicles; searching, ideally, for a level of consistency akin to that of ripe plums. We were then

18

instructed how to manipulate and expose the ram's penis, making it available for semen collection. There must have been thirty people in the queue and when the thirtieth and last person, Carol-Anne, knelt before the ram, squeezed his testicles and gingerly sought to release the penis from the prepuce, he pulled a face and promptly ejaculated copiously all over her.

4

Dances with Sheep

'D'you think that might be him there?'

'Hmm, possibly ... he's certainly a farmer of some sort. Whether he's ours, though...' I tailed off, warily eyeing one of the many rotund gentlemen in tweed jackets who were bobbing across the forecourt of Exeter St David's station.

'Hello, Mr Bentley?' ventured Sam in his best Formby English. 'Sorry lad, no!'

'Poor guy,' I thought, 'he sounded really disappointed.'

As he melted off into the crowd my quiet musings that railway stations can conjure both sheer bliss and gut-wrenching sadness, were interrupted by a large, weather-beaten hand being extended in my direction.

'Sam Winters, is it?'

It was a pattern I would come to recognise on a daily, or even hourly, basis during the forthcoming three-week spell we were to spend at his disposal. Give David Bentley a strangulated yelp of distress from the darkest recess of the lambing shed and our hero would effortlessly divulge the life history of the ewe's nearest and dearest, right up to which corner of the field her grandparents first achieved intromission. 'Yes, I adopted her on ... part of a super little double. Her mother is SG17? Remember? That pedigree Texel I was telling you about? The one that's outperformed the index for three years running now...'

But give him two polite, well spoken vet students whose first names both happened to begin with the same letter, and cue a misunderstanding every time.

* * *

20

Gritting my teeth and fighting the revulsion in my stomach, I forced a football-socked foot into a bitingly cold wellington boot and began the gravel-crunching hike up the hill to the lambing shed. My body protested feebly at the indignity of being roused at such an ungodly hour, but my sights were fixed on the dimly lit shed which sat swathed in early morning mist at the brow of the hill. My breath hung languidly in the freezing air, as all around me the cawing of crows reverberated across the valley. I peered tentatively into the shed, allowing several seconds for my senses to become accustomed to what was greeting me. A cavernous, hangar-like structure, packed as far as the eye could see with what seemed like a million sheep, huddled like boulders in the deep straw. One of the boulders swivelled, rustling in the straw, and greeted me.

'Hello!'

'Ah. Mr Winter, fancy meeting you here. Had a good night?'

'Not as bad as I'd been expecting, except I had to get Bentley up once.'

'Shit! Was he all right about it?'

'Yeah, he seemed to be. I mean, he acknowledged it was a really tight one and didn't, like, deliver it in seconds or anything.'

'Cool!' I said, relieved for my friend.

The whole point of the exercise seemed, at this point, to hinge on not incurring the wrath of Mr Bentley. If, in his eyes, we were deemed capable of lasting the pace, then this surely would be praise indeed. Except the praise never actually came. Only greater expectation, and greater disappointment when this was not met. It seemed to be a slight on him and his perceived ability to impart knowledge if the correct knot wasn't deployed at the right time, or the clammy presence of a lamb afflicted with watery mouth went unnoticed until too late. But Mr Bentley's wounded pride and battered ego healed all too quickly and was replaced by a harshness and belittling that would crackle and resonate with the despair of battles lost elsewhere. It was almost as if he hated himself for believing in us. He positively bristled with impotent rage as I stumbled over my feet in a desperate attempt to meet with his approval. 'All you can ever do is your best, son,' I told myself, wearing the words like an invisible cloak. The very notion provoked a scathing response from a scornful Bentley.

'People say that they *just do their best* and that's it? No, as far as I'm concerned that's just a cop-out!' I braced myself for the *coup de grâce.* 'You don't *just do your best,* you *just do it,* end of story.'

'So, Dave, how d'you see me coping with nights, then?' I asked Mr Bentley.

The prospect of being at the front line, throughout the night, alone with a shedful of ewes positively bursting to lamb seemed to terrify and exhilarate me in equal doses. It didn't matter how much petroleum jelly I smeared over my swollen hands, it was often impossible to squeeze them into the ewe's pelvic cavity. This applied especially to Bentley's prized pedigree Texels which had only recently begun lambing in earnest. Assisting their delivery had been testing to say the least, and more than once I had floundered, helplessly casting glances over my shoulder in the hope of communicating my predicament to someone, anyone. In delivering a candid 'It looks like I'm going to have to be woken up an awful lot,' Bentley had succeeded in stoking the fires of my anguish.

'Got enough layers on there, boy?'

'Not really sure ... six? Should be enough.'

'Six *including* long johns?'

'Oh yes!'

It was Sam's last night in the shed and he was having great difficulty concealing his glee. The relief transformed him. Suddenly a huge weight was on the verge of being lifted from his shoulders and would, all too soon, pass to me. The evening had passed in identical fashion to the previous eight. The nightly ritual of a barely satisfying 'supper', which never failed to disappoint, could not end quickly enough for me. My alarm clock was set for 5.25 am and all the post-supper pleasantries served to do was to eat remorselessly into the already meagre time I had to rest my aching body. But sleep provided little respite. Muffled murmurings from the shed would waft insidiously back down the hill to the cottage, permeating my subconscious and creating a haunted delirium in which borders of house and lambing shed became blurred and indistinct. In the semi-darkness, polythene bags were lambs, lost and in need of urgent attention, and the extension cord was a head rope strewn in the straw.

So my turn in the lambing shed came. Now Sam was tucked up in bed and I was alone in the shed. I busied myself with the myriad of small, time-consuming tasks that constituted a night shift: making up adequate quantities of powdered milk for bottle and stomach feeding any orphaned lambs, bringing in several bales of straw for future bedding and collecting all the shed's water buckets and scrubbing them clean, all of the while forcing myself to forget time, deliberately averting my glance from the digital display on the dusty clock radio. Nightfall seemed to distort the thread of time; elongating it wildly as if morning lay at the end of a bungee cord. I hoped that by avoiding the clock I'd be in for a pleasant surprise when I eventually checked and saw how many hours had elapsed. The eerie darkness smothered the shed like a blanket on a cage, swallowing sound with its stifling stillness. I was to turn 31 at midnight and would go on to spend much of my birthday as well as the two following days confined to barracks, stricken with cryptosporidial gastroenteritis.

Scrubbing the congealed mixture of blood, afterbirth and petroleum jelly from my hands and forearms, fresh from having delivered unexpectedly bright triplets from a rangy Jacobs's ewe, I eventually caught a glimpse of the time. It was 3.30 am, which was most encouraging, as it meant only two and a half hours to go. The only other pressing item was to ensure that a big Texel single I'd spent 40 minutes wrestling from her exhausted and protesting mother, had fed. I swung my legs over the wooden gate and into the pen. I was keen to tick this off in my notebook so I could pop back down to the house for a re-energising cup of tea and toast. Supper, as ever by this stage of the night, seemed like light years ago. Moreover I would need to be galvanised for the advent of dawn, which acted as a parturition trigger, characterised more often than not by widespread passing of water bags.

The ewe had ample milk in her udder, I noted, steam rising from the small amount of colostrum I expressed onto my hand. I cupped my other hand around her lamb's abdomen, cursing quietly to myself when I realised how empty her gut felt. The ewe backed away to the other side of the tiny pen, allowing me a better view of the starving lamb. She had a hollow, gaunt appearance and hungrily licked the colostrum from my proffered hand, butting me gently with her head. Kneeling painfully I held the achingly thin lamb beneath the dam's hindquarters and carefully placed a teat in her mouth, milking it in order to encourage sucking. Every time the visibly weakened lamb was on the verge of coordinating her

23

sucking with the presence of the teat in her mouth, the ewe would simply move off, leaving the lamb gasping on thin air. At the eighth or ninth attempt the pain in my knees was increasing as my chances of a warm drink before the dawn rush dwindled. On the tenth failed attempt something inside me snapped.

'Right, you,' I whispered, grabbing hold of the skittish ewe by the scruff of her neck, 'something obviously took the time to feed *you*; otherwise you and I wouldn't be having this conversation, comprendez?' Still with a tight grip of her thick wool, I pinned her to the corner of the pen, physically restraining her with my body weight. I closed my eyes, panting with exertion and listening to the sweet music of the lamb hungrily guzzling. Content in the knowledge the lamb had enjoyed a decent feed I released my grip on the ewe, playfully rubbing her head, overjoyed that the next time junior needed feeding I'd be tucked up in bed and it'd be Sam's problem.

'I find it ever so ironic, you know...'

'Oh right.' I braced myself for the latest instalment of Bentley's unique brand of painful honesty and unabashed self-adoration.

'My father spent his whole life attempting to get to where I am today. At thirty eight. *Thirty eight!* Everything he's ever tried in his life and failed miserably at, I've made a success of ... I think he finds that very hard to come to terms with. But I'm not sure what I'm supposed to do about it. I really can't help it if I keep succeeding where he's failed can I? But I won't lie to you Steven, I really do find it awfully hard.'

Our self-effacing hero furrowed his brow in silent contemplation of the double-edged sword that was his life. In the awkward moments that followed I briefly thought about indulging him further. I found Bentley's penchant for painful analysis and self-praise tiresome to say the least, but my impending departure for a night in the shed loomed large on the horizon. I saw in a reflective Bentley a possible stay of execution.

'Genuinely tough break, Dave,' I countered, stroking my chin, 'but d'you not think if the old boy couldn't do it himself he'd see it as the next best thing that his son had?'

Sadly, this ploy failed, serving instead to shatter his reverie. Lazarus-like he leant forward, wordlessly scooping up the last remnants of steak pie, which had been lying untouched in the middle of the scrubbed wooden table. Sam and I had spent most of Bentley's soliloquy shifting our gaze from the pie to each other and back, hoping it might play a small but key role in our quest to eat a satisfying meal. I looked across at Sam as he stared in disbelief at the spot where the pie had been, then at Bentley as he licked the last of the puff pastry from his lips and belched contentedly.

'Now, boys, have you both had enough supper?' Lorraine, patient and sincere as ever, seemed oblivious to her husband's utter lack of social grace, choosing instead to focus on his less tangible qualities.

'Oh yes!' Sam and I chimed, as one.

'Couldn't eat another thing' I added for effect, patting my stomach and grinning inanely.

'That's good,' Bentley said, his mouth still full of the pie, 'because I'm really tired tonight and, if you're comfortable with it, I'm going to ask you to go on up yourself tonight. Hmm, in fact you'd best make a move now; that Suffolk with the torn ear and that partial vaginal prolapse we repaired ten days ago? Remember that old girl? Yes. Well, she'll no doubt be ready to lamb now.'

In all of the previous nights Bentley had religiously accompanied the night person up to the shed to help ensure things at least began on a relatively even keel. Leaving the shed unattended for supper's hour or so would often lead to chaotic scenes on returning. It was imperative that any newly born lambs were penned with the correct ewe and received a gutful of colostrum, through natural means or otherwise. Problems began when there were large quantities of newly born lambs aimlessly wandering around the shed, with the constant danger of mismothering. Pandemonium could ensue as this fundamental process was carried out against a backdrop of general duties; delivering new lambs and ensuring bedding, food and water were constantly being replenished.

I trudged alone up the hill almost incandescent with rage.

'So I'm not *that* fucking incapable then, am I!' I ranted, hoofing a water bucket halfway across the shed. As I bent to retrieve the now empty bucket, a wave of reassurance engulfed me, until I felt my heart was going to explode. The night passed in a haze and, before I knew where I was, dawn had broken, sprinkling shafts of watery sunlight through the slats of the shed. Sam was standing bleary-eyed in the doorway and the log-book told of 14 lambed pedigree Texels.

Free from the good and bad of Bentley, my confidence grew nightly. I became aware of subtle hand manipulations that reaped dividends. Every single ewe that presented herself to me I found I could lamb, with the exception of the Suffolk whose head I cradled in my lap as she underwent a caesar. The solitude focused my mind, giving me a resolve I'd never felt before. This was *me*. Up to my elbows in a ewe struggling in labour, I'd implore her to help me. Grasping life in my hands. In the nine nights I spent alone in the shed, Bentley remained undisturbed in bed. By the end of the three weeks, *lambing* had become normality and it was the outside world that now seemed unpredictable and unsettling.

Standing shivering on the windswept platform, we willed the train to come. Lambing had become our lives, but now we wanted our old lives back. Previously I had imagined our departure from Exeter Station as akin to being winched to safety from the upturned hull of a shipwreck, but when the moment arrived, I found this was not the case. Instead I felt grateful for the privilege of walking this path. The experience changed me, and part of me remained forever in the lambing shed. Bentley never did say thanks. It didn't matter.

5

School's out for Summer

It's hard for me to describe how I passed first year at vet school
without using the word 'skin' closely followed by the word 'teeth'.
Hurdling those end of year exams was how I imagine jockeys in
the National feel when they stretch every sinew to scrape over the
top of Becher's Brook. Only after I'd hit the ground on the other
side did I realise how many had fallen.

For my part I was sitting bang on 50% for Vet Biology which
meant I'd be required to sit an oral exam, a so-called pass/fail
viva to determine whether or not I'd get the green light to progress
into the second year. The tradition in such cases was for a couple
of members of staff to sit with you for 20 minutes, often choosing
to discuss the questions you *didn't* answer. The two I wouldn't
have touched with a ten-foot cattle prod were on the contractility
of the heart and the anatomy of the dog pelvis. Our anatomy
lecturer, Dr Parsons, had left the university at Christmas so, foolishly
some may say, I gambled, putting all my ECGs in one basket, and
only revised the cardiac question in any great detail.

I turned up 20 minutes early for my oral but, instead of waiting
in the common room, tapping into the aura of blind panic, I stood
alone in reception next to the skeleton of the cow, and fiddled
nervously with my tie.

'All right, Steve, when are you up, then?' I looked up and saw
Danny standing in front of me.

'Twelve forty.'

'Don't worry, you'll be grand.'

'Are you done?'

'Yep, just out, lad.'

'How'd you go?'

'Yeah, probably did enough.'

'Great stuff mate, well done.' I reached out and patted him gamely on the arm, adding, before I could stop myself, 'So, what did they ask you then?'

'Started off with question 6, why I never answered *that* one … moved on from there…'

Question 6, question 6 … I could feel my heart sink. 'What? The *pelvis* question?'

'Yeah, thankfully I'd had a look at it.'

The colour drained from my features and I slumped against the wall, self-belief ebbing like blood from an open wound. I stuttered, barely able to get the words out, 'I … I … never looked at that, mate … I'm totally fucked.' I turned away, not wanting him to see me cry.

'Na, don't be silly, piece of piss, mate, listen…'

For the next 20 minutes, Danny sat with me on the floor in reception and, using the cow skeleton as a prop, delivered a revision lecture on the anatomy of the pelvis in the dog; which muscles attached where, general bone architecture and the course of the femoral nerve. All around us was a bustling hive of activity, students and lecturers going about their business, occasionally tripping over us. But Danny ploughed on, oblivious to the scrum and patiently imparted the knowledge I'd need to answer the question. By the time he'd finished I felt familiar enough with the topic for the sick feeling in the pit of my stomach to be quelled.

'Good luck, lad, you'll be grand.'

I shook Danny's hand, struggling to find the words to thank him.

'One I owe you.'

'You'll be doing the same for me, lad.'

He turned away just as I heard my name being called. I strolled down the corridor, determined not to show any fear and to present an air of calm confidence. Coming towards me was Karen, whose name lay before me in the alphabet and who'd just had a pass/fail viva of her own. She was quietly sobbing. Catching sight of me, she tried in vain to put on a brave face, only more tears came and her face dissolved. 'They're bastards, Steve…' was all she could muster. I turned, watching her stumble past me and out of the door, before straightening my tie and continuing my passage down the corridor. At the end I entered the door being held open for me and took my seat at a cheap Formica table facing two members of staff.

'Hello Steve, how are we today?'

'Ask me in 20 minutes.'

'Ha ha. We're not ogres you know. Anyway, I see from your exam paper that you didn't fancy the question on heart contractility.'

A couple of days later I stood impatiently in the same corridor, next to the same cow skeleton, awaiting the pass list. Had I known the future heartache the putting up of these lists would bring I might have been more reticent and hung back, allowing the crowds to clear. As it was I needn't have worried.

It was no longer bad luck to acknowledge that summer was here, stretching gloriously through to mid September. My girlfriend Isla and I had booked four nights in Paris in August and, at long last, I finally felt free to look forward to it, the worry of potential re-sits now lifted. However, the summer would not be entirely our own. By the start of the second year each student was expected to have completed twelve weeks of pre-clinical extra mural study (PCEMS). Sheep dancing had eaten up three of those, but that still meant a hefty chunk of summer would be taken up with a variety of these activities. My own particular agenda consisted of one week of equine, one of poultry, four inexplicable weeks of pigs (two indoor, two outdoor) and three weeks on a dairy farm

My week at Croxteth Park Riding School passed fairly uneventfully; I learnt how to clean and polish tack, how to groom a horse properly and how to feel comfortable enough around horses to prevent any obvious sense of disquiet transmitting itself to them. I never quite worked out whether the old 'they can sense fear' adage was actually true. Seemed a greater truth to suggest that I'd be put at ease by a calm horse than the other way around. Possibly the most valuable lesson I learnt that week, though, was in getting my PCEMS form signed on the Thursday instead of the Friday. I'd been invited to spend the weekend at Isla's parents' home in Oxford and the extra day's preparation would come in most handy. I'd met her parents, Roland and Clara, once before, but a brief lunch in Chinatown exchanging spring rolls and banal pleasantries would be nothing compared to this.

Isla's father swept the door open with a flourish, effusing bonhomie and sweat in equal amounts as he dabbed intermittently at his bald pate with a polka-dot handkerchief.

'Steve, *do* come in.'

The previous day I'd sidled obsequiously up to the manageress of Croxteth Park Riding School, searching for a literal and metaphorical stamp of approval as she poured over my appraisal form. This occasion felt disturbingly similar. Once again here I was, searching for approval, affirmation that I'd measured up to the required standard, and reassurance that I'd be welcome to return for more experience at a later date. Roland, Isla's father, immediately appeared most keen to present himself as a self-styled bon viveur, raconteur extraordinaire, regaling me with lurid, long-winded tales from his colourful past. I could tell he was keen for me to like him, as he was hitting me with what I assumed were all his A-list stories. I was more than happy to reciprocate, laughing at the appropriate moments, looking suitably thoughtful whenever the mood dictated and generally dancing to which ever tune Roland hummed. During one particularly rambling anecdote, based loosely on his recent successful completion of a wine-tasting course, I'd drifted out of concentration, rejoining the conversation to hear him utter the immortal phrase, 'and do you know, Steve, I got the grape to within the *next village*. They'd never seen anything like it. The *next village...*' How those words would come back to haunt me.

By the time Sunday evening arrived it was clear that, had the need arisen, Roland would quite gladly have ticked the relevant boxes on my sheet. I'd listened politely to a series of interminable anecdotes, I seemed to be making his daughter as happy as they'd seen her in years and all in all I'd come across as a quiet, respectful young man. I stretched back in my seat on the 18.07 to Liverpool Lime Street and exhaled extravagantly. During the journey home and through much of my following week at a battery chicken plant in West Kirby, the words 'to the *next village*' continued to ring in my ears.

My week of poultry experience involved mercifully brief periods with the actual poultry. On one occasion I'd had to accompany the owner into the bowels of the operation as he sought to remove a dead chicken. We traversed narrow aisles which cut a swathe between stacks of teetering cages, reaching from floor to ceiling. Within seconds of entering the barn my head was swimming, an acrid stench of ammonia clawed at the back of my throat. I stood adjacent to the cage containing the ex chicken and willed the owner to recover the body so I could get the hell out of there. As would often prove to be the case during PCEMS, the owner had us over a barrel, in the knowledge that a steady stream of vet students were duty bound to come and see practice with him. He was faced with a choice, really. Either make these visits worthwhile for both parties, putting students to good use but also divulging useful facts concerning, for example, disease control, nutrition or the merits of battery farms versus free range or deep litter systems. Or simply view this endless supply of eager-to-please vet students as a ready source of free (slave) labour and hand them a broom.

It would, sadly, have taken a bigger man than him to not exploit the situation fully. The upshot of this was that I was required to take two buses and a train in order to reach West Kirby in time to begin work at 8.40. I'd then spend the whole day, with the exception of a half-hour lunch break, packing eggs first into boxes and then onto a giant conveyor belt. At 4 pm I'd return home, taking the same two buses and a train. For this I received the princely sum of zero. Furthermore, such was my zeal in getting my form signed, conveying the message that I'd been nothing other than exemplary, that I even went as far as playing the bringing-in-cakes-on-the-last-day card.

By the end of the week I was more than happy to take up Isla's offer of a return weekend visit. She'd been suffering a torrid time of her own at the hands of a sadistic equine vet. So much of vet school's hardship is made bearable by the knowledge that someone somewhere else is suffering at least as much as you are. On the way to the station I slipped into Oddbins and picked up a mid-priced bottle of Chianti for Roland, choosing to ignore the voice in my head inviting me to explain the difference between this and buying cakes for the staff at the poultry farm.

'Hmmm, this is *very familiar*, it has plenty of *nose*. Let's see now shall we? Well, the specific gravity and the sedimentation positively *shouts* New World at me ... Steven I'm going to stick my neck out here and go for a Chilean Cabernet Sauvignon?'

I'd arrived at Isla's place just after eight and no sooner had I pecked her self-consciously on the cheek, dumped my bag and said, 'Hey big man, let me know when you want to take the taste test again,' than the whole family were sitting around the dining-room table with Roland studiously swilling the wine I'd brought, as if it were a post-prandial brandy. I shuffled uneasily in my chair. My choice had been governed purely by opting for a wine I was sure he'd readily identify.

31

'Not so New World, Roland,' I mustered, weakly.

'Ah, some of these southern hemisphere reds can be a real bugger to tell apart. OK, its either Australian or New Zealand. Right?'

I coughed embarrassedly and shuffled my chair forward, unable to meet his gaze.

'It's not from the southern hemisphere. It's European.'

'Oh. You see, Steve, I should have let it settle more. Ah well, my mistake. Right, that's better,' he gushed, holding the half-empty glass up to the light. 'Bulgarian! Speaks Bulgarian to me.'

'Er, no, not Bulgarian.' I just wanted him to get it right and release me from this torture.

'Romanian?'

'No.'

'Spanish.'

'No.'

'Not French is it? A St Emilion or a Fleurie perchance?'

'Not ... really.'

To the next village, Steve.

Each guess had followed a lip-smacking gulp of wine and now the glass lay as empty as my hopes of us ever getting along again. All I'd succeeded in doing was humiliating him in front of his wife and two daughters.

'It was Italian, Roland.'

'Good Lord, good old Chianti! Not really one of ours...' he conceded sniffily, keen to regain a smidge of honour through the vague suggestion that my choice somehow slipped beneath his class radar.

'Another glass?'

'Oh go on then.'

In many ways this cringe-inducing exchange summed up my relationship with Isla; well meaning but ultimately clumsy and ill suited. I'd begun vet school shyly taking stock of my surroundings in the failing light of my relationship with Michelle. Isla, on the other hand, was naturally subdued in company, not being the most gregarious member of the year. It had suited us both in those early socially daunting weeks to form an alliance. Sadly, the more I found my feet socially, the more gaping the holes in our relationship appeared.

The long-awaited holiday in France not only proved a wonderful antidote to the summer's toil but it also succeeded in bringing our differences to a head. These were encapsulated one fateful morning in the grounds of the Palace of Versailles. We'd had this 'when in Rome' attitude to our holiday, immersing ourselves fully in both the culture and language of France. We conversed with the locals in French at all times and sampled as many local delicacies as possible. Paté de foie gras, snails, frogs' legs and Pernod had already been ticked off our list, with only crêpes still missing. We were strolling romantically through the Palace's impeccably coiffured ornamental gardens when Isla stopped abruptly in her tracks and turned to me.

'Oh ... would you like to go for a crêpe now or would you rather wait and have one after we've seen Versailles?'

You set 'em up and I'll knock 'em down, I thought, before delivering the ill-conceived riposte, 'No, you're all right, love. I went first thing this morning.'

Isla met this with a withering grimace, the chill of which ensured that I spent much of our flight back to Manchester later that day still shivering at its recall.

We were deep into August; the leaves were now the same golden shade as the Premiership footballers' suntans. I couldn't help feeling I had to end things with Isla before we both got re-entrenched in the familiar furrow of vet school. I'd begun the previous year in an emotional tangle and it wasn't something I was keen to repeat. I wanted second year to begin with the clean slate I'd missed in first year. I may have been on the verge of losing a girlfriend but I'd gained a wad of signed PCEMS forms and half a bottle of semi-decent Chianti.

6

What Does the 'L' Stand for Again?

Second year kicked off with a brand new education initiative referred to variously as Problem Based Learning, PBL, or 'fuck off and find out yourself'. The upshot of this trendy new policy was that from now on the topic of reproduction would not be taught the old-fashioned way, by means of lectures explaining the intricacies of the subject, highlighting salient points and the inconsequential fluff we may disregard; instead our year was sectioned off into small groups, assigned a facilitator and invited to solve the mysteries of reproduction ourselves via a programme of informal seminars and workshops.

Displaying my usual impeccable sense of timing, I'd finished with Isla right on the cusp of starting back at school. As far as I was concerned FOAFOY couldn't have come at a better time. First of all we were working in groups of six to eight people, and each group had a completely unique timetable, and secondly specific study areas had been set aside, which meant the whole year was dotted all over the university. These significantly reduced the risk of accidental meetings. This regime was due to remain in place until mid November, by which time myself and Isla's demise would be old news.

This new system definitely suited my social requirements at that moment down to the ground. Unfortunately the same couldn't be said for my *academic* requirements. There was no actual curriculum as such for PBL, just a series of open-ended scenarios of the *Ms Hillyard has her pregnant mare scanned revealing what she thinks might be twins. Discuss the implications of this as her vet* variety. The intention was that the ensuing group discussion would not only help to work out what was best for Ms Hillyard but, more

34

importantly, uncover enough pearls of wisdom to justify never having taught us any basic reproduction in the first place. Furthermore, there was no exam at the end of the exercise, thus removing that most essential ingredient from the learning recipe: the *fear factor*. It is for this reason that many of this class of 2003 went to their finals of that year deficient in the fundamentals of reproduction. I don't include myself in that. Not because I had an especially firm grasp of reproduction, you understand, but because I wouldn't still be a part of that year by the time they came to sit finals.

Soon the last of the PBL scenarios were mulled over and put to bed. The Jack Russell straining to defaecate had his prostate examined per rectum one last time, the troublesome ewe with poor oestrus synchronisation had her last PRID implanted, and the Holstein Friesian with the suspected follicular cyst had it squeezed once more for old times' sake. Christmas and the upcoming millennium were a mere month or so away and Isla had reverted to being that attractive, dark-haired, slightly aloof girl who always sat fourth row, centre, left. From the faculty's point of view, second year was seen very much as an extension of first year, as opposed to a self-contained year in its own right. So much so that the second-year examiners reserved the right to examine us on absolutely anything that cropped up during the first two years. Frankly, this worried me. Certain topics, like the countercurrent multiplier system of the kidney and the horse's hoof, took on the guise of Glenn Close in *Fatal Attraction*; suddenly rearing up after having seemingly expired and terrorising me all over again.

The new topics consisted of digestion, the head, the central nervous system and exotics. The faculty had decided it might as well spend some of the £14,000 my parents had given them on actual teaching, as opposed to putting it all towards brand new laboratories for the pathology department. And so the period until the end of term was filled with lectures and practicals. One such practical formed part of the unit on digestion. It was designed, mainly, to elucidate the anatomy of the ruminant forestomachs, but also to help clarify the role of microflora in ruminant digestion. Unfortunately these organisms only tend to survive for a very short period outwith a healthy, living digestive tract and so, for an occasion such as this, only the freshest rumen liquor would do. This meant that when we turned up at 9 am one Thursday morning in late November for our practical, we were met by four live sheep, scuttling nervously around the laboratory and leaving little trails of maltesers for the cleaners. Ten minutes later any casual observer could have been forgiven for thinking they'd stumbled onto the set of a special Welsh edition of the Benny Hill Show; ten vet students farcically chasing sheep around a laboratory, tripping headlong over stools and slipping on small, chocolate-coloured treats.

The sheep were eventually cornered, gathered up and put to the knife. It was difficult not to feel a pang of remorse for their plight. Moments earlier they had been feistily giving us the runaround and now they lay unzipped and jerking on a cold stainless steel worktop. I'm not denying it wasn't illuminating to catch glimpses of microscopic protozoa, paddling through the still warm liquor. Without doubt, taking apart the sheeps' forestomachs led to a far more cogent understanding of ovine anatomy. It just struck me as deeply unsettling that our education had somehow warranted such a wanton act. I stood, lost in thought, inadvertently dipping the cuff of my lab coat in the pooling blood dripping from the table top. As my classmates jostled me for position I couldn't honestly say I was seeing anything that would make the following day's digestion exam any less of a mystery.

'These exams are really nothing more than glorified class tests!' I declared, keen to ascertain just how seriously they were being taken. 'Plus,' I added in response to the silence that greeted my previous remark, 'they're worth, how much? One and a half per cent overall? Jeez, I don't get out of bed for less than five per cent!'

'Aren't all four worth five per cent?'

'Listen, I'm really glad we've had this conversation. You'll have to excuse me, though, I've an exam to fail.'

Alex, exasperating in the extreme with his maddening good looks and propensity for getting 100% in these 'class tests', was impossible to dislike.

'I'm sure that won't be the case. Will we be continuing this conversation in the pub after, Stevie boy?'

'I'm supposed to be going on a date straight after.'

'Who's the lucky lady?'

'That girl, Phillipa. From Jenny's birthday last week?'

'Great stuff. Anyway best of luck with this.'

'And you mate.'

Now I know how that sheep felt yesterday, I thought, filing into the exam hall.

The format was the usual 40 negatively marked multiple choice questions; this was intended to remove the weapon of guessing from the student arsenal. I think, though, that if I'd only ever answered questions I was truly convinced about, I'd be lobbying for marks to be awarded for the correct spelling of one's own name. I felt like a compulsive gambler trying in vain to pick enough winners to make a better life for himself and his family. Having reached the point where whatever meagre tally I'd accumulated would have been eaten away to nothing if I continued guessing, I downed tools and left the exam hall.

I had arranged to meet Phillipa outside Blackwells at one o'clock. When I closed my eyes I found I couldn't picture her, something I found most disquieting. I hoped that meant I wouldn't accidentally blank her or, worse still, approach a total stranger. Given my truly heroic intake of cocktails at Jenny's party the previous Friday it wasn't surprising certain elements of that night were hazy. But what she *looked* like? It was, in truth, something of a minor miracle that I'd emerged from that whole blurry episode with the remotest chance she'd want to see me again.

The night had begun with Sam and I nursing several pints in The Old Monk. We quickly became immersed in conversation, and the faster we talked, the faster we drank until the lateness of the hour was impossible to ignore. It was well after midnight by the time we finally nudged past the bouncer and through the doors of the club, noting immediately that the party was in full swing. We pushed our way to the bar where we struck up a shouting, largely incoherent conversation with a girl in our year, Simone, and one of her housemates, Phillipa. The night progressed, swaggering and swaying drunkenly to an increasingly ragged beat. Phillipa and I exchanged a lingering kiss at the bar; I tasted the tequila on her warm breath.

Before long the four of us were rolling and bumping along in the back of a speeding cab home. We collapsed, laughing hysterically, over the threshold. Simone and Phillipa fussed around in their kitchen, chewing on toast and making cups of tea that never came. Sam and I, abandoned to our thoughts in the living room, sat and silently contemplated how hot the night's dying embers might still burn. Simone eventually appeared from the kitchen carrying a sleeping bag that she lobbed at Sam. Phillipa stood behind her and raised her eyebrows at me before turning and heading up the stairs.

'Shit. Am I supposed to follow her?'

'I think that's the general idea, Stevie.'

'Oh, OK...' I faltered, before regaining my composure. 'Well, I'll bid you goodnight, then,' and I followed the disappearing form of Phillipa up the creaking, paint-chipped staircase. The bedroom door shut with a dull clunk behind me.

I awoke an hour or so later and tugged a lifeless arm from underneath a quietly snoring Phillipa. The last of the evening's fluid intake had announced its presence in my bladder and had now become impossible to ignore. I clambered out of bed and walked slowly with my arms outstretched like Boris Karloff in *The Mummy* until I found the bathroom at the end of the hallway. After joyously relieving myself I re-entered the hallway and was suddenly struck by the fact that I didn't have the slightest clue where Phillipa's room was. The wall of darkness was so impenetrable that it seemed to make no difference whether my eyes were open or closed. I paddled the air like a drowning man, and shoved a heavy door open, quietly confident I'd found my way back. Tiptoeing across the threadbare carpet, rhythmic breathing alerted me to the bed and the shadowy form lying motionless within. I climbed onto the groaning bed and straddled the inert being. *It was Simone!* My heart missed a beat. In my attempts to scramble off the bed I nearly fell off it, dragging her duvet with me. I scurried to the door, not realising it had silently shut behind me, and thumped headlong into it. Madly scrabbling at the door for the elusive knob, I heard Simone stir, moaning quietly in her bed.

Over a subdued breakfast the next afternoon, a clearly fragile Simone mumbled, almost to herself, 'I had this really weird dream last night.'

I scratched at my chin thoughtfully, eventually venturing, 'It'll be that cheese on toast you had when you got in.'

'But I didn't...'

'Anyone tell me where the toilet is?'

7

Home is Where the Hurt is

I suppose I should have been thankful that it missed my head by inches, but at that precise second I wasn't feeling in a *giving thanks* kind of place. I'd been sound asleep in bed, taking advantage of a rare 10.30 start, when I suffered my rude awakening; a brick, hurled through the bedroom window, landing on my bed and showering me with stilettos of glass.

I'd noticed in recent weeks that my drug-dealing neighbour, having fallen on hard times, was turning up on my doorstep with increasing regularity. Ostensibly it would be to try and sell me some of his random possessions, ranging from a Blackadder video to a bench for working out. But I'd noticed with growing alarm how his eyes would greedily scour the contents of my flat. I began to worry that next time he might not knock.

As if this wasn't enough, I was fast tiring of the solitude I had so craved when I first came down from Edinburgh in 1995. The close-knit bonds harboured at vet school were making a mockery of my self-imposed exile. Solitude that had once soothed me now did the opposite, imprisoning me. At times I would restlessly pace my tiny living room like a caged tiger.

By around 3 pm the glazier left, having replaced the broken pane of glass. University had passed me by for the day. This week Teddy was stamping his inimitable mark on exotics. Diverting a topic as this was, exams-wise it was utterly irrelevant, and watching Teddy's honest labouring in the face of unbridled apathy seldom made for comfortable viewing. I decided to visit Rob. As far as I was concerned the only regret I could see myself having about leaving this place would be not being able to nip over at a moment's notice to see him. In years to come we would go on to become close friends, travelling the length and breadth of the country supporting Liverpool FC. Back then, though, I was just happy to have someone to talk to. Rob ran his own newsagents which allowed him to conduct lengthy conversations with a series of 'regulars'. Common or garden visitors often seemed more hindrance than valued customer. Over the years I lost count of the number of times I'd see Rob, in full flow in the back of his shop, stutter to a halt with an incredulous look of 'What now?' as some hapless soul wandered in for a *Liverpool Echo* or a can of Fanta.

'Hey Robbie!'

'All right, Scotty. I was just thinking about you actually.'

'Yeah?'

'Will Hearts win at Motherwell tonight? Need one more "away" for me coupon. It's *them* or Clyde away at Brechin.'

Rob was leaning over the counter, I peered inquisitively at his upside-down fixed-odds coupon. It was enough to jog my memory, triggering a stab of concern about the end of year exams and bringing our conversation to a premature end.

'Ah well Robbie, better get back to it.'

'Will you drop in tomorrow?'

'Definitely, mate.'

The extended Easter holiday, designed to accommodate first years' lambing commitments, stretched through to the middle of April, merging with the onset of exam leave. This afforded me the extra time I'd almost certainly be needing to take enough information on board to pass the year. The downside, though, was that it only served to magnify the solitude I'd been struggling to endure. I blocked this out as best I could and bullied myself into a strictly regimented study routine. The days fell like dominoes and it seemed like no time at all before our week of exams arrived.

I began the week keyed up, primed and ready to spring into action. However, such were the machinations reverberating through my brain that by night-time I found myself unable to switch my mind off, twitching and panicking in bed, staring at the backs of my eyelids trying to wrest back control of my thoughts. Lack of sleep began insidiously wearing me down. At the start of the week, during the written portion of the exam, I'd felt as sharp as a tack, ultra-confident I'd got some good points on the board. I felt my brain get woollier and woollier as the week wore on. So often during the practical and the MCQ days I'd chase pieces of information round my head like dander on a stiff breeze. As each day passed I'd sit alone at night convincing myself I'd done well enough in the first part of the week to cover these deficits. Cajoled and consoled I kept my head sufficiently together, ending up with yet another pass/fail viva. I didn't know whether to be happy or not with this outcome. I'd scraped through first year on a viva and was unable to escape the feeling I was living on borrowed time.

I'd learnt my lesson from the previous year's brush with defeat and had prepared scrupulously concise essay plans on each and every long and short answer question in the exam. During the six days' grace I had before the hot spot beckoned I left nothing to chance.

I was shown into the dissection room where my viva was to take place. When I realised I was to be examined by the Head of Neurology, Dr Stokes, and the external examiner, my heart leapt. In my exam I'd studiously side-stepped the spaghetti of Stokes's optic nerve pathways question, but had gone to town redressing the balance in the days that followed. We traded the accepted pre-viva platitudes and I barely felt able to contain my excitement. The words 'Go on, ask me about *your* question' repeatedly flitted through my head. *Perhaps they would transmit themselves into Dr Stokes's brainstem via cranial nerve number 8.* I eventually got my wish and Stokes asked me exactly what I wanted him to. Once I had the floor I was reluctant to deviate in the slightest way, shape or form, from this topic. Tiring of this ploy the external examiner eventually butted in, gently quizzing me on the types and causes of leukaemia for several minutes. By this stage it didn't matter. I knew I couldn't be caught. I hung around for the formality of the pass list.

Second year was rapidly disappearing. I noted with a sigh that the anxiety I'd had about coping with its rigours and the subsequent relief I'd felt at passing had now been superseded by worry concerning how much third year would ask of me.

In the pub afterwards Lesley asked how I'd feel about moving into the house on Penny Lane that she shared with three other girls in our year. The time felt right for a move; I'd had enough of solitude.

8

There Beneath the Blue Suburban Skies

The hallway smelt musty and damp and was dimly lit save for a slim crack of light emanating from under the living-room door. I heaved my bulging rucksack from my complaining shoulders, dumping it unceremoniously with all the other sundry detritus lodging in the space under the stairs. After composing myself and quickly checking my sallow reflection in the hall mirror, I pushed open the door, flooding the hallway with light. Over the summer I'd flitted back and forth to this new abode on Penny Lane, moving my belongings in much the same way as a sparrow constructs a nest. But this was the first time all the residents of our new home had been together in the house.

'Evening all!'

'Hey Steve!' Lesley replied for everyone, her eyes remaining fixed on the television. 'Be with you in a mo! Just need to see the end of this...' She tailed off as an unshaven guy with a bald head snarled at a younger guy with dark, spiky hair. A pretty, blonde girl was sobbing uncontrollably in the background, mascara running in rivulets down her face.

'*EastEnders* good, is it?'

'Mmmm,' came the reply, embellished with relish by four sets of lips.

During an interlude in the bickering Yvette piped up, 'Was Skye good?'

'Aw yeah, superb!' I enthused. 'Got, like, *this* close to a golden eagle,' making a gesture with my arms that no one saw. The arguing and crying had begun again.

'You should've seen it. It picked Sam up in its talons and swept him back to its eyrie up in the mountains. But the eaglets said he was wearing far too much hair gel for them and gobbed him out. Eagle was *well* pissed off. True story.'

'Mmmm...'

I retired, unnoticed, to the hallway, hoisted my rucksack on to my back once more and slouched up the threadbare stairs to unpack. I'd more or less finished when the distinctive closing drumbeats of *EastEnders* levitated through the floorboards followed seconds later by jangling and clattering from the kitchen, directly below my room. I sat on my freshly made bed and hoped, not for the first time, that I'd made the right choice.

'Steve? Tea?'

'Yeah!'

'How d'you take it again?'

'S'all right, Lesley, I'll come down.'

The five of us, Lesley, Yvette, myself, Andrea and Jane, sat with steaming mugs of tea in our living room. The novelty of this new arrangement still tickled me. We talked about the upcoming start of another year.

'I'm dreading parasites most,' declared Andrea, squirming. 'All those creepy crawlies, yeuch!!'

'Don't be silly, you're going to be a vet for heaven's sake!' snapped Jane haughtily, sending Andrea back inside the shell she'd spend the rest of the year in.

Fear of creepy crawlies, silence during soaps. Steep learning curve, Stevie boy.

'You've gone quiet, Steve.'

'Yeah Lesley, just thinking how much of an education this year's going to be. I've never lived with *girls* before.'

'Lesson one, then, always put the toilet seat down.'

'My last place was in Wavertree, not the Stone Age.'

'OK, lesson two; I take milk and no sugar in my tea.'

'Want another, then?' I volunteered wearily.

'Well, if you're asking...' Lesley offered her mug, a signal for the three others to do the same.

'Don't like this class' I pouted sulkily, dragging my feet into the kitchen.

Third year was generally thought of as the penultimate hurdle and the last opportunity for the faculty to weed out any miscreants. If

43

you were still left standing after third year, the chances were you'd go the whole way. Once you were into fourth year, it was a clear run to finals and beyond. The subject matter felt, without question, as if it had been cranked up a notch. Pathology, parasitology, infectious diseases and pharmacology combined to present a formidable barrier. The lectures and practicals began at a fairly leisurely pace, allowing the briefest of bedding-in periods before pushing the academic pedal to the floor. Pathology settled quickly into a routine that entailed taking apart an organ system a week, swarming fastidiously over it with a microscopic-tooth comb and swamping us with voluminous screeds of disease patterns. Parasitology was equally unrelenting; complex lifecycles racked up until our heads were as bloated and tight as the abdomen of a puppy with *Toxocara*. The other two subjects, infectious diseases and pharmacology, always seemed slightly less daunting prospects, but this had as much to do with the exceptional demands of pathology and parasitology as anything else. History showed that all four demanded equal respect.

The intense academic heat of these new subjects coupled with increased familiarity born out of the commencement of a third year together, had a distinctly warming effect on relations in the year. Like a bud unfurling its petals in response to the sun's caress, the cliques and prejudices that had carved our year into factions slowly began dissolving away. I welcomed this sea change. There was nothing worse than returning from a visit to the toilet on a night out in town and having to negotiate a minefield of cold shoulders and frosty glances in order to re-establish oneself in a safe, familiar social enclave. But the signs at the start of third year were most promising. There was an instantaneous upsurge in the quality and quantity of our nights out. New friendships emerged like clusters of snowdrops after a harsh and unforgiving winter.

In the first two years freshers' week made little impression on me, but this year was different. I'd always vehemently resisted the lure of the traditional Monday night ceilidh, cringing at the association between the country of my birth and the assorted collection of walking shortbread tins tripping over their feet on the dance floor. At last, though, I was free to begin an academic year untroubled by post-relationship baggage and surprised myself by having a superb time. As with only the finest nights, the five of us made our way home individually, each with a separate tale to tell. An impromptu party sprang up and became something of an endurance test, dragging on through until dawn. It wasn't until Prof Beech began his lecture on lungworm vaccination in cattle that we got some much needed sleep.

I had other reasons for welcoming this upturn in socialising. The alcohol helped to numb my rumbling worries about keeping up with the accelerated academic pace. Unlike first and second year, I was unable to actively contemplate the end of year exams. Our books of notes had past exam questions slotted in at the back and I'd felt the blood run cold in my veins when I'd unintentionally flicked to them. The chill shook me, re-awakening the arthritis from its latency. Niggling discomfort began gnawing indefatigably at the insides of my joints. Time was racing, exams were shooting into view at an alarming rate. Drinking also helped to take the edge off the pain in my joints.

In what seemed like no time at all our pre-Christmas pathology exam was upon us. I'd never felt so unprepared prior to going into an exam. My revision was spread so thinly it felt transparent. In previous years it had always been possible to predict, with a high degree of accuracy, which particular topics to have on board. It always made perfect sense to be familiar with the course of the radial nerve, for example, as it tended to pop its synaptic bulb of a head up fairly regularly. Similarly you knew it was possible to neglect, say, the hind limb of the dog, if it had been covered in the exam the previous year. Pathology was different. It was a law unto itself. So vast was the chasm it spanned that anything could crop up; and it frequently did. I never had that recurring dream about sitting in an exam hall and suddenly realising I was naked more often than I did that week.

The exam paper lay face down on the desk in front of me. I read the blurb on the back explaining there would be two hours to complete five out of seven essays, and the gravity of the situation struck me. I realised I'd struggle to come up with five questions of my own choice that I'd be comfortable answering. At the appropriate signal I turned the exam paper over and spent the next 80 minutes repeating, altering minimally and stretching out a very meagre repertoire of facts. I knew such a blatant attempt to maximise my paltry knowledge of pathology subtracted massive amounts of credibility from my performance. I didn't care. In the end I simply wanted to cobble enough points together to get me to the summer exams without having too much of a mountain to climb. I pinned my hopes on the arthritis having eased somewhat by then, cutting me some slack. It was fair to say the colossal effort of lugging my arthritic body this far into vet school had drained me beyond words.

I walked stiffly down Brownlow Hill to Lime Street station and could feel the resolve sapping from my bones. Home was where I craved to be but I doubted whether it would carry enough healing properties to take me where I needed to be. The future made me deeply fearful. Around half an hour from Euston I gulped the aspirin I had in my top pocket to galvanise me for the journey to Waterloo on the underground. At that moment the burden I was carrying extended way beyond a rucksack full of books and clothes.

9

What Price the Treble?

'I'm telling you, Ste,' puffed Rob, wheezing along beside me as we circumnavigated the outer perimeter of Cardiff's gargantuan Millennium Stadium, 'they won't start playing 'til *we* get there.'

It was 25th February 2001 and the Worthington Cup Final between Liverpool and Birmingham City was well under way. Horrendous traffic congestion on the M4 had meant we'd been stuck in a line of cars when the match had kicked off. We mounted the steps three at a time. The massive glowing scoreboard behind the goal opposite relayed the score poised at 0–0 with 28 minutes gone. Having located my seat, I sat, quickly drew breath and allowed my eyes to survey the vista spread gloriously before my very eyes. The first thing I saw was Liverpool's Robbie Fowler smash a dipping volley high past the Birmingham goalkeeper. The whole Liverpool end erupted all around me and Rob jumped on me screaming 'I told you, Ste, I told you they wouldn't start...' I responded by hugging him back and shouting 'First touch, Robbie, first touch' over and over again. The vast majority of our year were spending the weekend in the Cotswolds, revelling in the landmark of vet school's halfway point. I couldn't bear to be reminded of the reality of my life; the years of hardship that still lay ahead. Most days I wanted to forget I was a vet student at all. These snatched dalliances with Rob at Liverpool games allowed me to lose myself in the crowd – glad, albeit briefly, to escape this truth.

Liverpool eventually edged a nervy final 5–4 on penalties. I sat perspiring in the back of the car, still glowing from the effort of running the post-match gauntlet past hordes of jostling and kicking Blues fans. Rob turned, his face equally crimson, 'What price the treble, Scotty?'

'Can't see me passing pathology, mate.'

'Not you, soft bollocks, Liverpool! We've won this; quarters of the UEFA Cup, week on Thursday against Porto; Tranmere in the quarters of the FA Cup the next Saturday. Got to fancy it, we're on a roll.'

I couldn't see it myself. Too many potential banana skins. Barcelona and Arsenal to name but two. But Rob hated it when I displayed an ounce of pessimism on any subject, let alone the mighty Reds. Both him and his brother Al swivelled, staring expectantly at me, despite the fact that Al was approaching 90 mph on the sliproad to the M5. 'Well?'

My disposition at that moment didn't really lend itself to optimism about anything. 'I think there's about as much possibility of Liverpool doing the treble this season as there is ... as there is of me getting through third year first time of asking.'

Without missing a beat Rob turned triumphantly back in his seat. 'See? Didn't hurt too much did it? Dead cert, that.'

Third year exams sat, squat, on the horizon like a juggernaut. It became evident to me that the Christmas' trials and tribulations had merely been an opener to the brutal main event unfolding now. Arthritis was starting to seize me in a vice-like grip, grinding me monotonously to a halt. Exam-related apprehension only amounted to a portion of the stress I felt under. My relationship with the girls in the house was slowly disintegrating. They'd really seemed to enjoy hanging out with the fun, relatively mobile Steve they'd known at the start of term. The one who was bed-ridden because the stairs had got too difficult and hardly ventured outside because it hurt too much to tie shoelaces? Not so much. I felt staying in bed represented my best chance of passing. It took away many of the minutiae of tasks that drained my energy, as well as allowing my crunching, unstable knee joints a respite from the rigours of ensuring verticality.

I heard voices raised at the bottom of the stairs. This was followed first by the front door and then the doors of Yvette's Nissan Micra banging shut. *The girls were off to Tesco's.* I had, literally, no food and it hurt to know the girls were aware of this. This was more subtle than them simply reprising Kathy Bates' role in *Misery*, leaving me stewing in bed with busted legs and relishing the control. They were, in essence, punishing me for not asking if I could go with them. I shifted my legs painfully, propped up as I was on two pillows and told myself that if they actually cared for me, they'd have come up to my room and asked if I needed anything or would I like to go with them. They knew the state I was in. I had never felt so alone in all my life.

By spending a huge portion of the last two weeks studying in bed I had been able to cover acres of ground. It had also mercifully taken me out of the firing line of the girls. The run-in to exams had created a vile, poisonous atmosphere between them. Despite misgivings about my own perceived difficultness, I was male and therefore viewed as something of a neutral bystander. I began to lose track of who'd said what about whom and why. Barbed, personal comments and petty blow-ups ensured a relentless crossfire. I had enough problems of my own, but seeing the vitriol they reserved for one another made me almost grateful for the excuse of arthritis, limiting my forays downstairs.

Monday morning dawned dark and full of foreboding. I rose early, keen to get the blood flowing in limbs that had spent much of the previous fortnight redundant. Each day represented a mountain to climb in its own right: Monday, pathology written, Tuesday, parasitology written, Wednesday, pathology practical, Thursday, parasitology practical, Friday, infectious diseases. I thrust myself into the action, remaining as doggedly determined and upbeat as the shifting sands of my concentration would permit.

After a week crunching aspirin like sweets, Friday finally came and went and I heaved my aching limbs over the end-of-week finishing line. By the weekend I felt knocked senseless by the week's onslaught. My sense of identity had been pummelled out of me, leaving me punch drunk, a cracked and empty husk. I sat rocking on my bed, too sore to sleep but too tired to stay awake. We still had one more exam to go, pharmacology, on Monday. Resuming revision after such a gut-wrenching surge culminating in the week's supreme effort, made my head swim.

On the Sunday afternoon I took a break, timing it to coincide with the Liverpool FC treble parade crossing Queen's Drive at Allerton Road. I thought back to Rob at the start of Liverpool's run and his conviction this would happen. Its sheer improbability made my own prospects seem all the more weak. I bleakly surveyed the jubilant hysteria and celebratory abandon; it presented a stark contrast to the sense of impending doom festering inside me.

49

Pharmacology passed with blessed ease. Our lecturer, aware of the magnitude of our task, had plied us with enough pre-exam pointers to take the sting out of the exam. Three days of hanging on followed, in which I felt like I was on death row waiting to hear if the local gun-toting governor would grant a reprieve. There were guiltily hatched attempts to return to a semblance of normality in the house. Lesley and Yvette reverted back to pre-exam personae and we sat around drinking countless cups of tea and pointing out crucial flaws in *Neighbours* plotlines. But I couldn't escape the sense of betrayal. The manner in which they'd dropped me and cut me off meant I could never properly go back.

I suppose my luck had to run out sometime. I got 52% for pharmacology, 50% for both infectious diseases and parasites, and failed pathology. Immediately an unspoken barrier shot up between myself and a large percentage of my year who'd passed. They were free to talk at length about their plans for the summer. I couldn't. They could talk expansively about the implications of starting fourth year, sharing delicious frissons of anticipation at the thought of beginning rotations. I had to turn away from those conversations. When you fail and it's clear you're coming back for a re-sit in September, the nagging doubt, the knowledge that something excruciatingly unpleasant is due to happen to you in x number of weeks, haunts and torments you every inch of the way. It's impossible to truly escape this monkey on your back. The moment anything even remotely uplifting happens, the gremlins strike.

'*What are you so happy about? You've failed pathology remember, you've got to come back in September when, I may add, passing is anything but a foregone conclusion.*'

The rest of the year sees out the term's long evenings blissfully engaged in interminable games of rounders and a flurry of barbecues. By this point it has become virtually intolerable being around them. It's that look in their eyes; a loose amalgamation of heartfelt sympathy, condescension and ill-disguised irritation that your presence has made it harder for them to tactfully let their post-exam hair down.

After an all-too-brief respite we were conscripted back to university. Six weeks of official fourth-year lectures had been crowbarred in to take some of the pressure off the autumn timetable. My joints had flared up severely by now. I'd decided to subject myself to the agonising horror of rising from bed only on days when either a register was to be taken or notes were being given out. The girls had made it plain I could rely on them for neither. On one such visit there was a sequence of events which, although doing nothing to enhance my chances of escaping third year this summer, immeasurably improved my overall chances of surviving vet school.

I'd scrawled my signature on the register at the start of a two-week stint of small animal orthopaedics lectures. I'd also been fortunate enough to pick up the wad of notes helpfully left out for collection on the front bench. I was shuffling painfully back to the 699 bus stop, doing all I could to focus every iota of thought on the sofa back at the house and the extent to which I was going to enjoy collapsing on it. It felt as if each and every bone in both my feet was on fire. Whichever way I positioned my feet in making contact with the ground the agony was unspeakable. I stopped and rested a moment, levering my feet off the ground in turn, to relieve the weight. The intense throbbing made me choke back a sob and I pushed my head against the cold of the roughened concrete wall. I began to knock my head against it, gently at first, desperate for something, anything to take my mind off the intolerable pain. The bus stop suddenly seemed far further than a hundred yards away. My body gave up the fight to remain standing. I slumped against the wall and then down it, until I was crumpled on the ground and relatively free from the pain.

'Steve? What the fuck?'

I looked up at Alex, towering over me, a full styrofoam cup of coffee, swilling dangerously close to the brim, clasped in his giant paw.

'Mate, I ... I'm fucked.' I stammered, barely able to get the words out.

'Up you come.' He blew his cheeks out in concern and reached down, heaving me onto my feet with one linked arm. 'I hate to see you like this, buddy. Come on, I'll take you for a coffee and you can tell me all about it.'

Within half an hour I'd confessed how the condition had so drastically derailed me. I'd told him how I'd always been able to control the pain with aspirin but just recently they hadn't really been working, giving only an acute gastritis. As we talked it became clear I'd reached a watershed in my life. The time had come to look at things differently. I'd always shied away from admitting the condition to myself, let alone seeking the help of others. The days of self-treating my psoriatic arthritis with ad libidum non-steroidal anti-inflammatories had to stop. I even had the lecture notes in my bag to prove it. I'd been offered potent cytotoxic drugs over ten years before but felt reluctant to consign myself to the concomitant blood tests and immuno-suppression. Perhaps now, though, the pluses outweighed the minuses regarding this therapy. Alex listened intently, nodding quietly at the mention of cytotoxics. He'd been busily raiding the internet, reading up in advance for the upcoming orthopaedics lectures.

'Stevie, there's a whole array of drugs that could make your PA more manageable, there's...'

'And you know this from checking the internet?' I interrupted.

'Yeah, mate. There's two differ...'

'Checking the internet in advance of two weeks' lectures on the subject?'

'Yes ... and?'

I raised an eyebrow. 'The word "spod" mean anything to you?'

'D'you want to hear what I found out or not?'

'Sorry mate. Go on then.'

I made a doctor's appointment with the express intention of securing a referral to the rheumatology clinic at The Royal Liverpool University Hospital. Alex, standing with me in the waiting room, quietly offered to accompany me to the hospital when my time came.

I returned home on the train to my parents' house in Surrey. I was still in pain but felt far more heartened about the future. In my pocket was a referral letter I'd received that morning. My consultation wouldn't be until late September, by which time I'd know the fate of my pathology re-sit. I drummed my fingers on the table as summer flew unnoticed past the window. I allowed myself to fantasise about driving over from Leahurst for my consultation as a fourth year vet student, the window down and music blaring. I hoped events would pan out as they had in my dreams.

Could be worse, I suppose. They could have chained me to the radiator, I mused, surveying the bare austere cell with a derisory shake of my head. Four weeks had elapsed and I was back in Liverpool preparing for the dreaded re-sit. I remembered Catherine Street halls of residence from visiting Vincent in first year but, back then, they'd been a bustling, vivacious hive of activity. Now it was a rain-spattered concrete abomination, discarded crisp packets careering dementedly in the litter-strewn courtyards. The slate grey breezeblocks in my room seemed to be closing in, measly, pea-green curtains pulled grimly shut to limit distraction. The rickety desk rocked forward each time I turned a page.

The pathology re-sit was divided up in such a way that a whopping 20% was set aside for the oral exam. The logic was that by this stage students were probably being let down as much by poor exam technique as anything else. Some gentle probing was all that was needed to ease out the relevant knowledge. At least that was the idea. I returned to Catherine Street after a breathless practical in which my aching right hand had hindered me more than I cared to let on. I fought desperately to be upbeat, telling myself that any deficit would have been more than made up for by my performance in the written paper. Three days earlier I felt I'd handed in a paper which was more than competent. Alex had sent a good luck card, wishing me all the best and revealing that he'd been in touch with the housing officer at Leahurst and we'd be starting fourth year as nextdoor neighbours in Ritchie House. Everything was set up. I bemoaned the fact that I still had the oral to do. I felt I might have had around 40 out of 80 marks so far, but that could easily end up counting for nothing. An oral horror show would see this blow up in my face. I hoped beyond hope I'd be able to swing what was, in essence, a third pass/fail viva in three years my way.

As it was, my worst fears proved founded. I produced a calamitous performance; at one point responding to a question by smacking my forehead three times on the desk in front of me. Questions designed to begin moderately easily, getting tougher as the student, theoretically, took the strain, soon left the back-pedalling examiner with nowhere to regress to. My mind went completely blank. Every syllable assumed inflated importance in my head. Every time the examiner opened his mouth I felt cowed by the pressure of *needing* to know the answer to what he was about to ask. I could feel my mind putting up the shutters; as the examiner's words were being formulated I wasn't *expecting* to know the answer. The previous day Mrs Armitage, clearly viewing the oral as a formality, had assured me I'd get to know my fate the very second it finished. It was, therefore, somewhat less than promising when she could only muster the tersest thank you at the end. When, visibly sagging, I offered up the question, 'I've failed haven't I?' it was purely rhetorical. By way of response she mumbled, incoherently about proper channels and steadfastly refused to look me in the eye.

The wait was agonising, I just wanted to be put out of my misery. That way, I felt, I'd at least be able to begin the laborious task of picking up whatever fragments were still left. Dazed and preoccupied I clambered onto an 86 bus and headed out to see Rob. The pretext was that I needed to give him the money for my Aston Villa ticket, although it was closer to the truth to say I needed an escape, however fleeting, from this particular episode.

With Rob in tow I strode purposefully around to the main entrance. Our talk had raised my spirits and Rob's unshakeable enthusiasm and bubbling positivity had me believing I might just have snatched victory from the jaws of defeat. As I approached the door I cast a self-conscious glance across the square, catching sight of Greg chewing the fat with a second year. I stopped mid stride and sought to catch his eye. He'd know the fate of his own re-sit in parasitology by now and I hoped he'd come through it unscathed. On seeing me at the door he immediately lowered his eyes. I knew then I'd failed the year.

10

Practice Makes Perfect

I'd spent a large percentage of my first three years at vet school eyeing the year below with suspicion. In a trait not unique to this course, our year imbued the year below with all the characteristics we feared applied to us:

'They seem quite cliquey.'

'Bit quiet aren't they?'

'A *lot* of geeks in that year.'

'Hmm, they don't seem to go out that much.'

'Couple of decent people in there ... at a push.'

'Bit arrogant.'

'Fancy themselves don't they?'

Call it three parts siege mentality to one part unfortunate encounter with individual(s) embodying all of the above. I'd been happy to perpetuate the myth, choice meetings with unrepresentative social pariahs notwithstanding, and couldn't help but feel a mild twinge of remorse when I found myself the recipient of the warmest of welcomes. Then I heard my new third year housemates list the virtues of the year below *them* in similarly disparaging terms and concluded with a wry smile that this was simply the way of the world.

Although I'd been, for obvious reasons, the last of the five housemates to sign up for a year on Karslake Road, a hospital appointment and a league match against Spurs meant I was one of the first to move in. There were to be three other vet students in the house, two girls (Kate and Nina) and a guy (Brad). Our fifth Beatle, so to speak, was Paul, two years into a PhD in European politics. This hastily constructed hybrid of personalities took around half an hour to blossom into a harmonious unit; interactions which would whirr like clockwork all the way through to summer and beyond clicked into motion. A parity of sorts became established. Nina and Kate feasted on the delights of soap operas for which Paul and I dispensed the requisite number of soap tokens, making sure they amounted to no more than the football tokens the girls doled out for us. That way neither party felt short-changed. Brad often removed himself from the bartering, becoming unofficial arbitrator of any disputes.

One evening Nina and I were still smarting from a tempestuous house discussion/argument earlier that afternoon on fox hunting, an activity defended with equal amounts of restraint and eloquence by Brad. My mind flitted back to the flurry of Conservative party propaganda stacked up in the kitchen, addressed to our own Mr Bradley-Jones and decided the time had come for the party to take their association with him to the next level. Adopting my plummiest accent I phoned Brad on his mobile from the downstairs telephone, studiously avoiding eye contact with the rest of the house lest they make me laugh and blow my cover.

'Hello?'

'Hello. Is that a Simon Anthony Bradley-Jones by any chance?'

'Yes? Yes it is.'

'Good. This is Jonathon Coates from the Conservative Party.'

'Oh yes?'

'Yes. I hope I'm not calling you too late?'

'Good Lord no. Not at all. You've actually caught me at my desk working. I'm a third year vet student you see.'

'Really? How positively fascinating. You may be of some use to us. Might I ask a favour of you?'

'Of course, I'll see what I can do. Can't promise anything, extremely busy you know, blah blah blah, work and all that...'

'No, I understand entirely. It's just that you sound like a well-bred sort of a chap and I'm keen to ascertain your view on fox hunting. You probably know the blasted jocks are tabling a bill to have it banned.'

'As it happens I *am* actually pro hunting.'

'There's a good chap. How would you feel about addressing the party conference on the subject? A young vet standing up there, informing all those pinko do-gooders about the truth of hunting. You know? How the fox loves it, thrill of the chase and all that. How it's only old and sick foxes that get caught and how it performs a useful service, pruning the population...'

'Wow. It's very flattering to be asked but I...'

'Then you could go on to say that the tearing apart by foxhounds is so instantaneous that the little blighters don't feel a darned thing.'

'Well, I suppose...'

'Oh come now, don't be shy. You used exactly the same argument earlier today on Nina and Steve didn't you?' I blurted out, succumbing to an attack of the giggles and slamming the phone down before he could reply.

Brad, along with Kate, took on the role of surrogate parent in the house, diligently ensuring that all the bills got paid on time and espousing enough of an air of authority to make us all think twice about letting the dishes pile up to any degree. This was due, in part, to the two of them having lived in the house the year before but it also had its origins in Nina, Paul and I rapidly assuming the mantle of irksome siblings. Paul laid passionate claim to being Watford FC's most fervent long-distance supporter; often having too many palpitations to even take a quick peek at the latest score updates on teletext when his beloved Hornets were in action. Nina was our all-singing, all dancing, rugby-playing brat of a little sister whose party pieces ranged from belching the National Anthem to unbuttoning people's clothing with her toes. I think it's fair to say I loved them all pretty much from the start.

As a preamble to beginning my treatment with methotrexate I'd been put on a hefty dose of steroids. The ugly spectre of chronic pain was extracted imperceptibly from my daily life, lifting my hopes immeasurably and making my heart sing. As I eased my way back into pathology it felt like I was returning to a lukewarm bath after a very long phone call. The relatively slack academic regime was essential, allowing me to adapt properly to life with this new drug. The dose of steroids and the subsequent weekly methotrexate influx needed careful monitoring to gauge the appropriate dose. There were regular blood tests and appointments with my consultant, and a side-effect of the drug was that for a period of around 24 hours I was disorientated and nauseous. It slowly began to dawn on me that it wouldn't have been possible to have done this against the backdrop of fourth year.

A fourth freshers' week was now upon me. At around 10 pm on the Sunday night I eventually made an appearance in Dovedales

57

to meet my first year tutee. Alex and I had finally extricated ourselves from the chilled, convivial calm of the Penny Lane Wine Bar, reluctant to brave the jostling multitudes. I also felt vaguely reticent about facing my old colleagues, in many cases for the first time since failing pathology. As it was, the pub was hooching as expected and the worst I had to contend with were people very sweetly acting as if there'd been a death in the family, showering me with warmth and heartfelt condolences.

With this obstacle thankfully negotiated I was now free to play hunt the tutee. My duties as a tutor may have consisted of little more than scaring my tutee witless about initiation while simultaneously assuaging any fears she may have harboured about coping with her first year, but it would have been bad form to have left her dangling, tutor-less, for any longer. When I eventually located her in the scrum at the bar we exchanged the customary awkward pleasantries. Her doe-eyed innocence made it very hard for me to regale her with traditionally morbid tales of initiation. It often seemed there was no distinction made between boisterous rugby-playing farm hands eager for their perpetrators to do their worst and individuals of a more delicate disposition. I plumped for a benign downplaying of the whole event and left her to her new classmates. At the end of the night, as the pub disgorged drunken revellers, I hugged my old friends tightly, feeling this was a parting of the ways. Although Leahurst lay a mere 15 or so miles from Liverpool city centre I got a feeling that the onset of the clinical years would make it seem a very long 15 miles.

The initiation ceremony had been relocated to Leahurst. Liverpool's staff members had been loth to consign a newly refurbished lecture theatre to the undoubted trashing it would have received. I didn't feel ready to head over the water just yet. This year was offering me a heaven-sent reprieve. The noose I'd felt tightening around my neck as third year had edged towards its cataclysmic conclusion had slackened off to nothing. I could breathe easily once again and, for the first time, the thought of beginning clinical years at vet school didn't fill me with dread. Having said that, the thought of venturing out to Leahurst and seeing the people I'd stood shoulder to shoulder with for three years made me very sad. I'd hoped we'd progress all the way to graduation in summer 2003 as a group. The camaraderie had been so real you could touch it. I remembered Danny, back when we were barely even on first-name terms, taking the time to talk me through a potentially year-failing viva. Alex, picking me up and dragging me, kicking and protesting, from the depths of despair. I almost felt as if I'd let them down as much as myself. I'd wanted to march all the way to the finishing line with these people, hug them warmly on graduation day and tell them I couldn't have done it without them. The room next door to Alex, earmarked for me and still empty, served as a poignant reminder that I wouldn't be seeing this process through in the way I had hoped.

Pathology took up most of Monday and irritatingly tiny snatches of Wednesday, Thursday and Friday. It would have been less but pharmacology had been jettisoned into the second year in an attempt to lessen the demands of third year, and pathology had spread out, occupying this new space. It meant I was still blessed with a fair amount of free time and I had a keen sense I should use it productively. Besides, there really was only so much *Kilroy* and *This Morning* a man could stomach without questioning where it had all gone wrong.

So I scoured the Yellow Pages, discovering a vet practice near Speke that dealt in a 50:50 split of exotics and small animals and which agreed to me spending Tuesdays with them. This would be my first genuine stab at seeing practice as a fully fledged vet student. I'd done the Rolf-Harris-on-Animal-Hospital type practice where participation is limited to merely passing helpful comments and looking suitably doleful when patients 'didn't make it'. I became hugely excited as the days counted down. The previous summer had been designated as ushering in the *seeing practice* era. While my erstwhile classmates had been cutting their practice teeth I'd been preoccupied with my doomed re-sit. This year would offer the solace of restoring the balance.

I breezed through the waiting room on my way into the back of the surgery and the assorted exotic menagerie made me breathless with excitement. I nearly tripped headlong down the stairs after dumping my bag, such was my eagerness to get started. When the vet pulled the consulting room door shut behind us there barely seemed room for the two of *us*, let alone the steady stream of assorted humans and pets impatiently reciting their lines backstage. My nostrils were tickled with an aroma that would become synonymous with these sessions; the sweet tang of freshly dispersed disinfectant mixing incongruously with the obstinacy of two-day-old expressed anal glands. The vet busied himself logging on to the computer, filling in gaps in the protocol by absentmindedly sweeping the cat and dog hairs from his grubby tunic.

I sat in on my first consultation, a rabbit afflicted with dental problems, nodding in recognition at familiar snippets of the vet's smooth and winning discourse, delivered calmly, succinctly and without seemingly drawing breath. I could see the client's eyes glaze over occasionally as he lost the thread of the message, but each time the vet painstakingly came back for him, finding slightly different ways to repeat the same facts. I enthusiastically wiped down the table, savouring the sense of usefulness while the vet popped out to put the finishing touches to the client's prescription. I didn't want him to form the opinion I was unappreciative of this opportunity or the type of person liable to do the bare minimum so, in his absence, I took vigorous interest in the monumentally dull, laminated information poster pinned to the wall. I figured that when he came back and saw me utilising this spare time constructively he'd find my enthusiasm most impressive. After 20 minutes of reading about the frankly modest delights of ear canal pathology I was extremely bored and by the time he returned I was merely staring blankly at the poster so he'd at least know I'd read it.

'You should've come through, Scott. Just been stomach tubing a Burmese python. Big bugger. I'd have got you to help if you'd been around.'

I swore quietly to myself. I thought he'd gone off to tinker with the previous client's medication. 'Oh?' I said, trying to mask my deflation. 'Will you be doing it again any time soon?'

'We'll have to see, bugger nearly strangled me.'

I'd been pointlessly reading a stultifyingly dull poster on ear canals over and over again to seem *keen* and missed out on a snake nearly throttling the vet. I could have throttled *myself*. I silently pledged that this would never happen again.

After the next consultation, a rather poor prognosis for a hamster that sported a tumour so voluminous you'd have been removing the hamster from the tumour as opposed to the reverse, the vet glided out of the room without a word. I instinctively went after him. Three paces out of the door he suddenly remembered he'd forgotten something and turned, blundering into me. We did that narrow corridor dance where you jink from side to side to let someone pass you but they synchronise their movements with yours and you end up continually blocking each other, until he squeezed by me in vaguely irritated fashion, picking up a journal from the room. He slipped by me again and I continued my pursuit, this time ensuring there was a discreet distance between us. I shadowed his purposeful gait all the way to the gents, where he turned to close the door behind him, only to see me standing, poised with a notepad and pen in my hands.

'Sorry, I ... umm ... thought you might be stomach tubing another snake.'

He coughed embarrassedly, 'Not in here, the acoustics aren't right' and slammed the door.

The rest of the morning sped by. My only regret was that I'd be stuck in pathology lectures the following day and unable to follow up the cases I was seeing, including a vitamin-deficient African Grey parrot that the two of us wrestled into a towel in order to perform a clinical examination. The dripping blood on my gouged knuckles felt like a badge of honour. It reminded me of my football-playing days when I didn't feel I'd been in a game unless I was caked in mud and the opposition centre-forward had raked his studs down my shins.

'Right. Last case of the morning!'

'OK, it's gone very quickly.'

'Oh.' The vet seemed pleasantly surprised to hear this and thought for a moment. 'Well, good, let's see if we can't involve you a bit more in the proceedings, then, shall we?'

Shit.

'Amber Dempsey is a ten-year-old female spayed golden retriever. The owner has noticed she's been passing small amounts of blood when she urinates. Have a peek at the history and I'll go and fetch her in.'

The client, a middle-aged woman, appeared at the door as the vet opened it. She was dragging an obese and inanimate retriever along the floor, the dog's claws making a scraping noise like nails down a blackboard. With the help of the vet she tugged Amber into the room and squeezed the door shut behind her ample frame. She then repeated exactly what the vet had told me ten seconds previously.

'Any thoughts, Steven?'

61

The client, noticing me for the first time, shifted her gaze and fixed me with an expectant glare.

'From the history...' I began, nervously, 'I see Amber has quite a long history of bladder infections. I think we might be seeing a recurrence of this ... of this...' *Why did the words always escape me at times like this?* 'Condition!'

'Good! I agree! Treatment?'

'Antibiotics!' I declared, feeling the hard part had been done.

'Antibiotics? *Antibiotics?* This time next year you'll be doing written finals!'

No I won't, I'm only a third year!

'*What* antibiotic?'

'Ampicillin?'

'Ampicillin's as good a one as any!'

He left the consulting room to put the client's prescription together and I breathed a massive sigh of relief. Mrs Dempsey began fussing with her dog's collar to pass the time and I put my hands in my pockets and pretended to gloss over Amber's history on the screen, blowing out my cheeks. Our eyes met and the awkward silence broke.

'Training are you?'

'Yes. I'm a third year.'

'Ooh very good. Which one are you at?'

'Liverpool.'

'Ah. A woman in my calligraphy class has a niece at Cambridge. Jill, I think she's called ... or Gillian? Jill or Gillian?' She looked enquiringly at me.

'Sorry, I don't think I know her. There's upwards of a hundred people in our year alone.'

'Ooh my! Long time isn't it? Seven years.'

'It's actually five.'

'Oh is it?' She looked at me doubtfully as if sizing up whether or not to believe me. 'Still longer than a doctor, though.'

'I think it's about the same.'

'Mmm-hmm, *harder* than a doctor though, isn't it?' She thought for a moment. 'I mean they can't tell you what's wrong can they? Or even say *thanks* at the end.'

We had a parrot ten minutes ago that did!

'No. I know.'

The vet returned with a small childproof bottle of tablets,

interrupting Mrs Dempsey as she was informing me I'd no doubt end up on television like that Trude even though what she did to that poor defenceless kitten was just plain evil. He took her through the treatment regime. 'One tablet. Crushed in food. Twice daily.' As an afterthought he added, 'How are you off for wormers?'

'Yes. You'd better give me some of those, too,' she sighed. The vet slipped out again and Mrs Dempsey began complaining to me in a vaguely reproachful manner. 'The prices they ask for a few tablets! You just seem to charge whatever you bloody like. We come here because I like him, he's always been very good. But the prices...' she shook her head ruefully, seeming to lose the train of her thought. 'You know,' she smiled, brightening considerably, 'my granddaughter is going to become one of you!'

'Really? Brilliant, good for her!'

'Oh God, yes. Loves it, always has. I've bought her *all* the books for it, you know.'

'Fantastic. Has she begun applying to any colleges yet?'

'No!' Mrs Dempsey met this question with a look of utter incredulity, 'She's only six and a half!'

With morning consults drawn to a close, the vet's attention turned to the day's surgical procedures. I felt deeply self-conscious about my lack of manual dexterity and often found these slightly intimidating. On the one hand I wanted to appear keen to help, knowledgeable and capable, but on the other I was mortally afraid of being asked to perform a difficult or impossible procedure or, as was more likely in the early weeks, locate an item integral to the plot. This was in case (a) I didn't have the slightest idea what it was I'd been asked to fetch, I couldn't spell the word, far less picture what the blasted thing might look like, or (b) I'd know what it was I'd been asked to get but couldn't for the life of me find it, irrespective of how many cupboards I'd swing open or drawers I'd pull. The latter's discomfort would often be compounded by the misery of the 'opposites' game. In it a nurse helpfully offered directions to where the desired item resided and I would do the opposite of what she commanded. 'Left-hand cupboard, top shelf. No, *left*-hand cupboard. Top shelf. *Top* shelf.'

From my first Tuesday I was placed on anaesthesia duty; monitoring the heart beat and breathing of a series of surgical patients. The trust that had been placed in me spurred me on, making me strain my ears all the more for the merest hint of a muffled heart beat or wheezing breath. I'd thought the day I'd get to use my shiny new stethoscope would never come. The pristine sheen and fresh-from-the-packet smell were dissipating at long last.

The afternoon wore on and I realised I'd lost the vet again. I stood around, fiddling obsessively with my brand new stethoscope, relishing the sense of achievement on having christened it and getting in the nurses' way as I read more of the helpful posters. For a change of scenery I ventured down to the kennels to check the in-patients, poking my fingers through the wire of the cages and pretending I hadn't seen the glistening globoid cat turd sitting proudly in the litter tray like a cherry on a Bakewell tart.

Gutted that this diversion had eaten up only four minutes since I'd last checked the clock, I caught the eye of the nurse.

'He's consulting now.'

'Oh ... right.'

'Just go in, he won't mind.'

That's easy for you to say, sitting there folding your surgery kits.

I stood uncomfortably outside the consulting room, trying to pick the most opportune moment to butt in on the hushed conversation. I knew I had to move fast because there were nurses milling around and I was getting in their way again. I was concerned it would be construed as rudeness to simply blunder in uninvited. The vet may have been on the brink of bearing bad news. He'd *have* to look upon it unfavourably if I invited myself into the room just as he was on the verge telling old Mr Duggins that Trooper had chewed his last slipper. I took a deep breath and plucked up the courage to sidle, as inconspicuously as possible, into the tiny room. On entering the vet stood up from his stool, shook hands with the client and ushered him out. 'Consults over for the time being, don't look so worried, you didn't miss anything vital.'

Some Tuesdays saw a manic cascade of wonderfully exotic animals and diverse conditions. My eyes would steadfastly refrain from flicking clockwards and I'd be bitterly disappointed when the day drew to a close, knowing I'd have to wait another week to feel this way again. Other days I'd be repetitively updating cases on the computer and see the day I wished I was having flit past me from the next room. Some days I felt like nothing more than a well-meaning hindrance, yearning to be able to press a button and overnight become a crucial member of the practice team. Sometimes I'd feel clued in, intuitively doing everything asked of me and hungrily baying for more. Gradually I became more surefooted in this alien environment. Improvement came in the form of weekly reductions in the number of avoidable mistakes I'd make, of being asked to do more and having to seek assistance less. The beauty of the experience was the manner in which lecture material dovetailed with what I was seeing in practice. These tiny, mesmeric glimpses of the holistic nature of veterinary medicine kept me going back each week.

The first Tuesday I didn't attend was the last week of term and I spent it gleefully racing through my pathology paper. I'd relented at long last and been afforded an extra forty-five minutes on account of my arthritic hand. I couldn't help grinning to myself as I finished 15 minutes early in an exam for the first time in my career as a vet student. As I mulled over whether or not I dare leave early, my mind pictured the state I'd been in this time last year and I shivered, despite the fetid sweatiness of the exam hall. I reflected on how I felt a different person from the one who'd fallen apart twelve months previously. This year had been so rich, allowing me to take stock of my condition and face up to my limitations. It had loosened me up sufficiently to feel confident facing the now inevitable grapple with 4 am checks and out of hours duty that lay a little way down the line.

The most valuable lessons are often the most painful and I'd been starkly reminded of how far I should push my arthritic body in the early weeks of January. Paul and I took to spending Thursday afternoons playing football in the local park. It allowed me to rekindle my love of goalkeeping and gave Paul shooting practice prior to matches for the vet first-eleven on Saturdays. He wasn't a vet but living in vet houses for three years had granted him special dispensation to beaver away tirelessly in the vet midfield. I knew the moment he asked that it was beyond me, but yet ... I couldn't resist it. The lure of the dressing room, the pre-match banter, the smell of Ralgex, the clacking of metal studs on concrete giving way to the spongy resistance of grass. I missed playing. I wanted to be the same as everybody else. So, against my better judgement, I agreed. During the warm-up Paul fired a barrage of close-range shots at me and in clawing the last one to safety I fell heavily in the sanded goalmouth, dislocating my right shoulder. Paul kindly accompanied me to the Royal. I'd learnt a valuable lesson about not pushing my body too far. It was a warning I'd sadly fail to heed on upcoming clinical rotations.

The clock ticked down so slowly it almost seemed to be going backwards. I wondered, idly, what the end of exam celebrations would be like this year. Last year, fearing the worst, I'd retreated to the sanctity of home, battle weary and pinched with concern. I'd spent the weekend reading James Herriott books in the garden, washing the unpalatability down with extra-cold Guinness. Today was still only Wednesday. I'd need to wait until Friday to enjoy the festivities, as the rest of my year still had infectious diseases and parasites exams to sit. I'd make do with a night in front of the Champion's League final. It didn't seem to matter. I was relishing the novelty of a trauma-less hike up the vet school ladder and anyway celebrating had come to mean less and less as the year had gone on. In an attempt to maximise methotrexate's pharmacokinetics I'd been persuaded to give up alcohol. I'd found the oxymoron of being a teetotal vet student strangely liberating. Often in the past I'd sought oblivion to deal more comfortably with socialising, but with this mask now off-limits I became more confident.

I only ever once bemoaned my sobriety that year. At extremely short notice back in late January I'd been asked by my old year to address the haggis at the annual Leahurst Burns Night. The only kilt I'd been able to lay my hands on was that of the year's quasi-Scot, Bob Cartwright. Born and bred just outside Birkenhead, he may have had a 32-inch waist like me but at only five foot two he was significantly shorter than my six-foot frame. The only true 'pudden' on show that night was me. I donned a kilt so criminally minuscule that it instantly ruled out any queries about Scottish authenticity. I crossed my legs and recited Rabbie Burns in gabbled fashion to a raucous dance hall, necking Red Bull in the pretence it was Grouse and chopping wildly at the much maligned delicacy with a butcher's knife. That night probably marked the first time I actually felt I belonged in the year.

'OK, put your pens down.'

I gathered up my pen, pencil and rubber and made my way down the stairs with the other members of the year who had stuck it out to the bitter end of their additional time. Mrs Armitage, who'd presided over my implosion the previous year and who'd religiously cast a protective eye over me the second time around, took my question paper from me and offered a smile, tentative and hopeful. 'How did you find that Steve? Added time helpful?'

'Yes, I'd like to think I did OK. Wouldn't have liked not having that time, would've got seriously fraught at the end.'

'Well, best of luck'

Third year had finally been vanquished and with it went my sense of dismay about having buckled under the pressure the year before. In one of my last actions as a third year I had a meeting with Ron Jackson, the vet in charge of welfare at Leahurst, and sought very deliberate assurances that neither my safety nor my ability to receive fair assessments would be impaired once the clinical years began. I explained how some days my manual dexterity was poor and if my knees were bad, kneeling was a no-go. He allayed my fears, promising to communicate with all my superiors on rotation to tell them of my predicament and to formulate a document expressing my point of view. My position was quite simple; I wanted to be given the opportunity to do as much as was humanly possible but was keen that an inability to perform certain tasks wouldn't be construed as a lack of enthusiasm. I also wanted firm assurances that when it came to exams, practical or otherwise, my disability would always be taken into account.

It felt as if all the threads were being drawn together. Summer was well and truly here and I was ready for what clinical rotations would throw at me. All I'd needed was a little extra practice.

11

Please Don't Eat Me

I pointed my panting Fiesta at the M6. It chugged laboriously south, laden with all my worldly possessions. The four-and-a-half-hour drive was punctuated by my mobile, butting obtrusively into pauses in the music to register receipt of a raft of text messages. Danni was doggedly pushing my buttons. I'd decided, after a particularly uncomfortable end of the year ball, to leave her summer's queries unanswered.

It had all begun harmlessly enough. I'd taken myself off to the pathology lab to wile away a quiet pre-exam afternoon tinkering with a selection of slides. Danni, as fate would have it, had had the same idea and took her seat opposite me in the laboratory. We had the place to ourselves and relieved the boredom of a singularly unrewarding afternoon's drudgery by chatting throughout. Her ill-disguised discomfort with a subject I'd had the best part of two years to get my head around put me in the novel position of being able to talk her through some of the topic's finer points. The fact that I found her mildly attractive just made the job easier on my part.

We swiftly made these sessions a regular occurrence, synchronising our arrival at the lab to ensure we'd always get to sit together. This continued right up to and including the successful negotiation of our exam(s) as well as the deliriously unhinged post-exam night out that followed. Skirting the thorny issue of Martin, Danni's long-term boyfriend back at home, we spent the business end of the evening deeply engrossed in conversation upstairs in The Blue Angel club. This flirtation with danger made me giddy with excitement; my head may have been in heaven but my fingers were in the mire. We came within a whisker of kissing, swept chaotically from the path of logic, pulling away only from the very brink.

The tension continued to build. There was a series of clandestine meetings in which she'd constantly confide that her boyfriend didn't understand her the way I did. As the six weeks of fourth year drew to a stuttering close I began to feel emotionally emptied by our involvement. There were a number of occasions on which Martin would visit, accompanying us all on vet nights out. I'd struggle in vain to drag my eyes from them, irrespective of how painful it was seeing them together. If anything, her habit of leaning into me to whisper that I was her soulmate, Martin unhearing and oblivious on the other arm, made these nights even more distressing. However prickly and incompatible they appeared, the end of the night would invariably see the two of them depart hand in hand. I felt more and more as if I were merely her substitute boyfriend. Essentially inferior, I would be beckoned over and pressed into action whenever work commitments resulted in Martin being unavailable for selection.

Feeling short-changed and disposable I took my grumbling misgivings into a summer ball at which they were both present. I spent an unappetising dinner dipping in and out of anodyne conversation and fiddling distractedly with my salmon en croute and brick-hard new potatoes. With the plates cleared I was then joined by both of them at the bar. After a while Martin loped off to the toilet.

'Steve, you really don't seem your usual self tonight, is everything all right? You look great in that tux, by the way, most handsome.'

'Yeah, right.' I acted as if I hadn't heard the last remark and stuck to the script. 'It's just nights like these, I suppose. They make me wish I had a girlfriend. You know, someone to share things with, someone to go home with at the end of the night and wake up with in the morning. You know the sort of thing...'

'Oh,' she looked troubled, and thought for a moment. 'I'd hate it if you got a girlfriend.'

I didn't know whether to laugh or cry. 'Explain.'

'Because it'd mean you paying *me* less attention.'

'You seem to cope all right, juggling the boyfriend and the *attention* as you call it,' I snapped, bristling with pent-up emotion.

'Yes,' her eyes were beyond me and I could tell Martin was returning. I realised it was an impossible situation. She *seemed* to be playing me for a fool but what if she genuinely did harbour strong feelings for me? Supposing she did leave him for me?

They'd been together for *four years*. I caught a disturbing glimpse of what life would be like on the other side. Danni and I an item, gamely attempting to conduct our relationship in the maelstrom of vet school; her retreating home as an escape from the burden of stress, nestling into the sanctity of a 'just old friends' drink in the village pub with Martin. The shoe would well and truly be on the other foot, with all of *my* foibles getting an airing. Our, admittedly brief, history provided me with very little confidence in her ability to show any kind of loyalty to whomever she happened to be with at the time. For my own sanity and personal safety I decided it would be for the best if I extricated myself, forthwith, from this deeply dysfunctional love triangle. Not responding to Danni's increasingly demanding texts over the summer struck me as a good start.

As I'd had two years in which to see third year's requisite six weeks' practice, I began the summer break in the enviable position of having completed my quota. The main crux of my experience had been slanted heavily towards the small animal side of things, as farm and equine practice were traditionally far more physically testing; I'd winced my way through a gruelling week of each, reaching the summer having successfully evaded the radar of the Clinical Studies office. I may have jumped through *those* hoops but two more in the shape of a week in an abattoir and a week in a laboratory lay ahead. Most students were omitting these from their programmes until Christmas of fourth year or beyond, but I had time on my hands and felt it made good sense to get them over and done with.

I found an abattoir within daily driving distance from my parents' house, on an industrial estate on the outskirts of Guildford. I was keen to be spared blood on my hands, literal *and* metaphorical, reiterating to anyone who'd listen that it'd only be a week of observation. It became harder to maintain this fanciful façade when a letter offering confirmation of my dates arrived complete with the request for a doctor's note testifying as to my fitness for a week's abattoir work. A week on carcase duty, dismembering sheep and brushing up on liver fluke spotting skills now appeared ominously likely. There had been a suggestion that a guy in my year, Jack, who'd go on to become my nextdoor neighbour at Leahurst, would

70

be seeing practice there at the same time. My mood was not improved on turning up for my first day and being informed by one of an indeterminate number of Spaniards that Jack wouldn't be coming along after all. 'We already have two ah *estudiantes*,' he communicated in heavily accented English. When it became apparent the second amigo was a vet student from Cambridge with only a morning's practice to see, thereby leaving me alone for the rest of the week, I was one seriously disgruntled *estudiante*.

I stood in uncomfortable silence with the Official Veterinary Surgeon, Pedro, at the back entrance of the building. Within twenty minutes, fifteen hundred one-year-old lambs had been unloaded with military precision. We waded into a sea of bouncing lambs, inspecting them for any obvious ailments that would render them unfit for human consumption. They butted, nibbled and nuzzled us as we flexed limbs in the search for overt lameness and kept an eye out for the merest hint of neurological disorder. My mind kept replaying excerpts from the episode of *The Simpsons* where Lisa becomes a vegetarian, Homer rebuking her at the Sunday dinner table, 'What are you talking about, Lisa? This is *lamb*. Not *a* lamb.'

Seeing the multitude of distinct personalities milling around, bleating curiously as to their whereabouts, was deeply affecting. I felt traitorous and queasy; smiling disingenuously as I encouraged lambs up the ramp to what I knew would be their certain death. Somewhere along the line I'd need to cease seeing them as individuals and view them as commodities. But at which point along the line would that happen? Would it be when electric voltage was passed through their skulls, filling the air with the pungent stench of melting brain? Would it be when, paddling reflexively, they had the main arteries to their brain severed and were hung, dripping profusely, onto overhead hooks? When first the head and then the hooves were hacked off? Gutting? My head swam.

I continued my passage through the building, splashing through puddles of blood and clinging strands of viscera. Clanking machinery competed throatily with blaring radios. I found what I'd been looking for. A crate of choice cuts of meat. Wrapped in cellophane, priced up and ready for shipping. *That* was my commodity. I wasn't speaking as a militant vegetarian barking 'meat is murder' at the very whiff of a bacon sandwich. I adore meat, lamb especially. But I knew the next time I swallowed a bite-size chunk of lamb roast I'd also have to swallow what I'd seen here today. It wasn't an issue of humaneness. As far as I could make out, each and every process was carried out in total accordance with appropriate legislation. The lambs all seemed to have been adequately stunned prior to slaughter. Their holding area wasn't overcrowded and all the animals appeared relatively calm and unstressed. It was just the futility of their brief existence that stuck in my throat. Was this what they were brought into the world for? I remembered my lambing experiences in the first year, how I'd collapsed, sweating and invigorated, next to a recumbent ewe, her newborn lamb blinking wide-eyed on the straw next to us. Was this why I'd fought for 40 minutes delivering her?

At the end of the day I might have been on the brink of beginning my fourth year at vet school but I'd always purposefully shied away from looking too closely at this end product of the farming industry. This experience was utterly necessary. I needed to rid myself of this sentimentality. Questioning the point of the existence of farm animals really was faintly ludicrous. On rotation next year I'd be actively perpetuating a cycle that, by definition, would always include this unavoidable link in the chain of life. If I didn't clear my head, this course would eat me alive. I took this newly found depreciation of life into my second and final placement of the summer; a week at a major veterinary laboratory.

I'd always thought the laboratory placement was a week in name alone. From the year above I'd gathered that a generally low-key approach could be assumed. I turned up on the Monday morning expecting possibly one solid day's aggressive pipetting before bidding the kind lab folk a hearty farewell. It therefore came as something of a surprise to be presented with a meticulously devised week-long timetable. *None of the people I listened to can have chosen a VLA centre for their week*, I reflected grimly, perusing the week's delights. I was despatched to the neuropathology department and thrust into a series of research programmes concerning the long-term effects of scrapie and BSE in cattle and sheep. I spent the whole of the Monday hunched forward on a shoogly stool peering at screeds of histological slides of brain smears. The motion-sickness-inducing eight-hour trawl left a legacy that haunted me all the way home that evening; each time I blinked at the wheel of my car, blobs of light engulfed me. It felt as if my *own* brain had been indelibly stained with iridescent viewing medium.

72

This world in motion was replaced by a new order the following morning. I clambered into a white van and set out with a project leader and an assistant to a holding area at the far end of the sprawling compound. It housed six one-year-old bull steers that had been artificially infected with BSE in order that the disease progression could be scrutinised along with prognoses for palliative or curative measures. The one-ton steers were released at one end of a long barn with a sloping roof. I stood at the other and watched with wide-eyed alarm as the steers came bucking and barrelling down the barn towards me, careering madly into each other. I had visions of a Steve-shaped smear on the wall, my remains scraped off with a spatula and delivered to my grieving and uncomprehending parents in a manila envelope. Once these galloping, lolloping steers had been assessed neurologically and had blood samples taken, two of them were taken up to the autopsy facility, euthanased and dissected. I had never seen such precise autopsy and organ removal in my life. There was a piece of paper pinned to the wall listing items that included adrenal glands (left and right), nodose ganglion and mesenteric lymph nodes. Watching the staff in action reminded me of footage showing piranhas stripping a body of flesh, except that this eclectic swarming spawned a crate of small glass bottles full of vital organs.

The sudden transition from live animal to carcase brought back memories of my previous week at the abattoir. I knew I had to dissociate myself from the perceived morality of what I was seeing. Does the vet for whom fox hunting is complete anathema refuse to mend the splint-bone fracture on the huntsman's prized gelding? Does the vet ethically opposed to zoos refuse to vaccinate jaguars against distemper? I wasn't suggesting for a second that strongly held views should be checked at the door with the wellington boots and Barbour jacket. But I would keep my counsel. The actual *reason* animals require our attention ultimately is completely irrelevant. All that is of prime concern is that they are under our care and as such they deserve our fullest attention. It had been a sanguine experience but I felt I'd emerged fully versed in exactly where my responsibilities lay.

PART TWO

The Clinical Years

12

Institutionalised

I'd never noticed all the fifth years before. All the other times I'd been out to Leahurst I'd maybe caught sight of the odd one, as you did a squirrel when you stroll down the exit road there onto the A540. This was something altogether different. I knew a major part of moving out here was to do my rotations, and subsequently found my attention drawn to the equine yard. I seemed to take almost perverse delight in forcing myself to study fifth years in action. They had a purposeful and strutting, sleeve-rolled gait and a honey glaze of wholesome sweat. Ultra-confident students were marching horses fearlessly across the yard while their colleagues talked at length with owners, jotting down massively truncated histories, nodding intelligently and interjecting with apposite comments of their own. Everyone seemed to know exactly what they were doing and, more significantly, exactly how to do it.

It gradually dawned on me: *this is what is expected of us*. I'd slipped away from unpacking my room in Ritchie House, revelling in a deep sense of achievement in having got so far, but slightly bored and in need of a break from the mundane quest to find a home for everything. It felt to me as if the time had come to return to the boxes. There'd be plenty of time to scare myself rigid about equine rotations in due course.

Fourth year kicked off in the lecture theatre; the fact that it was in a completely *different* lecture theatre from years one through three didn't stop the majority of people unadventurously diving headlong for their usual seats. I'd always plumped for a front-row seat during pathology version 2.0, as I felt it crucial that my attendance could never be called into doubt. From day one Brad very kindly abandoned the nubile young fillies he routinely flirted with on the back row and kept me company in spod row. Now free to go wherever the current took me, I allowed myself to be swept up towards the back by Jamie, his girlfriend Miranda, and another girl, Hannah. A week of 'Cattle' had been timetabled.

'You wouldn't think there'd be much more than a week of cattle *in total*. How much can there still be left to cover after that?'

'No, mate. Not really sure.' Jamie looked up uncertainly from his furious scribbling, unsure whether I was joking or not. I was relieved I'd gravitated towards the back of the theatre. The lecturer, Dr Bennett, seemed to harbour an unhealthy fixation with making the session as interactive as possible and was haranguing the front three rows. I had absolutely no idea which word or phrase he was trying to wrest from their lips and hoped he wouldn't come delving in my direction for the answer. His twenty-minute opening address had seen him say 'heefers' when he meant 'heifers' and 'yows' when he meant 'ewes'. I'd been laughing so much to myself at this that I'd become detached from his meanderings an age ago.

'Well, let me put it to you,' he pontificated, 'that if the URDP *can, indeed*, have a *huge influence* on diet. Then, ladies and gentlemen, is it *not possible* to then be open to the suggestion that . . .'

I nudged Jamie, restless and uninterested in where this rambling nonsense was going, 'URDP? Why on earth would a Northern Irish political party even *care* what cows ate for their dinner?'

'Undigested rumen degradable protein, mate,' he replied, his writing hand not drawing breath.

I sighed, 'Yeah, I knew that,' and shifting uncomfortably in my seat gave the lecture theatre a quick sweep with my eyes. Surely I couldn't be the only one losing the will to live? I seemed to have spent my whole life in lecture theatres being droned at by men in beards who always wore socks and sandals. Prior to my zoology degree I'd done a two-year HND and basically this meant I was now in my tenth straight year of life at university. Thankfully there were only seven weeks of lectures before the first rotation (in my case small animal) began. I needed an existence that didn't involve sitting confined in narrow seats and being told what to write down and what to think.

Dr Bennett finished trying to coax words or phrases from people and we filed out of the lecture theatre for lunch. His feeling had been that we were jaded and needed to mull over the subtleties of nutrition at lunch before reconvening at two to ruminate further on the topic. I'd decided to spend the afternoon reading our cattle nutrition notes in my room. As I'd previously spent three years with the then fifth year, I chatted freely with them on the subject and many verified my assertion that these chaotic interactive sessions were often largely unproductive. It was as if the year above took on the guise of wise old jailbirds, winking conspiratorially as they slipped us invaluable tips on how to see our time out as smoothly as possible. Living at Leahurst could seem even more like incarceration in a minimum security prison at meal times; we'd stand in line, tray in hand and await the doling out of bowlfuls of steaming, unappetising slop. And, of course, when we weren't occupied with any of Leahurst's daily activities programmes, we could generally be found holed-up in our cell-sized rooms; breeze-block walls plastered with posters of movie starlets interspersed with poignant snaps of loved ones.

Of course it would be wrong to paint a wholly negative picture of life at Leahurst. Having a large number of the year living on site created a wonderful camaraderie and it was very reassuring only to have to walk ten feet to ask one of your mates about a piece of work that was bothering you. I knew that once rotations began in earnest, and we were being asked to compile presentations on specific cases, you wouldn't be able to put a price on such a support system. Add in a 24-hour bar, for which you simply tallied up your drinks on a notepad and wrote a cheque at the end of the month, and a mouthwatering array of parties which, at long last, meant the rest of vet school came to us instead of the opposite, and you can see that it really wasn't a bad life.

Moving into Leahurst seemed with one hand to broaden our horizons, delivering passage into a vast and challenging uncharted territory and constructing circles of friends that could, at times, seem indestructible. Meanwhile, the other made a fist, squeezing the limits of our existence until it was almost as if Leahurst's grey perimeter fence represented the very boundaries of the free world. Despite grave reservations about the onset of rotations, I was grateful to be going over the wall soon.

13

Midnight is Where the Day Begins

'Fancy going over to the bar, Jacko? God only knows when we'll next be free.' It was nine o'clock on Sunday evening and after conscientiously ironing my week's quota of shirts, even waving the iron quickly over my lab coat, I was at a loose end.

'Can't, mate. I'm on call.'

'Rotations don't start 'til tomorrow, dopey!'

'Equine started last night, so *dopey* yourself and there's...' he broke off as his phone went. I remained standing in the corridor with my head stuck round his door, in a quandary as to what to do next. As it was the call ended abruptly and he leapt from his bed. 'Colic's coming in! Ten minutes, tops!'

'Can't believe you've started, already.' I shook my head.

'Why not come along? Got to be useful for when *you're* on equine.'

He had a point. I hopped into my overalls, dug my stethoscope from my neatly packed bag and marched along the side of Ritchie House to the equine yard with Jack. I loved the feeling of importance as we purposefully strode out to meet an emergency head on. When we got there the horse was already kicking wildly in stocks and sweating profusely. A whole entourage of students had had the same idea as me and I deliberately hung back as Jack fought his way through to take the gelding's temperature. A member of staff was barking very precise orders at the on-call students and I found it most disquieting that they all seemed to know exactly what to do. *Would it be like that when I was on?* She then began randomly assigning jobs to the observing, non-equine students and I suddenly caught an image of myself messing up some task or other and failing equine before I'd even officially started. I winked at Jack

80

as he wiped a dollop of shit from his thermometer and slipped away murmuring to myself 'and so it begins...'

Rotations had seen the year split, initially, into three equal parts; section A, section B and section C. The first rotation had duly arrived and all the section A people were bundled off to equine. Farm animal got the section B crew and C, to which I belonged, were designated as small animal people. In the early spring I'd move on to equine (gulp!), section A would be on farm and B would fill in on small animal; hence the term *rotation*. There would be two separate three-week stints in each of the three disciplines and in every one of the 18 weeks students would be assigned to a specific component of each; equine orthopaedics, farm reproduction, small animal dermatology and cardiology or whatever. These would, essentially, take us all the way up to the Christmas of fifth year and written finals. By which point, the theory went, enough cases should have been worked up and enough tutorials and presentations sat through to make us as ready as we were ever going to be.

Each third was then further split into smaller, more manageable sixes and sevens, in order to slot comfortably into whichever activity they'd been assigned. The draw for this was as eagerly awaited as the one for any World Cup I could remember. The Friday afternoon before we were due to start rotating, group listings were posted on the noticeboard. Surprisingly the draw had been pretty kind to me, steering me away from some of the more potentially troublesome opponents. I'd been assigned to the following team: Matt, a good-natured guy and astoundingly good goalkeeper, was someone I'd got on well with the handful of times we'd chatted. Then there was Megan, the *other* Scottish person at vet school, save for a foaming-at-the-mouth Aberdonian genetics professor with whom neither of us ever really associated. Next came Sophie and Natalie. All I knew about them was that when Brad wasn't expressing solidarity with recently acquainted re-sitting housemates, he'd generally join *them* for lectures in the back row. The sixth and final member of our group was Georgia. I'd only really had one encounter with her and it had been at the ball at the end of the previous term. She'd been a comedy drunk and had pursued me all around the interior of the marquee, madly zigzagging around tables and tripping over concealed folds in the tarpaulin. She eventually cornered me at the far end of the tent and, in a hiccupping impersonation of Clarence the cross-eyed lion, slurred lasciviously,

'It'd just be *rude* to turn me down now.' Such was her state that night that I felt fairly confident she'd have little or no recollection of dangling so tempting an offer before me. Or of my tacit refusal, rude or otherwise.

Our triumvirate of small animal topics were scheduled to begin with one week of general medicine, moving into a second week concentrating on soft tissue surgery cases and signing off with a week learning the tricks of the anaesthesia trade. That final week would have the added difficulty of also being the one in which Matt and I had elected to do our out-of-hours cover in the small animal hospital. This necessitated relocation to the micro-flat above the hospital and the three-person team contained therein would provide out-of-hours medical care for all the in-patients as well as being on duty in the event of any emergencies being admitted. Some students decided the best time to tough this one out was during the holidays, seeing practice in the hospital during the day. Matt and I fostered the opinion that living in the hospital for a week *during* rotation would not only spare us the horrors of twice daily tunnel traffic but also confer greater familiarity with the in-patients, which simply *had* to facilitate their after-care. It was a cunningly conceived plan but one which had failed to take into account that by week three Matt and I would be more or less dead on our feet.

We lined up in the corridor. I'd always pictured myself on the small animal rotation with my stethoscope draped rakishly around my neck in a manner reminiscent of Carter in *ER*. That lasted right up until I caught sight of our year's assorted Dr Greenes, Bentons and Elizabeth Cordays preening themselves and secretly smouldering at their own reflections when they thought no one was looking. *Possibly not, then.* I stuffed my stethoscope into my lab coat pocket as we stood idling in the corridor. Dr Britton strode over. There was a wad of client files wedged under his arm as he hurriedly tucked his shirt into his trousers.

'Right. At 9.20 there's a dog with chronic diarrhoea coming in, who fancies that?'

Oh me please. Do send it this way; I absolutely adore dogs that just shit everywhere.

Natalie politely surveyed our mute group, checking no one's toes were on the point of being stepped on and promptly volunteered for the first case. Sophie and Megan also booked themselves cases that were due to come in at 10 and 10.20 respectively. I didn't want to be the only one without a case and one glance at Georgia, poised like a coiled spring to my left, suggested she was of a similar mind. I flexed my hand, keen to be quicker on the draw.

'At 12 we have Candy Robertson coming in, she's PU/PD; don't know much else.'

'Can I have that one please?' Georgia and I mouthed the same words simultaneously, but as I was closer Dr Britton heard me first and nodded in affirmation.

'Good. Come and find me at half eleven and I'll brief you.'

'Great, thanks for that!' I smiled, reaching for the file.

'No, they need this at reception,' the impatient tone of his voice implying I should have guessed that was how they did things around here. 'You can check the history at half eleven with me.'

'Oh. OK.' I demurred, feeling vaguely foolish and hoping the gaffe hadn't cost me valuable assessment points. I spent the hour and a half before the Robertsons' arrival sitting in with the rest of the team on Natalie, Sophie and Megan's consults. I prayed that by the time my turn came to the face the public they'd all be way too busy to eavesdrop.

'Come in, Steve. Now, Candy's *not* a particularly well dog. It isn't a great outlook for her to be honest but we'll admit her, possibly run some tests, depending on what you think, and see if we can't make her more comfortable. I'd be surprised if we'll be able to do much concrete but, again, it depends on what the tests show. Anyway go downstairs and meet them, find an empty consulting room and discuss the progression of Candy's condition with the owners. Don't worry, they're very nice. Take a good, concise history, give her a thorough clinical exam and then admit Candy. Then come and find me. I want a list of your differential diagnoses plus a list of the tests, if any, you feel it might be worth our while running. OK? I'll be up here writing some reports if you need me.' He snapped the conversation shut like a tightly hinged briefcase.

'Umm, OK.' I couldn't think of any specific questions to ask and turned to leave, a thoughtful if somewhat pained expression painted across my face. *I wish the others were around.*

'Candy Robertson, please?'

I led a middle-aged couple and their desperately sick animal wrapped like a papoose in a blanket in the direction of a consulting room. Candy was a strikingly attractive six-month-old cocker spaniel puppy that just seemed to have given up the fight. Her owners already appeared resigned to losing her, although Mr Robertson allowed himself a tormenting sliver of hope and placed a firm hand on my shoulder. 'We just want to get to the bottom of this and then, well, we'll see...'

'Well, she's in the best possible place.' I caught his eye, desperately straining to catch wisps of Candy's thready heart beat with my stethoscope. She struck me as being dangerously anaemic. Despite the gravity of her condition she wagged her tail and affectionately licked at my fingers.

'Heartbreaking isn't it?' I found myself saying. 'At this age they should be chewing your slippers, driving you insane. They shouldn't be ... like this'

'I know, doctor, I know.'

I established that Candy had been urinating excessively for six to eight weeks, hadn't eaten a proper meal for as long as the Robertsons could remember and had highly irregular lung and heart sounds. My gut instinct was that Candy was in kidney failure but I silently prayed it was something with a more favourable prognosis. A persistent bladder infection, perhaps. It was the anaemia, the lack of blood, which really bothered me.

'Do your best for her son.' Mrs Robertson smiled as a single tear trickled down her ashen face.

'If anything *at all* can be done I promise you we'll do it.' I gave her a disconsolate smile, feeling hopeless and cumbersome and cursing myself for the lump that was forming in my throat. 'I...' I coughed, fighting to regain my composure, 'I'll call you later on, regardless of what's happening, and let you know how she is.' They both smiled sadly at me and left hand in hand, supporting each other against the bright autumn chill.

Not long after they'd left, Dr Britton prepared the treatment room for taking a blood sample and I went into the kennels to fetch Candy. As I entered I almost tripped over a kneeling Natalie as she was mopping a freshly hosed floor with flattened sheets of blue roll. Her patient with the sprinkler system attached to its anus had sprayed everything within a five-foot radius, for the third time that day.

'Toby been bad again, Nat?'

'How'd you guess?' she puffed, looking up briefly. 'Anyway, what are you up to?'

'About to take blood from Candy, my six-month-old spaniel and possibly scan her kidneys in a day or so,' I said, hauling her emaciated form from the kennel and holding her against my warm body.

'She doesn't look too good.'

'No. I know,' I sighed, as Candy gently whimpered and shrank into me with all her pitiful strength.

Dr Britton's rhetoric had led me to believe I'd be taking Candy's blood sample but one look at the virtually non-existent circulation in her leg vein made him clip up her jugular area and take a decidedly miserly sample himself. I was shown which forms to fill in and Candy's blood was sent off for analysis.

The blood results were posted back two days later and were hugely suggestive of chronic kidney failure. With a sinking feeling we took her into diagnostic imaging to ultrasound her kidneys. Unfortunately this bore desperately bad news. The scan delivered brief but unequivocal images of kidney architecture totally nondescript in appearance and lacking even the slightest tubular differentiation. Candy's limp frame failed to offer the tiniest amount of resistance as the scanner was repeatedly pushed up and down her bony hind quarters. She tamely rolled her head, searching for a comforting face amidst all the unfamiliarity and upheaval. I played with her lolling ears and she thumped her stumpy tail against the work top. It seemed irrefutable that Candy was afflicted with a particularly severe congenital kidney disorder which was incompatible with life.

'Steve, take Candy back will you. I need to talk to the owners.'

My heart sank. 'OK...' I began, unsure of what to say or do next. I'd been phoning the owners each night as promised and wanted to stay true to my word. I tenderly placed a sluggish Candy back in her kennel and brightened when I saw Natalie, still cleaning.

'Same spillage or a fresh one?'

'Fresh one, the little bastard...'

In the interim I helped Matt replace the catheter in his patient's leg; a fourteen-year-old male cat called Frodo that had lymphoma. The adrenaline buzz I got from being entrusted with the treatment and welfare of patients kept me from seizing up arthritically despite the length of the days and my constant footsore traipsing all around the hospital. The joints in my feet would invariably begin to flare up around two or three o'clock each day. I would smother their inflamed complaining with extra steroid tablets, figuring there'd be two weeks of post-rotation lectures in which to be kind to myself. There would be plenty of scope for limiting my movements then, if need be. It struck me as churlish to scrimp on effort, especially as we had cases requiring urgent and prolonged attention *and* we were being assessed. Dr Britton poked his head around the treatment room door. 'Steve, Candy's owners have arrived. Bring her along to consult room two, will you?'

'Come on, sweetheart. Not long now.' I gathered Candy up in my arms and carried her near lifeless form through the maze of corridors to the front of the building. Dr Britton was waiting outside the consulting room for me. I could see the Robertsons through the vertical strip of glass in the door, huddled together in the small, impersonal room.

'Good,' he said. 'Best if I do this alone. It's going to be upsetting for the owners.' He relieved me of Candy's imperceptible weight without even looking at me.

'D'you not want me to come in too?' I asked, already knowing the response but needing to satisfy myself that at least I'd asked.

'Best not,' he frowned, appearing irritated I hadn't accepted his taking over of my case with good grace. He pulled the door shut in my face.

I didn't know the accepted protocol. It was still early days. What I *did* know was that Candy had been *my* patient the whole three days she'd been in hospital. For that reason I felt I should have been inside with them all, not languishing outside in the corridor while Dr Britton recounted the little tales I'd told in rounds about how good-natured she'd been. He hadn't found that out for himself. I turned and slunk away. I hadn't even got a chance to say goodbye to her. I was probably being overly sentimental, getting far too attached to my cases. I thought that was the whole point, though. That we did care.

Later on during evening rounds each student delivered a succinct appraisal of their cases to the hospital's battalion of clinicians and I bit my tongue. This was the crucial embryonic stage of only my first rotation; I couldn't afford a reputation as a trouble-maker. Rounds ended and Matt and I drove back in grim and stony silence, sweeping through charcoal streets that still seeped with a day's accumulated rainfall. As was so often the case, the condition of our patients was reflected in our mood. Matt's lymphoma cat wasn't responding particularly well to treatment and he sat lost in thought as I fumbled for change at the toll. It was after half past eight by the time we finally pulled into the sodden Leahurst car park. During the previous seven weeks the bar had featured some or all of the usual suspects most nights, but since rotations had begun it sat deserted and in total darkness.

All the other small animal commuters had long since returned to Leahurst and dined, a fact made plain as only Matt's and my dinners sat untouched and cling-filmed on the shelf. I was too hungry to bother microwaving my watery casserole and scoffed it cold with a piece of bread despite the insipid gravy and soapy mashed potato. We tugged at the day's injustices and as we did I could feel the knots of stress unravel. This became an indispensable panacea to the chaos and uncertainty that governed so much of life on rotation. Our deliberations were halted occasionally by lone equine students on call drifting indoors during short lulls in their punishing agenda. I listened with only half an ear. We would nurse steaming mugs of tea in the dimly lit, half-empty dining room and trade tales of hardship like First World War Tommies stationed at different garrisons on the Western Front.

At rounds the following morning I presented Candy Robertson's details for one last time even though she'd been dead nearly sixteen hours. They drew to a close, signifying the true start of the day but without a case I felt like a gambler without any chips. I needed to get back in the game. I took the next case that came in; a three-year-old female spayed shih tzu called Misty that had a long history of intermittent vomiting. Dr Britton filled ten minutes taking me through a potted history of the vast array of conditions that could result in these symptoms. He concluded by stressing how imperative a concise and detailed history would be. I felt heartened by the fact I'd been viewed as fit for such a tricky and involved case and strolled emboldened towards reception to meet the Arnolds. En route I bumped into Matt and swiftly relayed the details of my impending new case.

'Any tips, Matty?'

'One. Roll your sleeves up!'

'What? Why?'

'It's Friday. Our last day on medicine. When they think back to us while they're doing our assessments it'll be the last day they'll recall. If they picture you with sleeves rolled up they'll naturally assume you were a hard worker who liked to get stuck in.'

'It's a bit *Miami Vice* but I could do with the marks,' I smiled, rolling up the sleeves of my lab coat to just above the elbows. As it was, Matt had a spare hour before Frodo's next dose of chemotherapy and ended up joining me. Our team had gelled stunningly well. It was on the back of this that all six of us assured one another we'd email the clinical studies office and request to remain together as a group for the next rotation, equine. With the exception of Georgia, and possibly Natalie, we were dreading the unholy rigours of equine. Knowing we'd do both of the three-week toils in a group where people looked out for each other, didn't get lured into the trap of trying to make each other look bad and were, above all else, easy to get on with, was one less thing to worry about.

I sat upstairs in the meeting room and scribbled extensive notes on all my cases for the students landed with being on duty at the weekend as well as the ones on medicine the following week who would be entrusted with their care. There was no point in rushing my task as Matt was downstairs with Frodo's owners, discharging him and I was giving him a lift back. I allowed myself a momentary reflection on how well the medicine week had gone. Despite the throbbing pain in my feet and the occasional need to seek help with fiddly tasks like fine-tuning the valves on intravenous drip bags, I felt I'd acquitted myself reasonably well. I didn't want to rest on my laurels, though, as the next week could easily see all that change. We'd be on soft tissue surgery. This would mean that on at least one occasion I'd be invited to cram my ill-fitting hands into tight latex gloves and push my manual strength and dexterity to its very limits. This week the soft tissue personnel had each done one castration and one spay. There was no escaping the nerves I felt when I imagined myself gowned up and in theatre but I wasn't going to let that troubling image spoil the rest I knew I'd earned this weekend. Just after seven I pulled my car into a space less than five feet from Leahurst bar; its twinkling lights a beacon that lit my way.

* * *

Matt and I may have been wrapped from head to toe in a mummifying ensemble of scrubs, hats and masks but the narrow eye slits afforded enough of a chink of contact for us to convey how impressed we both were. Sophie had taken the plunge first and in one fell swoop elevated the surgical stakes out of reach. The glinting needle holders and forceps were like an extension of her delicately gloved hands. She stitched the eight-month-old Labrador bitch totally unflustered in spite of the six pairs of eyes boring into her handiwork, tracing each loop of nylon with slavish devotion.

'Can't compete with that,' Matt's eyes said.

'Nope. Not a snowball's chance in hell, mate,' mine replied.

The Labrador was wheeled off to recovery. Dr Barclay filled the unplanned hour with a tutorial, detailing the many causes of incontinence. Feeling suitably enlightened, not to mention desperate for the toilet, we were discharged for a twenty-minute break. This week Natalie, along with two other students scattered throughout the other small animal groups, was doing her out of hours duty. Although this sentenced her to seven days' hard labour during which time she'd be horrifically overworked and constantly suffering the nagging effects of sleep deprivation, it was, for the rest of us, something of a bonus. It meant we had the privacy of the flat during the day for coffee breaks and lunch. The others had been held up, leaving the two of us alone upstairs.

'Listen,' I said, half turning as I filled the kettle from a spluttering tap. 'Matt and I are on duty next week, so we'll have the flat all the way through to the end of the rotation.'

Natalie said nothing.

'What's up, Nat? Can't be cream crackered already, it's only Monday!'

'Steve ... it isn't that,' she finally confessed, after a long pause.

'Oh, OK. What's up?'

'We never got a chance to unpack properly yesterday. You know how that Dalmatian came in as an emergency at tea time?'

I nodded, encouraging her to continue.

'Well, we had to stay up with it all the way through to eight this morning until you all got here and now *medicine* have her.'

'Right...' I said, unsure of where she was going with this.

'Mike Nugent's got hold of Chris just now,' she began to cry. 'He said he'd seen the state of the flat and that it was totally unacceptable. He told him that not keeping the flat clean was a serious offence. One that...' she faltered, 'could see an individual or group *fail* their *rotation*!'

'What!' I exploded. 'So the fact it was all hands to the pump last night and you were tending an emergency through 'til dawn is irrelevant here? You don't get thanked for that, instead you get threatened with failing because you *never tidied your room*!' I took a deep breath and thought for a moment. 'I know he's the head honcho, Natalie, but he'd never get away with that.' I placed a mug of tea in front of her. 'Here, drink this.' I could hear raised voices echoing in the stairwell. Sophie entered with Matt, her face still flushed with the heat and success of her surgery.

'You guys read your emails?' Matt inquired, by way of a greeting.

'No,' I said, still picking over the bones of Natalie's revelation.

'Mike's sent an email to the whole year warning us about the state of the flat!' Sophie announced with a flourish. 'He concludes it *if you do not follow this procedure, you will fail.*'

We sat sipping our tea, switching between consoling Natalie and sourly chewing over this latest aberration. There was no doubt the small animal team provided expert tutelage but they had the unfortunate habit of appearing truculent and ungracious, pettily picking holes with bureaucratic zeal.

In terms of numbers of in-patients the soft tissue week ended up as far less demanding than general medicine. Dr Barclay ensured any gaps in our schedule were filled with cadaver work, tirelessly lobbying the dissection room on our behalf and procuring two full sessions at the start of the week. These were spent lugging out three frozen dogs that had had their limbs butchered by first years in anatomy class. In pairs we perfected a selection of specialist surgical procedures. These ranged from eye enucleation to skin transplants and from ear resections to the application of chest drains. I relished these demystifying sessions of victimless surgery and began to believe that maybe I could stay afloat and survive the vet school tempest after all.

My right hand was hurting. The ache, brought on by the day's prolonged usage, came in oscillating waves. I winced and rubbed the inflamed and inarticulate finger joints in between reading Fossum's notes on how to perform an ovariohysterectomy. I'd been earmarked as the next one to go over the knife and wanted to be as prepared as humanly possible. I wasn't sure what made me more nervous; the thought of performing an entire surgical procedure on a living, breathing animal or that I'd be doing so with my five group-mates huddled expectantly around the table, gazing inquisitively at my every botched scalpel stroke and abortive knot throw. As I lay reading on bed I consoled myself that Dr Barclay would be scrubbed in with me, holding my latex-gloved hand. So far this week I'd seen her coax Sophie, Georgia and Natalie through their surgeries, her unflappable tones calmly featuring all the way from first incision through to final knot.

'All set Steven?'

'Yeah, just looking for Sarah.'

'Don't. She's not in today; she's on revision lecturing duty for the fifth year. Finals are in less than a month for them.'

I looked quizzically at Ruth Sanderson, an abrasive Australian one year into a surgical residency.

'You'll be doing your cat spay with me today. Although I say *with me*, I shan't actually be scrubbing in with you. I mean, come on, it's Thursday, you must have seen a heap of these already this week.'

'Would she have scrubbed in if it was Wednesday, then?' I whispered to Matt as she was momentarily distracted by a snatch of clumsy office banter. She pawed at the air in mock irritation, chiding 'Oh you guys!' her accent mangling the vowels beyond recognition.

'You still here?' she asked, turning back to face me. I'd already mentioned my arthritic hands to the head of welfare, Ron Jackson, as well as to Sarah and a smattering of other clinicians. Although I had no confidence that Ruth had been informed of my propensity to struggle with tasks dependent on manual dexterity, I couldn't bring myself to tell yet another person. All I seemed to do these days was spin yarns of excuses and telegraph my limitations to a never-ending line of pseudo-sympathetic members of staff. A tincture of my uncertainty must have permeated her consciousness. 'Natalie have you done one of these this week yet?'

Natalie looked up, sleepy from the soporific warmth of the clinician's office. 'Yes. I did a bitch spay with Sarah on Tuesday.'

'Well, this is a moggy, it'll be easier. Scrub in with Steve! You can each take a horn.' This wasn't what I'd envisaged for the day.

91

We vigorously scrubbed up and backed into the theatre, gowned, gloved, hatted and masked. To our surprise Matt and Megan were already in there, gowned up and deliberating in urgent tones across a draped lump of their own.

'What's under the drapes Matty?' I inquired, my words muffled by the mask.

'A bitch Megan and I are supposed to be spaying together but Ruth has just buggered off and left us. She says the two of you are just to get started, by the way.' He wagged his wrapped head at the clipped and surgically pristine feline spread-eagled on the table. I knew he was smiling at me from under his mask, and I smiled back at him. I made the first incision, recalling my previous evening's homework and leaning heavily on Natalie's helpful promptings.

'Nat, I've got the horn!' I winked triumphantly as I hooked the first ovary. 'Think you'll get it too?' I added.

'All right you guys, sorry I got waylaid.' I hadn't noticed Ruth come in and blushed deeply under my mask and hat. 'You're doin' great!' she cast the briefest of glances at our handiwork as she breezed past to check on the other duo. Natalie and I continued our rummaging; jogging and cajoling each other whenever a surgical impasse was reached. Ruth hovered around the outer fringes of both tables, peripheral enough to drive us to draw the answers from each other, but close enough should anyone stray from the notes and chop through something vital. She edged across, peeking over her trendy half glasses to see what stage we were at. After a moment or so she brusquely recited a monologue of instructions that would take our procedure through to its conclusion. She then exited the theatre, swinging the door shut behind her and wafting in a cool draught that chilled me through my sweat-sodden hat.

'Did you get all that?'

'Pretty much.' I lied, hoping the solution would come to me as we ploughed on. I knew we were nearing the end and sensed that between us we could do this. I screwed up the itchy nose I longed to scratch and switched my weight from one foot to another. When I took a breather from stitching up to allow the sensation to return to my hands, Natalie made a subtle enquiry as to my well-being before taking over from me, with the minimum of fuss. I allowed myself a wry smile. The cutting needle of Damocles had been hanging over me all week and here it was passing without leaving a blemish on my person. I shivered with relief beneath the clammy, sweat-soaked gown. The following day was Friday and I knew no new cases had been booked in. It promised to be a safe and untaxing day devoted to leisurely sifting through radiographs and discharging the previous two days' patients. With the procedure completed I tore off the skin-tight gloves and rolled my sleeves up in readiness.

'Haven't we just left here?'

Matt only grunted in response. It was shortly after three on the Sunday afternoon as we trudged across the windswept car park. Chris and Natalie met us at the door of the hospital, wedging it open as we heaved our week's belongings over the threshold. The incessant yelping from the kennels that filled every pause made my skin crawl. Sunday in the SAH was generally a rather sedate affair. The decks, more often than not, had been cleared in preparation for another manic Monday and the beginning of a week's fresh influx of shitting unfortunates. It therefore augured very badly for this upcoming week that it took close to two hours for Natalie's group to take us through the medical needs of all the in-patients. With the handover finished the three of them scuffed excitedly upstairs to have one last scout around for any errant belongings. Matt and I slowly followed, viewing their unbridled joy pensively. Satisfied nothing had been left behind, they kindly gave us their mobile numbers before almost falling over themselves to leave the flat, fighting and jostling their way down the winding staircase. Matt and I just looked blankly at each other as the words 'Thank God that's fucking over!' billowed upwards and seemed to hang in the air for an eternity.

'We'll be fine' Matt eventually volunteered, breaking the deathly silence that had engulfed us. 'No way will we have a week like they did.'

'No, that was a freakish one-off,' I agreed, glad of his optimism. I reached over to switch the kettle on.

'Hmm' Matt looked thoughtfully at his watch. 'Maybe we'd be better saving our tea until after we've finished what needs doing at six. Then we'll be done 'til the eight o'clock stuff!'

I looked at my watch which said 5.40 and reached for my lab coat, draped over the back of a chair. 'Sounds like a plan to me, Matty!'

It goes without saying that we should have taken that tea break when we had the chance. Not long after six our third person, Piers, arrived. This wasn't enough to stem the tide of tasks that continually amassed, swamping us and swallowing time. Six o'clock checks merged so seamlessly with eights that you couldn't see the join. Catheters were yanked out by dogs throwing tantrums, drip machines ground to a halt out of pure spite and the three of us didn't draw breath until finally extricating ourselves at the back of ten o'clock. We clambered the same stairs that five hours ago the previous group had descended in a state of sheer delirium. 'This time next week *we'll* be the ones done, guys,' I sighed, voicing what they too had been thinking.

I couldn't honestly believe it was only Monday morning. The rest of our group sat bright eyed and freshly scrubbed in the prep room, glistening with the promise of a new week. I yawned, rubbing my eyes and feeling dishevelled. I tried in vain to pull the creases from my crumpled lab coat. I couldn't believe how ill-prepared I felt. Grappling with a brand new subject, especially one that relied on a healthy commitment to alertness, ranked pretty low on my wish list at that precise moment.

'How was last night boys?' Sophie inquired brightly. Matt and I looked at each other, as if sizing up which one of us had the most energy left to cobble together a response.

'We got on top of things around half ten,' Matt began. 'Had a quick bite to eat. Then an emergency came in just after eleven. A border terrier in respiratory distress. We had to take turns sitting up with her all night. What with everything else that needed attention, we were basically all up the whole night.'

'Oh!' Sophie pulled a sympathetic face.

'We were shown how to do an emergency tracheotomy, just in case its condition deteriorated,' I chipped in as Matt flagged. 'I *was* going to use my pen, like on *ER* that time, but then I realised I wouldn't have anything to write my hourly checks with. Thankfully I was spared having to make that difficult choice, though.'

'Phew,' Sophie smiled pleasantly. 'So the dog made it, then?'

'Not exactly.' Matt rejoined the conversation with a long-suffering smile. 'Dr Britton took one look at her when he got in this morning and immediately pulled the plug.'

Matt and I started to laugh, the absurdity of the previous night's pointless vigil lending a tinge of mild hysteria.

Within fifteen minutes I was sporting ridiculously tight scrubs, which left nothing to the imagination, and embroiled in a seven-hour operation to repair a perineal hernia. The procedure is renowned for being extremely painful, and I was keen to spare the hulking German shepherd any unnecessary discomfort so kept the isofluorane relatively high. The need to constantly monitor a whole gamut of parameters kept me mercifully bright. I was anonymously squirrelled away on a small stool at the head end, skulking beside the blinking monitors. I couldn't help but eavesdrop on the final week's soft tissue group, offering silent prayers of thanks to the rotation gods for the group bestowed upon me; this group's niggly bickering formed a backdrop to the surgery as irksome as the bleeping pulse oximeter. The hours mounted up. At the back of one o'clock I felt a tap on my shoulder.

'Go and get some lunch, Stevie.'

'Aw thanks, Natalie.' I stretched, adding, 'I shan't be long' and getting unsteadily to my feet, rediscovering the use of my legs. I returned upstairs to the empty flat, fighting the urge to simply flop under the duvet, knowing that if I did I'd be as comatose as the German shepherd downstairs in a matter of seconds. I made do with chewing on my plastic Leahurst packed lunch, kindly ferried over by Megan, and tuning into the one o'clock news. I felt peculiarly disconnected from anything happening in the world beyond the confines of the SAH. It all seemed so distant and irrelevant. With lunch over I splashed water roughly onto my face and returned to the action. I assumed the rest of my disparate group were all beavering away downstairs and it felt wrong to lounge around in the flat while they were working. Natalie and I spent the rest of the afternoon jointly monitoring the hernia surgery, smirking at each other as the soft tissue group continued their snide sniping at each other.

'How was your day, Matt?'

It was half past five, we'd changed and were forcing down a lukewarm plate of pasta before infiltrating medicine's rounds to learn just how much of an ordeal the night was due to be.

'I had a dog wake up.'

'Nice one, mate. I mean, they're always going to wake up, at some point, you hope...'

'No. You misunderstand. I mean it woke up *during the surgery*. Just got up. I thought for a minute it was going to jump off the operating table.'

'And here was me thinking *I'd* be the first of us to join the wide awake club. Who was operating?'

He tried to suppress a grin. 'Terence Bains!'

'Oh fuck!' I guffawed, unable to help myself. Terence Bains was a pathologically serious surgeon who'd once famously frogmarched one of my mates from the year above, Clinton, out of theatre for not being familiar enough with the procedure for a bitch spay. Clinton's priceless response of returning, fuming, to the changing room and urinating in Terence's shoes immediately became part of vet school folklore, as well as ruining a perfectly decent pair of Italian loafers.

'So what did *old wet feet* do?'

'He went, *I think this dog is a little light,*' Matt replied, doing a passable impersonation of Dr Bains.

Our night was thankfully free of any emergencies, bogus or otherwise. The wipe-clean board listed procedures for 10 pm, midnight and 4 am. All three of us scurried through the ten o'clock duties and then stacked the washing machine with a mountain of soiled bedding for the next morning. I then went straight off to bed, setting my alarm for four while the other two sat up watching television until midnight before doing those checks together.

It seemed as if my head had only just touched the pillow when my alarm went off, shooting me bolt upright in bed. I gathered up my discarded clothes and, with my eyes still screwed up, made for the crack of light framing the bedroom door. Blinking like a mole I emerged into the beaming landing lights and padded along empty corridors feeling giddy and queasy from being ripped from my bed. I made myself take a groggy tour of each and every cage, checking all the patients still had pulses. With nothing on the verge of embracing rigor mortis I flitted through my list of chores. I gave a huge sigh of relief when I noted that none of the drip machines was playing up, and tiptoed around them reluctant to do anything they might object to. I gave a cat an intramuscular injection of pain-killing buprenorphine, infiltrated a drip bag with metronidazole antibiotic, flushed a handful of catheters and did a semi-decent job replacing a dog's bandage that had unfurled, losing its adhesiveness. In spite of the smoothness of my expedition downstairs it was still after five thirty by the time I returned to my still warm bed. *It's now Tuesday*, I thought as I wrapped the duvet around me. *Thank God. These days can't pass quickly enough.*

As a sizeable chunk of our week's assessment we'd each been set the task of preparing a talk for Friday on an aspect of anaesthesia of our own choice. Matt and I wondered idly where we would find the time to compile such a presentation. The days were long and stressful and merged into nights that offered little respite. Although the three of us found that by staggering our trips downstairs we got more sleep, sharing a bedroom invariably meant we all got roused anyway. I opted to do my presentation on anaesthesia in fish, my logic being that in choosing such an undeniably obscure topic, I was significantly reducing the odds of anyone actually noticing if I messed up any of my facts. By the time Thursday night arrived, Matt and I were virtually sleepwalking along to the seminar room in between ten o'clock and midnight checks, to throw our talks together. We'd scraped the bare bones together when Piers stuck his head around the door. 'Emergency, guys! RTA! Dog's been run over on Mount Pleasant!' I folded up my already dog-eared presentation and stuck it in my lab coat pocket.

'Let's do it.'

Once we'd resigned ourselves to losing another night's sleep, the sting was taken out of the episode. The hours melted away and Friday dawned like a long-held promise. Matt and I wearily pushed open the prep room door, visibly wilting but still in good spirits. In doing so we interrupted the other four members of the group enthusing wildly about the end of rotation party planned for that night. The conversation ground to a halt when we entered.

'Right, boys! When do you finish up here?' Sophie demanded, rubbing her hands as if she meant business. 'Because...' she continued, not waiting for a response, 'we've got a bit of a plan!'

'Sunday at some point?' I surmised. 'We'll miss tonight's party, but what are you going to do?'

'Well...' she began. 'I've booked Mr Chows for eight o'clock on Monday night for the six of us! We don't want to celebrate the end of the rotation properly, until we know you two are free to join in. It just wouldn't seem right.'

I didn't know what to say.

The official last day of rotation number one sped hazily by. Matt and I stepped up to the podium first and recited our paper-thin presentations. We then squirmed painfully as, one by one, the girls took to the floor with a dazzling flotilla of colour-coded visual aids and word-processed handouts. Part of me fervently prayed it had registered with our assessors just how arduous and time-consuming our on-call week had been, but a larger part had ceased to care. The week had been draining and exhausting, pummelling the life from us. The last thing I felt inclined to do was plead for clemency regarding any perceived lack of effort on my part. As the day ended everyone except the three stooges on duty clicked into party mode, smacking their lips in anticipation of the monumental shindig brewing and willing the curtain to fall on proceedings. Lab coats were balled up and stuffed away for the foreseeable future and people drifted out into the night in chattering clusters.

'All the best for tonight, boys.'

'Cheers Megan, you too. Think of us at midnight and four am. I'm sure you'll still be up...' I replied, pretending to be disgruntled.

'Aw hark at Cinderella!' snorted Natalie, seeing through my act. 'Don't know what all the fuss is about. It's nice and quiet in here now, at least you'll get a decent night's sleep. Leahurst will be bouncing and all I want right now is bed.'

'All in good time, Natalie! Certain things can't be rushed.'

As a softener for missing out on the festivities, the kennels had been more or less cleared, bequeathing us an undemanding Friday night and Saturday. Moreover with the rotation now officially at an end and no trio of students poised to relieve us at 3 pm on the Sunday, Ruth Sanderson benevolently discharged us shortly before midday. Piers drove Matt back to Leahurst while I sped off to meet Rob for the Liverpool/Sunderland game. I fought in vain to disengage from the most intense three weeks of my life but the monotony of the goalless encounter wouldn't allow it.

After the game I drove gleefully back over the water and slept for sixteen hours straight. Monday's mixed bag of lectures passed me by altogether, then I resigned myself to one last sleepless night before we broke up for Christmas, propping up the bar with my friends. As I stumbled back to my room, the birds had started singing and a milky dawn was studded with scudding clouds. A layer of mist was clinging to the field in front of the equine yard like a moist blanket. I stood for a minute, listening to the early morning sounds of the yard that never sleeps, and for the first time since beginning at vet school, I didn't feel worried.

14

Feeling a Little Horse

'So...' Natalie looked pointedly in the direction of an oblivious Georgia, 'is everybody happy with the on-call rota *now*?'

I leant back on my bar stool, surveying the piece of paper in my hand and gulped, my mouth feeling dry. Three weeks' worth of dates were listed and my name was highlighted five times, once with each member of the group: Tuesday and Friday of the first week, Tuesday and the weekend of the second week and Thursday of the last week.

'Everyone is down five times, including one weekend. I think it's fair,' she added testily. Georgia's complicated social calendar had led to Natalie having to rip up the previous two rotas and her obstinacy rankled with everyone. After a minute's silence I tentatively broached something that had been bothering me. 'Natalie ... it doesn't include the first weekend.'

'Yes it does!' she snapped. 'Look!' and jabbed her finger repeatedly at Matt and Sophie's names.

'No, sorry, I meant the weekend *before* we're actually due to start. Last time around they had to provide cover from four pm on the Saturday.'

We all looked at each other. 'I think I might be busy that weekend,' Georgia interjected.

'I'll take that bet!'

'Sorry?'

'I said *look it's all wet*,' and I held up my rota replete with offending coffee ring.

She pursed her lips, unconvinced.

In the end we did have to supply cover and as neither Matt nor I had been creative enough to invent a spontaneous subterfuge we were both landed with spending the whole of the Sunday on duty. I'd seen two weeks of equine practice near home over Christmas as a horse d'oeuvre to the rotational main event, and returned infused with greater self-confidence when it came to handling horses as well as a deeper understanding of the horsy set. Having said that, I'd seen Jack's first night on duty first hand and still recoiled at the memory. I'd vowed, there and then, never to put myself through that, steadfastly shirking any pre-rotation duty. The way I saw it, the first Monday of rotation had to feature some sort of introductory tour in which the system would be explained to us. Prior to that happening there'd be literally nothing. We'd just turn up unannounced and be expected to pick up instantly from where the last group left off. I tossed and turned in bed on the Saturday night, cursing the situation I now found myself in. Here I was on the brink of stepping into an almighty storm and, what's more, it was one I'd seen forecast three months previously.

'Did you get breakfast, Matt?'

'No, the staff hadn't bothered putting any out yet.'

'That sucks.' I'd been too nervous to stomach any food but the indolence of the kitchen staff never ceased to aggravate me, even more so now that our rotation had us based on site. 'They do know that's the only food we get?'

He shook his head, 'You wonder sometimes.'

The two other six-person groups in our section of orthopaedics, soft tissue surgery and medicine had also contributed two people, meaning that six of us converged on the yard shortly before eight o'clock on the Sunday morning. I blew on my stiff hands, my wispy breath trapping the sun's rays as they slanted acutely across the equine hospital's low tiled roof. As far as I could make out the yard was packed to the rafters. We all studied the wipe-clean board, silently pondering how long eight o'clock checks would hold us up and when we'd get our Sunday back. Matt and I were the first to break from the group.

'Me and Steve will take block D and block E, then,' he announced, unconcerned with the receipt of any confirmation. We then focused our attention on sifting through the relevant client files and filling our pockets with what amounted to a portable pharmacy. 'Don't want to keep having to come back for stuff,' he explained, as the other four looked on.

'Plus,' I added, following his lead and warming to the task, 'the sooner we start, the sooner we can get some breakfast.'

We were on the point of disembarking, our pockets bulging, when Jill, the resident on duty, turned up looking harassed.

'Hi guys! It's going to be a bit of a madhouse today. You've probably noticed how busy we are. We'll just have to muddle along as best we can.'

Matt and I exchanged a glance of hungry irritation and took the pause in her address as a cue to leave. 'Wait!' she shrieked, freezing us in our tracks. 'One thing I *have* to tell you, probably the *only* thing of any note I'll get to pass on to you today! Never *ever* enter a cubicle alone. If someone gets kicked the other person needs to be able to raise the alarm.'

'What if we both get kicked?' I whispered to Matt.

'Whoever regains consciousness first raises the alarm?'

'Gotcha!'

It became apparent that, as a bare minimum, every horse on site required TPR – temperature, pulse and respiration – to be checked twice a day. As I'd brought my digital thermometer, Matt and I quickly cultivated a system whereby he'd opt for heads, putting the head collar on and taking a pulse from the facial artery running beneath the chin, and I'd get tails, taking a rectal temperature and scrutinising the ribcage for the number of breaths per minute. It was extremely unusual for this to be anything other than the tip of the iceberg, though. Such was the expense of boarding horses that they were generally only hospitalised for specialist treatment. A clutch of horses on our beat were afflicted with one of a number of inflammatory conditions, ranging from abscesses to pedal osteitis to respiratory infections. They all required intramuscular injections of Neopen antibiotic in the rump. For these Matt clung on to the head collar for grim death while I punched the horse's rump three times before inserting the needle. It was clear which patients were past masters at suffering this indignity. As soon as we entered their lair the unfortunate souls would back into the farthest corner and kick out at us when approached. One in particular, a seven-year-old thoroughbred suffering with an upper respiratory tract infection, must have been a veritable pin cushion judging by the way she continually spun around with Matt hanging on to the lead rope. I knew that by remaining tucked in tightly at the animal's side it would be difficult to get kicked, but the horse spinning around, with Matt at the apex, rendered me very vulnerable. Twice I got the needle into position but applying the syringe proved more problematic. This bout of unarmed stable combat rendered us tousled and battered until Matt eventually plugged the syringe into her neck, receiving a head butt for his trouble.

'Nice work, Matty!' I gasped as we fought for breath.

'We'll make sure someone else gets that one at eight tonight,' he noted sagely, rubbing his swollen temple.

'No complaints there,' I grinned, bolting the door behind us. I'd been informed by Alex, from the year above, that breaks needed to be taken whenever the merest window of opportunity opened up. *Otherwise you'll never get away, Stevie boy! I kid you not.* With that in mind, Matt and I tiptoed past reception, having updated our two blocks in marker pen on the board, for a much-needed late breakfast.

Twenty minutes later we returned to the yard, self-consciously brushing the toast crumbs from our overalls, to be met by a scene of carnage. A boisterous foal was battling in stocks to resist being examined, blood gushing from a gaping head wound. Jill looked up in consternation from applying a tail bandage. 'Oh thank God, where the hell are the others?'

Matt and I looked guiltily at each other, 'Doing checks on the yard?'

'What? There's an emergency to deal with! Thank heavens *you* didn't go too far,' she panted, flicking a strand of hair behind her ear.

'Well we were...'

'Oliver here needs to go for colic surgery straight away, Prof's on his way in,' she bulldozed on. I filled a syringe with a couple of mils of xylazine that I'd stumbled across when searching for saline earlier that morning, while Matt located the components for an intravenous line and laid it on the trolley for Jill. We both then fought to restrain Oliver's head, Matt wrestling with the twitch, as Jill sutured the catheter into place, spurting more blood over Oliver's trembling neck. The others duly returned in time to see Matt and me escort a heavily sedated Oliver around the yard to the padded box he'd go down in.

As it was a Sunday no nurses were available to assist with the surgery, therefore all six of us were summoned into the fray. This was my worst nightmare. The theatre was cavernous and cupboards stretched as far as the eye could see. I kept my head down, hoping that the avoidance of eye contact would protect me from being asked to go and fetch any obscure items I'd never heard of. Oliver was flat on his back in sternal recumbency atop a raft of large inflatable cushions. I slowly and deliberately rolled my sleeves up, unsure what was going to be asked of me. Jill scraped a giant black bucket over to me with her clogged feet and intimated with a wave of her hand that I should take it over to the rear end of the prostrate foal. *Great, tails again!* Prof entered the arena and a reverential hush descended. He began growling inaudible commands at Jill, scrubbed in beside him. Great, steaming coils of intestine spilled out and were slit open to flush the suspected impaction. I ascertained from Prof's dancing eyebrows that my mission, should I accept it, was to hose the matted contents into the bucket.

The surgery progressed slowly and I suspended my fear that the bucket's stagnant contents would spill over the brim. However wet the task was making me I was glad it at least ensured I was sedentary. The others were constantly being despatched to ferret manically in the cupboards for a variety of items, skating in ungainly fashion across the treacherously wet floor. After several hours Prof grunted something unintelligible and Jill nodded before requesting more suture material. She then looked up at the clock, hesitated a moment and said, 'Prof's closing up now, can four of you go and do four o'clock checks?' I assumed I was no longer required for bucket duty and gladly splashed out of theatre with Matt, Chris and Hannah.

Four o'clock checks began late and dragged soul-destroyingly into eight o'clock checks. No one had eaten since mid morning. It was half past nine and pitch black by the time the four of us, joined latterly by Chloe and Ben, had completed all the yard's tasks. We stood, tired and disgruntled, beneath the board. As always duties were penned in for midnight and four am. I leant against the wall, savouring the minuscule relief it afforded my feet, and forcibly ejected from my mind the notion that our rotation had yet to even begin. Midnight checks appeared far more involved and time consuming than those at four, so we reached the democratic decision that four people should do midnights, with the other two getting up for fours. I couldn't face staying conscious until midnight and volunteered for four o'clock checks with Hannah, before limping dejectedly back to my room.

I felt dispirited and broken by the day. Every single joint in my body seemed to be screaming out in pain and my fingers felt swollen and useless. I tore my overalls off, leaving them piled in an untidy heap on the floor and was on the point of climbing, fully clothed, into bed when there was a knock at my door.

'All right, Steve?' Jack came into my room, looking concerned. 'You OK, mate?'

I collapsed on my bed, close to tears. 'I'm fucked Jack! Today was a joke! By the end my hands hurt so much I couldn't even undo head collars, let alone use a syringe or a pair of scissors! I felt like a fucking waste of space.' I turned to face the wall and roughly wiped away the tears, cool on my burning face.

'It won't always be like that, mate,' he said softly. 'That first Sunday night I was on, when you came for a bit? It was horrific. I got to bed at three and then had to get up again for four o'clock checks. I couldn't see myself coping with the whole rotation if that was how worn out I was going to be! Seriously, that's as bad as it'll ever get.'

I couldn't work out if I believed him or not but the sentiment was comforting and I really *wanted* him to be right. I took a deep breath. 'You're a good mate, Jacko.'

'Coming over to the bar for one, then? Matt's up for it.'

'I'm on fours, mate, so no. But we'll definitely squeeze one in later in the week.'

'Fair dos, g'night, then.'

'Yeah, g'night, mate.' I smiled as he let the door swing shut. 'And thanks.'

There was something undeniably reassuring about being reunited with the group. Seeing their faces, all together in one place again, reminded me of how we'd pulled together on the last rotation and prevailed; the tense aura surrounding equine seemed to lift as the seconds ticked by. We talked excitedly, Matt and I luxuriating expansively over our weekend's tale of hardship.

'Oh God, it sounds awful.' Sophie shook her head. 'Did you have to do four o'clock checks this morning?' she asked Matt, fearfully.

'No, Steve did. I was on midnights.'

'It wasn't too bad in the end...' I shrugged benignly, 'I'd got off to bed at ten and slept like a baby through 'til four. None of the cases were too troublesome; a couple of colic checks and a catheter flush. It ended up being fairly routine,' I heard myself and it sounded like someone else was talking.

There seemed to be a never-ending line of lame horses trotting disjointedly into our orthopaedics week. All six of us knew we'd acquire at least one patient each when we saw ten horses listed on the cases pending board. Leahurst boasted some of the finest equine minds on the planet. This often led to the large animal hospital taking delivery of referral cases that other vets had found beyond their capabilities. Prior to discharging such patients, the student assigned the case had to write back to the referring vet and elucidate the crux of the problem. I sat in the office and studiously prepared myself for taking delivery of one such enigma; Kieran Barnwell, a ten-year-old gelding with intermittent right forelimb lameness which was not responding to treatment.

A giant horse box drew up outside, blotting out the sun, and I slipped out to introduce myself as the owners climbed down from their behemoth. The three of us nursed coffees in reception and I probed for the subtleties of Kieran's condition. Satisfied that sufficient territory had been covered, I bid the owners farewell and stepped outside for a closer look at my new patient. Kieran had come across as mildly stroppy, valiantly resisting removal from his horse box. But now that his owners were nowhere to be seen he became even more petulant, biting, kicking and rearing. Our French orthopaedics resident, Gerard, took Kieran to one side and berated him, spraying the crisp Cheshire air with Gallic expletives. It took only the slightest of edges off Kieran's sociopathic tendencies, though, and ten minutes into his meticulous lameness work-up, he reared up again, ripping open a gash on Matt's right hand with a flailing hoof.

After a temporary hiatus to stem the bleeding and further chastise Kieran, the exam re-started. Gerard observed Kieran astutely from a distance as he trotted up and down the forecourt. He deployed nerve blocks with the precision of a master craftsman. As expected, right forelimb lameness was demonstrated and a lesser man might have left it there. Instead Gerard continued investigating, blocking that pain and unmasking lameness in the *left* forelimb. Still not

106

entirely satisfied he'd got to the bottom of the problem, he blocked this too, discovering previously unrecorded left *hindlimb* lameness. It was an extremely convoluted case and I frantically scribbled down notes as we took a series of radiographs that revealed frank osteoarthritis in the left hock; so-called bone spavin.

At six we finished rounds and, with the exception of Megan and Georgia who were on duty that night, were discharged for the day. 'Going in for tea now Steve?' Matt asked, as we walked briskly past rows of horse heads bobbing merrily above their stable doors.

'Matt, I'm on duty tomorrow night so I'm going to take the opportunity to do the letter for one of my cases now, while I've got the time. It's still fresh in my head so it makes sense, I suppose...' I could feel the resolve waning as my stomach rumbled in dissent.

'Is that *Kieran*?' Matt sneered disdainfully.

'Yes, the one and only! How *is* the hand?'

'Bit tender, still.'

'Sorry mate.'

Each morning, after students had performed eight o'clock checks on their cases, they were summoned to the seminar room, as our third of the year congregated for a thirty- to forty-minute tutorial. Every morning was devoted to a different facet of equine medicine and I was about to discover the hard way that Tuesday was always orthopaedics day. I arrived on to the yard around eight and unhurriedly TPRd my two cases before letting them stretch their legs around the yard. I then retired indoors to escape the whistling wind, update my patients' files and claim a decent seat in rounds, preferably one hidden somewhere towards the back.

'Ah Stefan, You are OK thees morning?'

'Good thanks Gerard, yourself?' I responded chirpily.

His reply knocked me sideways. '*Bon, merci!*' he nodded, continuing, 'Can you present Kieran at rounds please?' and handing me a manila envelope that contained all of Kieran's radiographs from the previous afternoon.

'What? Present it *to everyone in here*?' I railed, aghast.

'*Oui.* You weel be OK I sink.' He then swivelled on the tiled floor and left, his heels clacking down the polished corridor.

Oh. Fuck! I stood for a moment looking around me, and then began frantically padding at my pockets. *Please be there. Oh God, please be there!* My digging eventually unearthed what I'd been searching for. The rough copy of my letter to Kieran's referring vet, dutifully typed up the previous night. I unfurled it and lovingly planted a kiss on it.

'Love letter, Steven?' I turned quickly to see Sophie and Natalie standing laughing behind me.

'In a funny sort of way, yes. Will you give me a hand putting these up?' I asked, brandishing the envelope. 'Looks like rounds are on me today.'

I knew I'd gone bright red. The seminar room looked so much bigger when I stood to face the sea of expectant faces. After an abbreviated and slightly hesitant ad-libbed preamble, I dived into an ultra-conservative word-for-word rendition of what I'd typed. My grasp of equine anatomy probably wasn't as tight as it should've been and I peppered my address with ambiguous reference to the well-thumbed radiographs pinned behind me. Once I'd spluttered to a standstill, Gerard materialised by my side like the shopkeeper in *Mr Benn* and padded out my talk by firing random questions at individuals in the audience. From my epicentral vantage point I traced tiny tremors of unrest as they disseminated through the captive audience. After five or so minutes of interrogation, Gerard drew proceedings to a close and I returned, ebullient, to the yard, elated that my fifteen minutes had come and gone.

I'd acquired another couple of cases. Although both were of the low-maintenance, splint-bone fracture variety, they required radiography; an activity renowned for consuming inordinate amounts of time as students fumbled nervously to operate the clunky machinery under the waspish tutelage of Erica Thomas. As I was on call that night and resigned to spending much, if not all, of it on the yard, the delay didn't perturb me as much as it might have done. At seven o'clock I finally escaped the yard's clutches and grabbed a spot of dinner before returning shortly before eight for checks with Matt and the four other lucky souls also on duty. Matt and I restricted our checks purely to orthopaedics cases, the familiarity we'd built up with our patients' foibles and vice versa ensuring a swift resolution. We then baled out the overworked soft tissue duo, performing a trio of colic checks and drawing eights to a satisfying close.

I returned to my room relieved I'd secured midnight checks later, and not fours. I'd found it well nigh impossible to get back to sleep when I'd finally returned to bed after four am checks on Monday morning; the sun was up and birdsong had filled my head. This was my first time of officially being on call and I was unable to settle, rattling dementedly around my room. The peculiar mental torture of being on duty had its unpleasant way with me. *Is my phone fully charged? Does it still have a signal? It's not on silent is it? Is it? Should I take my phone into the toilet with me, just in case? What if someone else phones me while I'm in there, though? Not even my mother would appreciate an echoey conversation with me sitting on that seat!*

Midnight checks came and went, and I levered my heavy joints into position in bed, hoping I wouldn't be required to stir them again until after dawn. My phone kept its counsel, as it would go on to do for four out of my five periods on call. The one exception to this would be my gruelling last night of duty on the Thursday of week three; that bottomless pit of a night would more than make up for previously being spared, leaving a painful legacy that would haunt me all the way through to the following Christmas and beyond.

The following week, soft tissue surgery, was significantly quieter and didn't get off to the best of starts for me. The paucity of cases prompted Prof, in one giddy moment of light-hearted joviality, to advocate going out and knocking something down to bolster our paltry caseload. The diminished clientele created a shift of emphasis. Large segments of the week were spent fighting sleep during hours of interminable tutorials. We tried in vain not to disappoint Prof with the limitations of our anatomical acumen as he guided us through a spate of surgical slideshows. Sadly, the debilitating warmth of the seminar room along with his lugubrious delivery meant most of these were spent flirting with narcolepsy. During one such episode I was constantly re-opening my leaden eyelids in the middle of a session on the post-surgical complications of castration when Prof put a slide up featuring champignon; so-called because its bulbous lesions bear more than a passing resemblance to mushrooms. I rejoined the waking world to be greeted with the question, 'Anyone think why it's known as champignon?' Even the perennially taciturn Prof had difficulty keeping a straight face when I plucked, 'Is it because the discharge is champagne coloured?' from the sleep-induced ether.

I compounded this with an equally calamitous display later that same day. Prof had asked one of us to stir Dr Kris Douglas from his office in order for him to deliver his much vaunted suturing tutorial, in which he'd explain, among other things, the hidden art of one-handed knot tying. I sprang to my feet eager to shake the sleepy cobwebs from my head. Standing outside Dr Douglas's office I composed myself before knocking. As I did I saw through the wired glass that he was flat out on the floor, writhing demonically, his beetroot face contorted beyond recognition. Convinced I was seeing someone in the throes of a grand mal seizure, I burst into his room and knelt beside him, leaning forward with the intention of loosening his buttons, lugging him into the recovery position and unplugging his tongue from his gullet. I laid a hand on his top button, at which point he sat up and I realised he'd simply been going through his morning's exercises.

'I thought you were having a fit!' I bleated squeakily, scrambling to my feet.

'It's nice to know you care,' he chuckled as I blushed red. I informed him we were now ready for his tutorial and dived headlong for the door.

Although admittedly pedestrian, the week still endeavoured to deliver all six of us to theatre to scrub in with Prof. The case I'd plumped for was already twenty minutes late by the time Jill took me aside and briefed me as I flicked through the case history. Sandy Dennison was a twenty-eight-year-old male Welsh cob with a diffuse, infiltrating flurry of suppurating sarcoid tumours that were spreading rampantly across his inguinal region.

'He's been through an awful lot and he's fairly old for surgery,' Jill began, 'but his owner is very attached to him and has begged Prof to take one last look at him and do what he can.'

I looked up from the file. 'It says here Sandy had surgery to remove these four months ago...'

'I know,' Jill's eyes flicked to the window as a modest horse box pulled up. 'They recurred with a vengeance. This will be the last time he'll go to surgery; we'll also be trying some experimental post-surgical treatment with tazarotene ointment. But it's touch and go.' Her last sentence had been uttered under her breath, as Mrs Dennison had spied her through the glass door and come into the office. Jill got to her feet and smiled broadly, extending her hand. 'Mrs Dennison, lovely to see you again! This is Steve, a fourth year here, I'm going to leave you in his very capable hands.' Jill shook the client's hand and gestured at me with a sweep of her other hand.

'Nice to meet you,' I said, getting to my feet and standing awkwardly as they chatted. Jill departed and I pulled up a chair for a deeply distressed Mrs Dennison. As Sandy's condition had relapsed there was really very little to add to the pre-existing history during our short and harrowing exchange. Mrs Dennison clutched at me like a drowning woman as I shepherded her towards the door.

Sandy had eaten earlier that morning and so he wouldn't be going for surgery until the following day. I walked him slowly to his appointed stable and scrawled 'food out at 8 pm' on a plaque which I attached to the door. I was struck by how docile and amenable he was despite the agonising discomfort the brushing motion of his hind legs must have caused. He advanced genially to the stable door before I'd even finished bolting it shut and I gave him a polo-mint, ruffling his fluffy grey mane. 'You're a good lad, aren't you? Let's see what tomorrow brings...'

Despite the brevity of the procedure and its lack of invasiveness, it had come as no surprise when I was asked to scrub in with Prof the next morning. The upshot of this was that I'd now be required to meet his curt requests with instantaneous placement of the relevant instrument into his gloved and expectant hand. I knocked the tap shut with my elbow and reached for the sterile towels partially unwrapped for me by Janet the nurse. The previous night I'd borrowed Jack's catalogue poster of surgical instruments, furiously testing myself until my head spun. As I dried my hands and forearms I closed my eyes and fought to visualise the distinguishing features of all the scissors, forceps and needle-holders I'd need to be able to tell apart.

I leant so far forward, craning to listen, that I was in mortal danger of tipping headlong into the drapes I'd only just clipped into place. Prof's mask and my hat conspired to smother his already clothy delivery.

'Muh ... muh ... maum scissors?' I felt like I was receiving a

111

plea for assistance from Lassie. *What's that, Prof? There's a horse from near that old, abandoned mine with dodgy sarcoids? And what's that? You need a pair of Metzenbaum scissors to help you with the surgery?* A combination of avidly following the surgery, trying to forecast each move and Janet's surreptitious sleight of hand, ensured Prof took delivery of the desired instruments with little fuss and he drew the procedure to a close with a gruff 'thanks everyone'.

Jill had spoken of an adjunct to the surgery and I was instructed to apply a semi-experimental ointment, tazarotene, to Sandy's tender inguinal area. The skin in this region was gritty and thickened almost beyond recognition. It was hoped daily application of this ointment might thin the skin as well as delay, or even postpone, the re-appearance of the larger sarcoids. These thrice-daily forays into his highly sensitive nether regions must have been unimaginably unpleasant. Sandy would automatically begin twitching the moment I entered his stable and put my latex gloves on. We geared ourselves up for the worst, such was the horrific dermatological distortion that had plagued Sandy for so much of his twenty-eight years. And anyway don't low expectations save you from greater hurt and disappointment? But we had to give him the best chance possible and I religiously smeared the oily substance over a designated area during the three days he remained in our care, post surgery. Sandy was beautifully natured and took my regular poking and manhandling with heart-wrenching stoicism.

Friday arrived and Sandy's surgical wounds had healed sufficiently for him to return home. Jill and I cleaned him up for Mrs Dennison's noon arrival, scrubbing at his blood-stained fetlocks with clumps of cotton wool and Hibiscrub. We took him from the constant twilight of the stable, tethering him on the yard and using the natural light to help assess the state of his underside. I couldn't believe it. There'd been a positive reaction to the cream. The specific area we'd targeted was clearly delineated and significantly mollified. On cue Mrs Dennison pulled up and I could see her preparing for the worst as she left her daughter to stew in the van with a stern shake of her head. I couldn't help but break into a huge smile as she reluctantly walked over to us.

'Please tell me he's OK' she begged, tears welling up. Jill quietly took her through the surgical procedure, deliberately injecting a note of cautious optimism as the upturn in his distressing skin ailment was discussed. They both turned to me when she'd finished. 'It's Steve who's been putting the cream on every day, though. So you need to thank him!'

Mrs Dennison smiled at me through the tears. 'He's the sweetest horse imaginable, you know!'

'I know,' I beamed back at her. 'I had to leave myself really vulnerable in order to apply the cream properly. He could've kicked me to kingdom come! He never touched me once, though.'

'Oh, thank you!' she choked and gathered me up in a huge embrace.

* * *

'See you back here at...' Sophie stopped walking and checked her watch, 'quarter to eight, then. God, that's not even two hours!'

'Not if I see you first,' I retorted, stupidly tempting fate, as I yanked my fleece over my overalls and zipped it up. Our paths diverged, her's to the car park and a drive home for a shower and a bite to eat, and mine to the Leahurst dining room for a plate of lukewarm slop. Unlike the previous two weeks I was only on duty once this week and that night had duly arrived. The fragrant hint of spring hung in the air and this, along with the fact I'd yet to be called out on any of my other spells on duty, filled me with optimism regarding the rotation in general and the night in particular. The finishing line was so close I could almost reach out and touch it.

Not long after six, my overalls' sleeves still knotted around my waist, I dumped my plates and formulated a plan to check my email before nipping back for a shower prior to meeting Sophie for eights. But I wouldn't even reach the door of the computer room.

'Hello?'

'Hi, is that Steve?'

'Yeah! Who's this?'

'It's Hannah! Something's come in...'

'This a wind-up? It hasn't even gone six yet!' I lied. I took the tangible air of exasperation from the other end as a no. 'Right, Hannah, I'll be along in two minutes, OK?'

A Shetland pony foal born twenty-four hours previously was showing signs of gastro-intestinal discomfort, more commonly referred to as colic. I scratched my head as I studied the tiny

113

patient, and couldn't see beyond either an impaction caused by retained meconium or a ruptured bladder. The case was further complicated by the foal's relative young age, meaning wherever he went, mother had to go too. Regardless of the problem the key to a successful outcome was stabilising the foal. There was a distinct possibility the foal had excessively high potassium levels and we knew if this wasn't addressed swiftly it could precipitate the foal's premature demise. Sadly the fiercely protective mare could only see the distress we were causing her offspring and lashed out violently, bucking and double-barrelling as we held the foal tightly to take our blood sample. It took four of us to pin the mare down while Hannah and Sophie efficiently relieved the foal of the requisite blood.

The blood was run for analysis and in the interim the resident on duty, Trudy, arrived. The mare and foal were then frogmarched through to radiography as there was a slight possibility x-rays might clarify the aetiology. It was 7.50 pm and the six of us and Trudy fought to contain the situation; Trudy and Chris were occupied with operating the radiographic equipment and processing sheets of inconclusive films. Sophie and I were strapped into lead aprons and manipulating the uncooperative, uncomprehending foal. Hannah, Chloe and Ben were wrestling to subdue the increasingly agitated mare that seemed constantly on the verge of breaking free from their clutches and running amok in the enclosed space of the radiography room. During one of the countless long pauses in the operation, I turned to Sophie. 'Are you OK to be left holding the baby?'

'Had enough already?'

'I think I reached that point an hour ago. But no, I was just thinking I might nip off and make a start on eight o'clock checks. It's going to be a while before we finish up in here.'

'On your own, Steve?' Hannah queried, shifting the strap of the cumbersome apron across her shoulder.

'Well, no one else can really be spared and they need doing. It'll be fine.' I pulled a face as I strained to free myself.

'I'll come out and give you a hand as soon as we're done in here,' Sophie promised, smiling and altering her grip on the foal's lead rope.

Rushing around struck me as pointless. The chances were we'd be here for the duration. Foals in that state always required round the clock surveillance and aggressive fluid therapy to restore normality. It may even be that Prof would be called out if surgery was indicated. Either way it was shaping up to be a very long night. I stepped on to the yard, veiled in near darkness, and had a feeling reminiscent of my last night on-call in the small animal hospital. I felt that the night could throw all it had at me, tomorrow would be the last day of the rotation and after that I'd be home free. I knew this was nothing more than a mirage, but there was no escaping the fact that these false horizons made vet school palatable.

I perused the needs of block A from the sanctity of stocks before steadily working through them; one basic TPR, one colic check, one small bran mash to be laced with ventipulmin and phenylbutazone and a couple of bandage checks with suggested yard walks. *Suggestion noted!* I knew block B contained a particularly obstreperous two-year-old, seventeen-hand thoroughbred with a devilish habit of taking liberties with anyone brave or stupid enough to enter. I took a deep breath, shot the bolt and stepped, tentatively, on to the flattened straw at the stable's threshold, the head collar looped over my arm. I leant back over the stable door and, with a deep sense of misgiving, bolted it shut behind me. We both eyed each other suspiciously in the flickering light, my neck craning to meet his crazed, sidelong gaze.

'Come on, Dennis, I don't like you and you don't like me, but let's just get this over and done with.' I edged forward with the intention of dropping the collar over his obsessively rocking head. It was my plan, thereafter, to tether the lead rope in a slipknot and then perform an exceedingly brief colic check. But Dennis had other ideas and, as soon as the head collar brushed at his forelock, he reared up, jarring my wrist with his right hoof and smacking into me with his full force, tossing me against the wall as if I were a piece of straw. Winded, I staggered unsteadily through the stable door and clamped it shut behind me with a grimace. My head was singing and my arm and ribs ached, but most of all I felt foolish. I limped back to stocks to get my breath back before addressing the realistic needs of block C and beyond.

It was ten-thirty by the time I returned to stocks for the last time. I caught a glimpse of my image in the glass of the pharmacy cabinet and was reminded of the perspiring, workaholic fifth years who had so intimidated me on my arrival at Leahurst back in September. Despite the intense pain in my ribcage whenever I took

115

a deep breath, I suddenly burst out laughing. It was nice not to be scared any more.

'You didn't do the lot did you?' Sophie suddenly popped her head around the door, making me jump.

'Ah. I need to talk to you about that. Dennis still needs his colic check, I learnt the hard way that it's a two-person job.'

'You didn't go in did you?'

I nodded, feeling chastened. 'Plus there's a couple of drip bags close to running out...'

The two of us stepped onto the yard to put the finishing touches to eight o'clock checks and make a start on midnights. All the while Sophie was filling me in on the progress of mother and child. Apparently the radiographs belatedly showed that the bladder was almost certainly still intact, but the potassium levels were almost through the roof. The foal would require round-the-clock attention throughout what was left of the night. Unfortunately that was only half the problem. The mare had been pacing around throughout the whole episode, appearing highly distressed. Everyone had automatically assumed this was merely due to unrest regarding her infirm offspring. Sadly, a brightening of the foal's spirits had only been greeted by an escalation of the mare's malaise and she'd spent much of the last hour pawing at the ground and rolling. In other words, displaying textbook symptoms of colic herself.

'And so we called Trudy back out. She'd gone home after instructing us how to manage the foal,' reported Sophie as we sped through the last of the midnight colic checks – the redoubtable Oliver, on his way to receiving the all-clear for a morning return home. I absent-mindedly stroked his head as Sophie auscultated his gut sounds.

'What did she say?'

'That we were probably over-reacting...'

'In other words she'd just got into bed.'

'Pretty much.' Sophie and I plodded back through the engulfing darkness, savouring the sweet smell of silage lilting across the fields. When we got back Trudy had arrived after all and was drawing up a measure of xylazine, a sedative, for the obviously colicking mare. The other four students were trading puzzled looks. I sidled up to Hannah. 'What gives?'

She leant over and with a careful eye on Trudy, whispered, 'I think she's reluctant to call Prof out.'

'What's delaying the inevitable going to achieve? Didn't she see the mare rolling and pawing at the ground?'

Hannah shrugged and we all stood in silent bewilderment until Trudy had finished injecting the mare and left once again. The six of us looked blankly at one another, unsure what to say or do next until Chris broke the silence, launching into a furious tirade. 'If she'd phoned Prof now we could have had this all fixed by three! This way all that'll happen is that the xylazine'll mask the discomfort *until* three, at which point it'll return, worse than ever! This is a joke!'

His words would prove prophetic. It was three-thirty am and Sophie, Hannah and I were taking turns to infuse oral fluids into the foal, monitoring his parameters. Suddenly Chloe, Chris and Ben burst in. They had taken the drugged-up mare for a stroll around the yard in the hope of untangling or loosening up whichever portion of gut had seized, and the symptoms had resurfaced with brutal vengeance. She began violently throwing herself against the padded walls of the box and spasmodically rolling on to her back, kicking wildly at the air, her eyes deranged. Trudy was phoned again and before long the three of them were helping her to prep the mare for surgery in sullen, grudging silence. All four of them then accompanied the recently arrived Prof into theatre, leaving Hannah, Sophie and myself to tend the foal until dawn. The constant kneeling meant my knees were pleading for mercy. Stomach tubing the foal required one person to manipulate the tube and two others to hold the increasingly energetic foal down. In between these tortuous but sadly unavoidable interludes we sat in the deep straw of the box and chewed the fat like hardcore party animals keen to push on through to dawn.

By the time dawn's pastel shades had given the yard definition, and our foal had become heartily sick of his lot, we could hear noises emanating from down the corridor. Chris stuck his head through the box's hatch and stared down at us, sitting together in the straw. 'Rise and shine, campers,' he yodelled, far too brightly for me at this hour. 'How's the patient?'

'Pretty good,' I replied. 'Other than missing his mum. Speaking of which?'

'Epiploic foramen entrapment. Prof's just closing up.'

'Hear that, junior?' I smiled, scratching the foal's velvet ears. 'Told you everything'd work out, didn't I?'

Mare and foal were groggily reunited around eight, just as the first dribs and drabs of students began filtering dozily on to the yard, for the first checks of the day.

'Tired, mate?'

'That's one way of putting it.'

'Go off to bed for a few hours; you guys have earned it!'

'Hmm. It wouldn't be right, Matt.'

'Aw come on! Don't be so virtuous, we can cope!'

'Oh. It's not that...' I prevaricated, momentarily lost for words. 'It's just that tomorrow's the National and rumour has it rounds this morning are devoted entirely to Douglas revealing his cast-iron tips. Can't miss that!'

'Wild Shetland ponies wouldn't drag you away?'

'Quite.'

The day seemed to drag dreamily along. Shortly after ten Sophie and I were excused duties for a couple of hours to allow us to shower and grab a change of clothes and a bite to eat. Before returning to the yard I drove to Ladbrokes in Neston and backed all four of Dr Douglas's tips. As I depressed the clutch I realised how sore my knees were.

As the afternoon drew to a close I knelt one last time to take the foal's temperature and felt a gruesome tweaking of ligaments in my right knee. I yelped in anguish and hobbled to my feet. I found to my distress that I was unable to straighten my right leg. Grabbing on to the wall I hopped, incapacitated, into the seminar room and tried in vain to fully extend my leg. Matt and Natalie volunteered to TPR my three cases at four and I limped back in the direction of my room, virtually dragging my right leg behind me. It was the last day and I'd pushed myself way too far. By 4.10 I was propped up on my bed, shell-shocked. I couldn't believe that such a momentous, all-consuming three weeks had climaxed so inauspiciously, with me just quietly limping off into the sunset.

The television room in Leahurst House emitted a giant gasp as the Grand National entered the final straits. Douglas's tips were sensationally accounting for four out of the first five horses placed. Every single person in the packed room had swallowed the gospel according to Kris and backed his choices to the hilt. I reclined in my easy chair and savoured the novel experience of winning

118

handsomely. In the whooping celebrations that spilled over into the evening, I finally got the opportunity to lay the three weeks properly to rest. We sat on Leahurst lawn content to bathe in the spring sunshine and share the spoils of victory. We all told stories, trading triumph and mishap. I looked around at the group and could instantly recall a fleet of incidents with each and every one of them. Times in the heat of battle when a selfless gesture or a kind word had warmed the soul. I had a support bandage on my right knee which hurt whenever I flexed my leg, and I was up at seven in the morning for the drive to Kendal and two weeks farm practice, but as I looked around me I didn't want to be anywhere else in the world.

15

Close the Gate Behind You

I could not believe it! Five years to prepare for my first day of farm rotation and I turn up with wellies that leak! I squelched through the ankle-deep mud and focused all my powers of concentration on not dropping the ultrasound scanner. Once inside the dilapidated outhouse I stepped over a partially unwound hose, coated with twenty years worth of accumulated dust, and set the scanner down on the uneven stone floor. Everyone I'd asked about farm animal rotation had offered the same, unequivocal riposte; *it's definitely the most laid back of the three, you'll love it!* I ran my hand through my drenched hair, unable to quite see it, myself.

'Cheer up, Stevie! It could be worse, we could be in smallies sitting through one of Mike's tutorials on how to get the best from your microscope!'

'That's true, Chloe, he could be handing round the antiseptic wipes as we speak...'

It wasn't just the incessant downpour that was responsible for ruining my mood. After this three-week rotation was over we'd go straight into our mock finals. This in itself didn't worry me too much as it only accounted for a measly 5%. What worried me was that the same week as we were being mocked, the fifth years were undergoing the real thing. They'd get their results at the end of that week and then that would be that. Above us there'd be only sky. No more protective senior years buffering us from the business end of the course; we'd be top of the food chain and next in line when it came to written exam papers. A squirt of ice-cold rainwater dribbled down my back and I shivered miserably as a drip of water formed on the tip of my nose. I wondered what would become of me.

'Right! Who's had a go at pregnancy diagnosis per rectum before, then? Steve?'

'I've had a quick in and out, nothing more.'

'Uh-huh ... and what about the pregnancy diagnosis?' Roddy doubled over, screwing up his schoolboyish features.

'No. Just the in and out.' I smiled. So far I was finding the sopping squalor of the farm extremely disagreeable but Roddy's sense of humour was infectious.

'No matter,' he winked, enclosing the scanner's cable in an arm-length glove and plugging it into an overhead power point. 'Just dive in and we'll see what you can feel, yeah?' He consulted his muddy notebook, 'Matt, you take 291, Chloe, 818 and Steve ... 336.'

'Should we be able to feel much, then?' Chloe had pulled her long glove up to her shoulder and finished the task of squeezing liberal amounts of lubricant over the fingers. She was standing poised like a suspected drug trafficker's worst nightmare.

'Definitely, Chloe,' Roddy sidled over to her. 'The rectum in the cow passes very close to many readily palpable structures: ovaries, uterus, cervix, left kidney, rumen, bladder...'

She nodded and then made her hand into a point by forcing all her fingers together before easing it into the cow's rectum, a profound expression inscribed across her features. She went in up to between her elbow and shoulder and then turned to smile broadly at Matt and me, informing us helpfully, 'It's very warm and squishy!' The cow then flicked its shit-encrusted tail, catching her full in the mouth. As she spluttered in indignation, Matt and I exploded with laughter as we donned gloves of our own.

I'd read somewhere that deprivation of one sense leads to a compensatory enhancement of the others; in much the same way blind people often have very sensitive hearing. I closed my eyes as I entered, figuring it might make me better equipped to visualise shapes and structures. Matt, Chloe and I were standing in a line, each of us with one arm plugged inside our cows. As I'd been the last to enter, Roddy was coaching the other two in the art of rectal palpation. I listened in on their exchanges and tried to make use of them for myself. I kept hearing Roddy make mention of ovaries and follicles. It didn't seem to matter how deeply I burrowed, nothing even remotely close to those shapes or sizes entered my zone of exploration.

Eventually he squelchily disengaged himself from 291 and edged around her to me. 'So, Steve, how was it for you? Fulfilling?'

'*Nearly* ready for that post-coital fag, Roddy! Umm ... but before that, I don't seem to be feeling anything that the others felt.'

'Really?' Roddy frowned, before taking a step back and fighting to suppress a smile. 'You aren't in the rectum Steve. You've found the, err ... the *other* hole.'

I felt my shoulders sag. I knew this would now follow me all the way through vet school and beyond. 'Oh no!' I looked over at Matt and Chloe who were clinging on to each other, doubled up with laughter. I removed my arm to a very noticeable sucking sound and seconds later 336's vagina emitted a massive watery fart that rang out belligerently in the confined space of the dripping outhouse.

It was difficult to keep a straight face throughout the remainder of the routine visit. These visits were a staple of the general practice week, as well as on reproduction which made up week two and clinical studies which we'd go on to do after the summer break. Each morning, after a forty-minute tutorial, van-loads of students shuttled between farms dotted across the Wirral peninsula. In each establishment the farmer would cordon off any members of his herd that had a breeding profile which was giving him cause for concern or any individuals that he felt might be in calf. The team would strive for a definitive diagnosis in each instance and perform a drug-induced tweaking of the reproductive system where necessary.

'Right, Steve, ready for another?' Roddy's mouth was threatening to break free from his face.

I sighed heavily in mock despair before perking up and declaring, 'Keep 'em coming Roddy.'

'That's the spirit.' He smiled warmly and patted me on the back. 'Good lad! Take 161. The farmer says she's not been seen bulling this week. Let me know what you come up with.' I eased my hand and arm in and scooped out the accumulated faeces that would only complicate my examination. They spattered on to the stone floor with a sound like a slow handclap and Roddy looked over approvingly. 'That's it! Stay in the *brown* pocket, remember.'

Right ... Thanks for the tip!

A few of the possible reasons why a cow may not be observed to be in heat passed through my mind as I re-entered: *So, she might be cycling normally but farmer Joe's just missed it, she might*

122

not be cycling at all, so-called anoestrus, or she could be in calf...
My fingers strummed at the doughy uterus and I tried to work out
what I felt about its condition. It felt slightly *fluidy* to me, which
made me think she might be in calf, but I knew I'd need to locate
the ovaries before I could take anything back to Roddy. I pulled
my hand slowly back to the bifurcation and then traced the right
horn all the way to the ovary.

'Any joy?'

'Well...' I thought for a second as my fingers fiddled with a
nodular mass on the ovary. 'The uterus has definite tone and I
think I can feel a corpus luteum on the right ovary. I'd say she's
in calf.'

'Right. Very good. Out you come then.' Roddy clasped the head
of the scanner in his right hand and passed both into 161. All four
of us stood and watched the constantly swirling, mutating image
on the screen. 'Good call, Stevie. There's your CL.' Roddy ran
the head back and forth over the ovary, relaying images of a fluid-
filled sac onto the tiny screen.

'Nice one, Steve.'

'Cheers, Matty. Anything would have been an improvement on
being in the wrong hole.'

The routine was over. We cleaned up, wiping down the scanner
and scrubbing our waterproofs and wellies with disinfectant before
climbing back into the van. I stared out at the lush, verdant
countryside bouncing past the window and craned to make out
Roddy's utterances from the driver's seat.

'This afternoon we're foot trimming and de-horning, yeah?' he
yelled, fighting to make himself heard above the buffeting wind
and the best efforts of Radio 2. 'That really was good work this
morning.' he persevered, half turning to catch my eye as we pulled
into Leahurst. 'Joking apart. Really good work!'

Our group differed ever so slightly from the team for equine/small
animal. Matt, Georgia and I were still together, but we'd lost
Natalie, Sophie and Megan. As Matt and I nosed around the farm
building after lunch we'd bumped into our three former compadres
and it had taken a huge effort of mind not to simply tag along
with them the way we always used to. In their absence we'd
acquired Chloe, who'd not only been present for many of equine's
more memorable episodes, but had also been one of Natalie's two
out-of-hours buddies threatened with failing the all-important module

123

on flat cleanliness during our soft tissue surgery week on small animal. Our group tally was boosted to seven by three other new members who tended to keep themselves to themselves. Fortunately Roddy favoured very small groups for farm visits and, as Georgia preferred to go with the new trio, it invariably left Matt, Chloe and me together as a team. After twenty minutes of fruitless meandering, Matt and I eventually unearthed Roddy. The plan was that he would take our threesome to do some de-horning while Lester foot-trimmed with the other quartet. Around three-thirty the groups would switch over.

I helped Roddy load up the van while Matt and Chloe went off in search of a couple of bottles of lignocaine with adrenaline for use as local anaesthetic. As the two others were nowhere to be seen, it would have represented very bad van etiquette for me not to get into the passenger seat next to Roddy. He seemed a tad preoccupied.

'What's up Roddy, run out of jokes about me entering the wrong hole?'

He grinned, casting a quick look from side to side before turning to face me. 'No, nothing like that. Just thinking ... Chloe's a good laugh isn't she?'

'Yeah, mate, she's brilliant.' I caught his eye for a second and then glanced at the side mirror. 'Here she comes now, in fact.'

Roddy stuck his head out the van window and hollered, 'Get it, guys?'

'Of course Roddy, I'm not just a pretty face you know!' Chloe fired back, placing the two brand new bottles into the wooden medicine box located at the back of the van.

'Hear that Roddy? Not *just* a pretty face,' I winked at him as Chloe climbed on board and yanked the sliding door shut with a grunt.

'OK, guys. Let's make use of this time we've got and have a quick tutorial, yeah?' declared Roddy about ten minutes into the journey. 'Abortion in sheep! Let's go round the three of you and see how many causes you can come up with.'

'We can't really hear you very well in the back, Roddy.' Chloe protested, unconvincingly.

I swivelled in my seat, catching sight of her nudging Matt, her eyes smiling and I suddenly felt horribly exposed in my front berth.

'Looks like it's just you and me then, Stevie,' acknowledged

Roddy philosophically. 'Their loss,' he added, nodding backwards in the direction of a sniggering Chloe and Matt.

I began listing conditions starting off with the two main culprits: toxoplasmosis and enzooitic abortion.

'You've got the big two there, excellent, but how could you tell them apart from looking at the placenta?'

I could feel a boot, either Chloe's or Matt's, playfully kicking at the saggy underside of my seat and, as I considered my reply, I slouched back and quickly snaked an arm around the back of my seat, grabbing hold of a writhing foot and tugging hard.

'Well, isn't it that in enzooitic abortion the intercotyledonary area is clearly thickened?' I replied, my voice competing with a now howling Chloe.

'Yes, that's right,' nodded Roddy seemingly oblivious to the commotion behind him as he indicated to turn right and we bumped up the winding farm track.

'Who's not done an injection yet? Matt?'

'Yep, just done one!'

'Chloe?'

'Uh-huh.'

'Steve, have you done one?'

'No, can't say I have.'

'Well, bring that syringe of local. We'll hold her down for you, yeah?'

I advanced on the calf, taking a firm hold of the head being grasped for me, and pressed the underside of my thumb across the frontal ridge, searching for the distinctive depression.

'Happy?'

'Ecstatic,' I replied, removing the syringe from my pocket and pulling the cover off the needle with my teeth.

'Don't let Won Jackson see you doing that!' Chloe chided. Ron, a senior member of the university's farm team, was a renowned stickler for hygiene protocol.

'Is your mouth stewile? I don't think so!' I responded, giving a vague impersonation of Ron, before injecting my six millilitres of local into the vicinity of the cornual nerve. I repeated the trick on the other side and by the time I'd given both my injections enough time had elapsed for the first anaesthetised calf to go under the flame. Although only around ten weeks old, the calves were leggy and unruly and it took two people to subdue them adequately for disbudding.

'Here's where we find out if that local's been effective,' Roddy stated glibly as he lit the flame of the disbudding iron and thrust it into one horn bud and then the other, with all his strength. The hairs were scorched right down to the bone and the stench of smouldering animal matter seared the air. A quick spray of alamycin antibiotic and the slightly frazzled calf scampered off to join her suspicious mates. Soon my turn came and I grabbed hold of the lit iron.

'Go on Steve, best shot!'

I couldn't work out if Roddy had forgotten my hand problem or whether he had enough confidence in my ability to perform this task in spite of my debilitating condition. Either way I was glad it had been left unsaid. I felt up to the task and adored the spirit of togetherness as we pooled resources. I gripped the handle of the iron with my left hand, as it had a tighter grip than the significantly more damaged right one. Being right-handed, though, the left was slightly less effective and I had to forcefully depress the nozzle into my calf's skull several more times than had Matt and Chloe. Thankfully my dispersion of the local had been successful and after a couple of strained efforts I finally scraped out the charred plug of horn, flicking it, still smoking, on to the walkway.

A total of ten calves had required disbudding and Matt, Chloe and I took three each, with Roddy doing number one as a demonstration. With the job done we quickly cleaned up and set off in the van for West Kirby and foot-trimming. I shut my eyes as we sped along the A540 and, unnoticed, rubbed at both wrists as they nestled aching in my lap.

Our silent partners in the other half of the group had worked very diligently, meaning only two lame cows remained. I feigned disappointment but was secretly quite relieved. In the end Matt and I were given the last cow to do between us and took a hind foot each. I pared the heel down, repeatedly switching hands and stances. Lester, the burly foot-trimming expert genuinely loved by students, guided me painstakingly through the whole laboured attempt.

'I definitely want you to try and do as much as you can, Ste.'

'You and me both, Les,' I panted, looking up at him for confirmation that I should persist in my gouging of the foot with my hoof knife.

'That's it, keep going, you want to bring *that* down to *this* level,' he directed, passing his hand over the suspended foot to illustrate his point. The strapped-up cow kicked out three times before seeming to accept her fate and standing stock still. I was beginning to lose the sensation in my right hand from gripping the knife and fought with my left to even up the foot paring. 'That'll probably do you...'

'Really? Cheers Les!' I gratefully tore off my protective gloves and chucked them into Lester's box.

I ended up developing quite a taste for these general practice farm days which blended effortlessly into reproduction for week two. The mornings always consisted of pregnancy diagnoses and once I'd mastered the art of putting my hand in the correct hole I became adept at detecting many of the subtle indicators of pregnancy. Afternoons generally presented more of a challenge. Foot-trimming required a hand grip I simply didn't possess any more and there'd be the odd day when Lester would catch my eye and I'd slowly shake my head. Disbudding depended very much on the size and strength of the calves we were dealing with. That said, I could virtually guarantee I'd emerge smarting from some aggravated injury or other. Holding the restless, pugnacious calves for my colleagues often meant my tenderised feet were trodden on and my hands and wrists would ache in the restraint of anything even remotely feisty. I fared slightly better when others were pinning a calf down for me to disbud, although I seldom delivered an even amount of pressure to the horn, meaning I was never the quickest. In the end I was relieved it would soon be time to herald in week three, investigation. I assumed this would be a quieter and far less physically demanding week. As it was, I ended up being completely wrong in this assumption.

The investigation week had been created to allow students to undertake the in-depth analysis of a specific problem a local farm had been having. The end of week presentation they gave would ideally contain the odd pointer on the best way to manage this problem. In the two weeks we'd been on practice and repro, the first group had infiltrated a nearby farm afflicted with chronic respiratory disease, while the other had been posted out to a farm in mid Wales with a drastic and unexplained drop in milk output.

Our group turned up for rounds on Monday none the wiser as to what we'd be investigating.

'Hi guys, fancy a spot of TB testing?'

'Roddy! Always a pleasure,' I beamed. 'Probably best not, though, we need to find out what our investigation's going to be on, don't we?'

Roddy's fondness for our group in general and Chloe in particular had resulted in us spending the majority of the last two weeks in his company. He seldom partook in the investigation week, though and we'd assumed the love affair was at an end for the time being.

'No! It's actually *on* TB testing.'

'You're kidding!' I must admit I was pleased to be working with him again. He was easygoing, the banter always batted pleasurably to and fro and he explained what we needed to know in a code that was always painless to decipher. Furthermore he was easily a far less daunting prospect than some of the grizzled, old-school members of staff who would have spent the week barking abrupt questions at us.

We arrived at our nominated farm shortly after ten-thirty. En route we hatched a plan whereby every single cow would be inoculated during this visit, irrespective of how long it might take us. This would not only shift this thankless task out of the way once and for all but also facilitate the assessment of our inoculees once the allotted seventy-two hours had passed. We disembarked from the van and Roddy immediately strode off in search of the owner, leaving us free to explore.

The farm was spectacularly ramshackle. Not ramshackle in the way you might expect after entering a time warp that had you whisked back to the 1930s or something. It was more like the sort of ramshackle you'd see in a post-apocalyptic war zone. Foliage spilled out from beneath derelict buildings, piles of rubble and jagged rusty fencing. Matt and I rounded a corner, marvelling at the sheer decrepitude and almost blundered straight into a recumbent bull, dozing on a strip of pockmarked grass. The colossal Hereford had been sleepily dribbling in a patch of sunlight, perched on his haunches, until we shattered his peace. He sluggishly came to life, scrabbling to his feet and exhaling loudly through his nostrils. A pitiful, flattened fence was all that lay between us and him. I turned sharply to find Roddy bringing up the rear. 'Don't worry lads, the farmer *assures* me he's lame!'

'It's not lame farmers that concern me Roddy!' I retorted, skipping past him as the bull bellowed, pawing aggressively at the ground. 'Probably best if we give the old boy a wide berth, yeah?' Roddy shook his head incredulously as he shepherded us back the way we'd come to begin testing.

It became apparent that this would not be an isolated incident, as the farm was desperately understaffed and hopelessly disorganised. There were calves and milkers dotted around the farm in inappropriately small paddocks where the accumulated layers of bedding had piled so high that the perimeter fence appeared absurdly low. We systematically targeted each of these in turn, climbing over the fence and forming a human barricade to separate animals we'd inoculated from those yet to be tested. On a number of occasions calves would become unsettled by the herding and manhandling process and break free from our clutches, clearing the perimeter fence and galloping for the hills. This would precipitate a sudden frenzied pursuit with either Matt or Roddy hurdling the fence and charging after the escapee, wrestling her back to the sanctity of the paddock. This would all be carried out under the haunting spectre of the marauding bull, as he patrolled the farm, limping from shadow to shadow. It was a scorching May afternoon, summer finally burning through Tupperware skies. Sweat-stained, battered and bloodied, the eight of us stuck to our task until each and every cow had been accounted for and spiked with our two jabs.

After a slight delay, caused by the ambulatory bull sniffing inquisitively around the van, we dragged ourselves painfully on board and made good our escape. A quick stopover at Leahurst to shed overalls, waterproofs and testing equipment and we decided to head virtually en masse to The Wheatsheaf in Raby. Matt declined, citing a need for a bath to ease the sting of a clutch of painful knocks. In the end there were several more late withdrawals and only Roddy, Chloe, Georgia and I made the trip, with Natalie joining us around eight. The Georgia of the previous year's summer ball resurfaced, choosing to harbour a drunken infatuation with a wincing Roddy. She was utterly oblivious to his fondness for Chloe. I toyed with an extremely rare beer, watching the drama unfold.

'I've got heaps of pizza back at my place, Roddy! Why don't we go back and eat *that*?' she gabbled with a knowing look. 'I mean everyone *else* is welcome!' she added as an afterthought, as our table had fallen deathly silent.

Roddy tactfully procrastinated and retired to the bar for another pint. From my relatively sober vantage point it was clear chaos was in the pipeline. Natalie arrived with a smile and a gin and tonic and squeezed in next to me. 'It's going to end in tears, Nat.' I confided with a nonchalant flick of my head at the increasingly unhinged Georgia. The conversation circulated in ever-decreasing drunken circles. We revisited the topic of religion which no one had really cared for at the first time of asking.

'Aw this is boring!' yawned Chloe in her finest Lancashire drawl.

'God, Chloe, you're so *common*!' bit Georgia, unsubtly.

'*What* did you call me?'

Roddy, Natalie and I all began talking at once to try and cover Georgia's tracks. Roddy engaged Georgia's attention while Natalie and I began joking loudly with Chloe about her propensity to sample vodka intra-ocularly when a certain point of the night was reached. I looked up and saw Roddy manoeuvre a leaden Georgia out of her chair and out towards the car park and her long-overdue taxi ride home. Before long he returned to our table via the bar and rather unsteadily set down a tray bearing four more drinks.

'Thank heavens for that!' he sighed. 'She was just going to get more and more offensive wasn't she? Wasn't she? Steve? What's wrong with your face?'

'Roddy, I cannot believe you turned down the opportunity of free pizza! It's half ten. I'm starving!'

'Just have to make do with another pint then won't you!'

'Go on then, what harm could one more do?'

I stirred in bed, it took only the merest hint of head movement for the throbbing to register. I was about to roll over and continue my losing battle with the light that was cascading into my room through anorexic curtains, when the body curled up next to me moaned gently, and a mop of blonde hair bobbed into view. 'Good night last night, Natalie...' I croaked, half statement, half enquiry.

She nodded and then slowly began rubbing her head. 'I think I might head back to my room,' she began.

'Sure.'

'Before anyone, you know, sees me leaving your room.'

130

'Yeah no bother.'

She kissed me lightly on the cheek and emerged fully clothed from my bed to force her feet into her trainers. 'Thanks for letting me snuggle,' she turned and looked down at me, suffering beneath my crumpled duvet.

'Any time, Nat,' I smiled drowsily, relishing the warmth of the bed I now had all to myself. I rolled over as the door clicked shut behind her.

I dozed fitfully for an hour or so before giving it up as a bad job and reaching over for the sheaf of anaesthesia notes in the cabinet next to my bed. Students had begun worrying about the impending mocks to the point where they were scrimping on their rotation duties and using the time to cram. Dr Helen Sutton, her finger as ever on the pulse of the year, sent us all an email stressing the far greater importance of getting the most from our rotations. When this did little to appease our year's resident population of clucking hens, she went further, offering heartfelt assurances that the exams wouldn't overly tax us and then posting up the essay questions we'd face. That was for all except the small animal mock. They'd steadfastly refused to play ball, offering up only the vaguest of essay title clues and circulating an email distancing themselves from the word *mock*. Thankfully equine had been more forthcoming and I knew they were featuring, as one of their two essays, a question on alpha 2 agonist use in general anaesthesia. I elected to read that over for a couple of hours before facing the world. That was until my mobile began to ring.

'Hiya Steve!'

'Hey Chloe?' I gleefully dumped my notes, glad of the excuse, and stretched out opulently in bed. 'How are you this fine morning?'

'Fine.'

'And...?'

'Well, you'll never guess what happened last night.'

'Go on.'

'Roddy stayed over!'

'Really? I knew he really liked you, you little minx! Well best of luck with it, Chloe. I really mean that. He's a nice guy.'

'Aw thanks, Stevie.' She went quiet and I knew there was more. 'Nat rang ... said she stayed over but nowt happened. What's the matter with you?'

I sighed. 'She wanted to cuddle and it was nice just having her

131

here. She's not over Andy yet and to be honest I can't see that changing any time soon.' Natalie had undergone a painful split, with her boyfriend in the year below, in the midst of the equine rotation finale/Grand National night of celebration.

'I'm sorry, Stevie.'

'Don't be. Hope you and Roddy continue making each other happy and see you Thursday.'

'All right, see you then.'

Thursday duly arrived and we returned to the farm to carry out the statutory post 72 hours check for delayed hypersensitivity on all the inoculated cows. It was imperative that we re-checked each and every cow from Monday for the test to have any validity. Roddy stiffened when we scanned the empty paddocks for our subjects.

'Right, that's it, I've had enough of this! Stay here!' he fumed, stomping off in the direction of the owner.

'Look!' Matt pointed out at the banks of fields backing on to the farm. 'There's our bad boys out there.'

I shook my head. 'No wonder Roddy's irate.'

'Think he'll be OK?' Chloe inquired, almost inaudibly, her face pinched with concern.

'I'll go and have a wee look shall I?' I volunteered and set off after him. I reached the peak of a hillock and in the dip below spied Roddy and the owner engaged in a heated exchange. The owner furiously jabbed his finger at Roddy as they stood toe-to-toe. Roddy remonstrated with him all the more vociferously and I could hear his shrill voice above the chirping of the grasshoppers. 'Sort it! Sort it! Or I'll call the ministry in! Got that?'

I clambered down the dusty embankment back to my friends. 'He's OK.' A minute or so later he came down the hill himself. 'Well?' we uttered, as a collective.

'He's got no staff other than himself. We're going to have to get the cows in ourselves before we check them. It means we basically go out to the *back* of the furthest field and walk them all back in. Sorry guys, it's far from ideal, I know.'

We stood in a circle, mulling this over. 'How many fields, Roddy?' I queried, breaking the silence.

'Seven, I think.'

'Well we'd best set off then, hadn't we?' declared Chloe, planting her hands in her pockets as if she meant business.

We reached the back of the seventh and final field. In the middle of the lively patchwork quilt of Holstein Friesians a very distinctive rusty brown form continually announced his presence by mounting various cows. He was like a younger, more virile version of the bull we'd encountered shuffling around the barns and outhouses earlier in the week. His rippling folds of muscles were plainly in evidence.

'As long as he's interested in them, he won't give a jot about us. We'll need to keep an eye on him, though.'

'OK, Roddy, you're the boss.'

We marched down through the fields gathering an ever-increasing mass of bovines in front of us. Matt, Chloe and I became detached from the rest of the group, lagging behind, deeply engrossed in conversation. I would throw regular glances in the direction of the bull but as Roddy had predicted he was far too happy humping his way around all the fields to bother himself with a little light sport with any of us. We were halfway across the last field by the time Roddy and the rest of the team reached the wooden gate at the bottom. Roddy turned to look back at us and suddenly became extremely agitated, signalling furiously that we should hurry. I quickly turned, panicked by his actions, but relaxed when I saw the bull innocently nibbling at some grass.

'What?' I shrugged. 'We're coming! What's the rush?'

He said nothing, but his eyes widened and he signalled even more furiously. There'd been *another* bull in that group. He was black and white and perfectly camouflaged, escaping our attention. Matt, Chloe and I hadn't escaped his, though and we turned to see him standing several feet behind us, snorting and pawing at the ground.

'Guys!' I yelped, 'I think he's good to go!' We broke into a sprint and scrambled over the fence with the bull in hot pursuit.

All our cows were gathered into a gigantic barn. They were to be flushed into a narrow race which would funnel them into a crush where they would be restrained, allowing measurement of any reactive lumps with regulation callipers. Chloe was designated scribe, noting down cow serial numbers and measurements in millimetres relayed to her by Roddy. Matt and another team member, Viv, remained in the barn and fought to propel cows down the passageway and into the race. I worked the crush, trapping each cow at the withers and forcing a cast-iron pipe behind each inmate to prevent them backing out. In the depth of the battle, in the caking mud and oppressive mugginess, the team pulled together like a dream. We were totally absorbed by our task and hadn't noticed the skies began to darken ominously.

We'd got through about three-quarters of the herd when an explosive clap of thunder shook the air. We stared at each other, transfixed, and after an imperceptible delay the heavens gaped open and we began to be pelted with gobstopper-sized hailstones. We elected to plough on through the storm but as conditions worsened so did the fragile mental state of our cows. They became increasingly spooked as the thunderstorm took hold. Matt and Viv took a beating in the barn as the cows switched between smacking themselves against the corrugated walls and stubbornly refusing to be moved anywhere. Once in the crush they reacted badly to the notion of entrapment and vehemently deployed reverse gear. This often coincided with my attempts to pin them in position with the heavy piping and on a number of occasions their violent attempts to exit backwards swung the pipe outwards, thudding it into my legs. Just as the hailstorm began to abate Matt and Viv appeared at the top of the run, shoulders pinned against a particularly obstinate cow. 'Last one!' Matt hissed through gritted teeth, his voice heavily distorted with the effort of heaving the uncooperative cow towards us. At great length she was shoved through the crush and given the all-clear.

Our work done, we sludged, bloodied and bowed, back to the van through glutinous mud. We'd completed another rotation. I rubbed at a hand-sized bruise on my hipbone, discovering two more I had no recollection of receiving. I was in dire need of a steaming hot shower and, if it ever stopped raining, I had a new pair of wellies to buy.

16

A Dress Rehearsal

Even though we'd all just notched up another three-week rotation, the third of six, it was the following week's mocks that were uppermost in the minds of some.

'It just seems totally unnatural to me.'

'Right ... sorry, *what* does?' I'd been hijacked midway between my room and the shower. What had started out simply as a casual exchange of end-of-the-week pleasantries had degenerated into a charged debate.

'Well, I'm about to spend a whole weekend putting together a series of essays that I *know* I'm only going to *regurgitate* next week. In *real* writtens they can ask you absolutely anything.'

No shit, Sherlock! I pulled my slipping towel tighter around my waist and took a deep breath. 'But we've had no time to revise! If they were to ask *absolutely anything*, as you put it, most people would fuck up the entire paper. Isn't the point of these exams merely to give us a slight idea what writtens are going to be like?'

'Yeah, but they won't be like that!'

'Hence the word *slight*. And anyway won't the MCQs be like that? How many real clues have they given away on those? Umm ... none!' I snapped, losing patience with this unresolvable conversation. 'Anyway, I'm in danger of exposing myself here so...'

'Sure, maybe see you at dinner.'

'Yeah mate, maybe.'

I stepped into the shower bemused by the exchange I'd just had. Questioning the point of the mocks struck me as totally pointless. In my eyes the exams would be offering a little taster of what would be in store for us at Christmas. Others seemed more worried that the giving out of essay questions had affected their chances of demonstrating superiority over the rest of the year. *Fucking high achievers! I'd take 50% now if you offered it!* I squeezed my eyes tightly shut and prayed for just such an outcome.

I spent Friday night at my desk putting the finishing touches to rough essay plans on sheep abortion and foal medicine. Not long after ten I ceased in my scribbling and shivered as the memory of a discussion I'd had earlier in the evening flooded back to haunt me. I'd encountered Danny and Sam from the year above, while checking my emails, and both had appeared genuinely shell-shocked. I'd thought orals and practicals weren't due to begin until the Monday but one look at them and I was left in absolutely no doubt they'd already begun in earnest.

'What have you just had guys?'

'Farm practical.'

I didn't want to ask my next question. The thought of how they might reply scared me witless. 'So ... how was it?'

They both quietly shook their heads. 'I don't know what they were playing at. I hadn't *even seen* half of that stuff, let alone be in any position to answer questions on it...' Danny petered out, staring into the middle distance.

'Shit! I'm really sorry.' I flicked my gaze from one to the other before asking as casually as I could muster, 'What's the format again?' I'd buried my head in the sand concerning this specific portion of finals but our dialogue was stirring me into action. Sam began talking in a detached monotone.

'There's ten props. You've got a few minutes at each to answer a number of questions. Then a bell goes and you move on to the next one.'

'*Fuck.*'

'Yeah.' Sam had always come across as honest and level-headed and certainly not one to blow anything out of proportion. 'It was *unnecessarily* hard.'

'So what's next up for you boys, then?' I thought it might be best if we moved swiftly along.

Sam thought for a second before reciting in a tight voice, 'Equine practical on Monday, small animal practical on Tuesday, farm oral on Wednesday, equine oral on Thursday and then on Friday it's ... it's...'

'Smallies oral?' I finished for him.

'Well, yes, but *results*.'

'Oh.'

'The list goes up shortly after six.'

I felt a wave of nausea engulf me. 'Well...' I fought hard for the right words. 'You've both always struck me as being really capable and knowledgeable here. If it's occurred to *me*, then you'd have to think the people who really matter must have noticed, too.' We all put so much faith in the powers-that-be and their perceived omnipotence when it came to evaluating who in the year *had it*. It was far more comforting to view our destiny in this light. 'So, all the *very* best.' I concluded, patting them both on the back. In the end I couldn't escape back to my room quickly enough.

The following week the farm animal and the equine mocks both managed to impart two messages; each one delivered a potent wake-up call in terms of how much information we'd need to acquire prior to *Showtime* at Christmas, while also handing us a welcome confidence boost in the shape of the two well-crafted essays we were able to transcribe for each subject. As far as I was concerned Friday's small animal mock delivered only the wake-up call. Overall, I struggled to get my head around the fact that by Christmas I'd need to have assimilated enough to sit these written exams without the benefit of any essay pointers. Even more galling was the notion that in exactly one year I'd need enough on board to be deemed safe to be let loose on the general public.

I joined a small cluster of fourth years lending moral support from the sidelines and watched in silence as, shortly after six o'clock, the whole of the fifth year piled into Leahurst House. Some linked arms with whoever was closest and squeezed out the tersest of grins, others did their best to appear unfazed but made such a show of this act as to render it meaningless. I imagined myself, had it not been for two measly pathology percentage points, moving indoors with them all, encased in my own private hell. I envisaged a frantic desire to check the list for my name, offset by an equally breathless, unbearable fear of it not being up there. I shook the image from my head to release the tightness in my chest and reverted back to the role of impartial observer.

Gradually people began to filter back out into the sunshine. It

137

became impossible to tell who'd passed and who'd failed, as one by one they'd emerge sobbing uncontrollably to friends and/or mobile phones. Curious, I pressed past people and up the stairs into Leahurst House. It was complete mayhem. The air resonated with hysterical screams and people deliriously leaping on their friends and weeping with unrestrained joy. All except one person.

I saw Danny standing alone in front of the board, staring in unblinking disbelief. The hordes around him seemed oblivious to his plight as he stood amid the euphoric abandon. I remembered back to the end of first year, four years ago, almost to the day: Danny, in the days when we'd been complete strangers, taking the time to stop on his way to celebrate the viva he knew he'd breezed, to check I was OK. He'd seen the worry on my face and come forward, talking me through the fundamentals of what I'd need to know, were they to ask. All I could think, over and over, was *not him, anyone but that guy*. I didn't know what to say or what to do.

As I stood in the doorway, two of Danny's best mates brushed by me, evidently searching for him. They put a consoling arm around him and he crumpled, sobbing. I turned and wandered preoccupied back to my room to wait for the party to start. I knew I was borderline in most of the exams I sat at vet school. I hoped I wasn't seeing my own grisly destiny.

17

Three Nights, Four Days

The dust slowly settled on the latest in a long line of hedonistic Leahurst parties and days' worth of detritus was stacked away for the bin men. During the long weekend's revelling, the fifth year metamorphosed into nomads, unable to lay claim to Leahurst any more. Still hungover they cleared out their lockers and, by close of play on the bank holiday Monday, had jetted out to Majorca to crystallise all their last goodbyes. In their absence we assumed the role of lords of the manor. The wheel *had* rotated, though and, as if to emphasise the point, our section was on the verge of revisiting the topic of small animal studies for the second and final three-week stint.

Our remaining subjects were first opinion, dermatology and cardiology and, finally, orthopaedics. First opinion offered up a choice of venues and, back in October, Matt and I had plumped for a busman's holiday in Manchester for a week of practice with a registered veterinary charity a mere brick's throw from Old Trafford. The bank holiday meant our presence wasn't requested until the Tuesday morning. Keen to keep our time away from Leahurst to a bare minimum, thereby saving money, we drowsily set off for Manchester at half past six on the Tuesday morning.

The posting would offer our first genuine opportunity to take consultations alone, as well as affording us a glimpse of life in a place where lavishing money on household pets simply wasn't an option. We unpacked hastily in the newly refurbished upstairs flat before knotting our ties and presenting ourselves downstairs at twenty to nine. A steady stream of Liverpool twosomes had previously made their way along the East Lancs Road to Manchester and the staff barely batted an eyelid as we loitered in the narrow corridor. It was the sort of scenario which, faced alone, was often

139

slightly nerve-racking; self-consciously shedding cool points with every simpering half smile and shy attempt at eye contact. With two of us, though, it was distinctly untroubling and Matt and I conversed happily while the staff took their time choosing how best to deploy us. A middle-aged man with hair greying at the temples and a lab coat buttoned tightly across an expansive gut approached with a cool and laconic air.

'Matt and Steve?' he inquired, referring to a clipboard which he returned under his arm when we both nodded. 'One of you consults while the other stays in the back and helps out with procedures. You switch over after lunch. Got it?' We both nodded again. 'Good. Who's first, then?'

I looked across at Matt, 'You drove, mate. You choose.'

'I'll do the afternoon. You go and consult now.'

'All right, cheers for now.' I followed the vet, known cryptically as Mr J, as he weaved his way through the building and into what may once have been a large-ish consulting room but which now had a partition dividing it into two. Mr J logged on to the computer which served both halves and spent several minutes scrolling through the waiting clients to find something suitable for me.

'Fancy this one?'

'*Kittens with respiratory infection*' I read off the computer. 'Sounds fine. Probably an issue of vaccination?'

'Or lack of it,' smirked Mr J, superciliously raising a single eyebrow and putting me in mind of Roger Moore during one of his later, more avuncular Bond reprisals.

'Jessica Collins, please?' I opened the door of the packed waiting room and the mere action of requesting a client of my own was enough to send an exquisite quiver of excitement running through me. 'So, what can we do for you today?' I inquired brightly, on returning to my side of the table. Ms Collins said nothing, instead tipping up the battered cardboard box she was carrying, and unceremoniously dumping two scraggy kittens onto the table before me. According to the file both were around ten weeks old. I carried out a brief clinical examination but the problem was obvious. Both kittens had severe upper respiratory tract infections characterised by runny noses, watery eyes, coughing, sneezing and an overall poor condition and lacklustre demeanour. After taking both animals' temperature, noting a slight pyrexia, I broached the subject of vaccination.

Ms Collins proved incapable of grasping the significance of this and our conversation kept disappearing up blind alleys. I very quickly found the exchange infuriating. Both her pets appeared clogged up with cat flu and it had all been totally avoidable. I fought to remain diplomatic, painstakingly outlining the concept of vaccination when all I felt like doing was wrenching my hair out. I seemed unable to get through to her at all. I stood back from the table to gather my thoughts and hopefully summon an explanation that would be greeted by more than a vacant expression and a shrug. Out of the corner of my eye I caught sight of Mr J desperately trying to catch my attention. I looked across and he was gesticulating with both hands in a manner that left me in no doubt. *Leave it!* I prescribed a course of antibiotics to treat both kittens symptomatically and made sure the client left with a leaflet outlining the basics of vaccination. I was left harbouring a deep sense of frustration.

The practice was generous with breaks and before long Matt and I were back up in the flat drinking tea and discussing the colour of Philip Schofield's hair.

'It definitely *wasn't* that colour when he came out to Leahurst and made that documentary for BBC 1!' stated Matt authoritatively.

'Perhaps he found being out there severely traumatising? Wouldn't be the first.'

'Anyway, how's consults going?' asked Matt dragging his eyes from the television which had cut to a nappy commercial.

'Weird, really, because we're in quite a rough area and it's a charity, I was expecting to see caseloads of neglected, mistreated animals.'

'Right.'

'And, I suppose I've seen *some*, but in the main the clients have been totally devoted to their pets. If anything ignorance seems more of an issue than malevolence.' I told Matt the vaccination story, gulped down the remnants of my tea and then headed back downstairs for a case that would blur the distinction between the two.

'Can I please have Joe Dempster?' I let my eyes flit across the waiting room for any signs of movement. A young mother rose and escorted three pre-school children and a decidedly groggy-looking Staffordshire bull terrier puppy over towards me.

'My husband really hates these places,' she announced, I assumed by way of an explanation for his absence.

'Yeah, I'm the same with dentists,' I replied, smiling at the morose children clinging for grim death on to their mother.

'He absolutely *adores* Cole, though.'

I wondered who she was trying to convince. 'Glad to hear it. How *is* Cole?' I squinted down at the rather withdrawn puppy, chewing on his leather leash and drooling over the floor.

'My husband...'

'Your husband?' I prompted, hoisting Cole gently up and on to the table to save me from having to bend my knees to examine him.

'He was fitting these brand new radiators in the house when one ... sort of ... fell!' She lowered her eyes and almost apologetically stroked at her unresponsive puppy's mottled and downy coat.

'Okay.' I took my stethoscope from my pocket and felt my heart sink when I saw the bruises around Cole's midriff and the tennis ball sized implosion at the back of his skull. 'How's he been since your husband ... since the incident?'

'He hasn't eaten anything and he keeps bringing stuff up.'

As she spoke I shone my pen torch into his glazed eyes and he blinked back me, uncomprehending. 'He also, like, circles around and he's had a few funny turns and all.'

I nodded and turned away grimly to try and catch Mr J's eye as he consulted to my left.

'Will he ... will he be OK, doctor?' she looked beseechingly at me.

'As my name badge says, I'm just a fourth ... sorry, final year student. In my opinion Cole's in quite a bad way but I'm going to see what the vet has to say.' I turned to see Mr J in quiet attendance, on his side of the partition. 'Excuse me one second, please.' I moved over to him and recounted what I'd seen and heard. Then I stood back as he first re-introduced himself and then went on to explain why Cole wouldn't be leaving with them.

'Won't he get better?' the eldest of the children suddenly burst out.

Mr J regarded him with careworn sincerity. 'He's got very bad damage to his head. He's a very sick dog, who's in an awful lot of pain. I'm afraid this is by far the kindest option.'

The family trooped out sadly and rather reluctantly.

'I'll raise the vein and you can do the honours.'

I exhaled deeply, 'Sure.'

'He isn't her husband by the way.'

'No? I wasn't sure,' I murmured, plunging the needle tip into the bottle of pentobarbitone. 'I'm also guessing this little guy *wasn't* hit with a falling radiator.' I looked up from drawing the requisite volume of drug into my syringe. 'Not unless the radiator happened to have the exact same dimensions as a steel toe-capped boot.'

'You don't know that. They've been bringing their pets here for years and this is the first time anything like this has ever happened.'

I paused as he finished talking, altering his grip on the puppy's upper right forelimb.

'Ready?'

I nodded and pierced the pliable skin, entering the vein and clouding the interior of the syringe with blood which mingled wispily with the blue pentobarbitone. 'Right. Inject slowly and keep drawing back to check you're still in.'

Cole slumped languorously into Mr J's arms as I ejected the entire contents of the syringe into his obscenely young body. 'Sorry, Cole. It's not turned out the way I'd have chosen for you, boy,' I whispered, as he took his last breath. Mr J verified that Cole was dead and gave me back my stethoscope.

'Will anything be done?' I asked, despising what I'd just had to do.

'I'll file a report and inform the relevant authorities. If they pursue it I'm happy to help. Listen...' he began, as I'd turned away. 'Our priority is to deal with what is presented to us, what animals come through this door. The rest...' he waved an arm in the vague direction of Greater Manchester, 'is someone else's problem. We have enough on our hands as it is.'

My mood stalled in the doldrums for the remainder of the day and failed to lighten as I eased into Wednesday. 'Agnes Carson, please?' A frail elderly gentleman was tugged to his feet by a sprightly mongrel that possessed a baffling montage of differing breed traits. I held the door open as the man doddered passed me and into the room.

'Agnes was my wife but she's past away now.'

I tutted sympathetically as his dog sniffed around the floor and leapt up at him.

'He was always *her* dog. That's why it was in her name.'

'Aw that's no problem. We can easily change that for you, if you like. I guess he's *your* dog now, aren't you boy?' I switched my attention to the dog and he licked eagerly at my hand.

'Won't be any need for that, son,' his gnarled hands rolled and unrolled the dog's lead. I hadn't even been aware he'd unclipped it.

'Sure, we can keep it registered as Agnes,' I said gently, ignoring the tone of resignation in his voice. 'I'm sure she'd like that.'

'I mean, we shan't be coming here any more. Like I said, he was always her dog. She always said she couldn't bear the thought of Billy having to cope without her.'

Please don't ask. Please.

'It's what she wanted ... if you could please? It's not fair on Billy; having to cope without his mum.'

'I understand,' I said evenly, stroking at the wiry hair on Billy's oversized head. 'You know, he's still got a good few years left in him, a bit like yourself.' Mr Carson looked weary and downcast; his hands bound by a pledge that left him powerless to act. 'He'd be good company for you, too. I beg of you, *please*, don't be hasty...' I found my mouth had gone dry and I swallowed hard, acutely aware of the desperation in my voice. '*Please* ... he'd want to keep going.'

There was no turning him. 'It's what she wanted,' he said flatly.

'D'you want Billy's body for burial or anything?' I found myself saying.

'Just his collar,' he replied faintly, a large tear landing with a plop on the dark table. He shuffled quietly from the room and left me alone with Billy wagging his tail and throwing looks of bemusement up at me and at the door that had now swung shut.

'Can we not just *say* we did it? Give the old boy his collar back and let the dog live? Re-home him or something? *Surely* one of the nurses...'

'It's the owner's wishes. Apart from anything else it's a striking-off offence, not to carry out his request.'

'What? Even if the owner's request is needlessly cruel?'

'It isn't needlessly cruel; he's fulfilling his dying wife's last wishes.'

'But...' I was losing the argument and knew it. 'No one needs to know.'

'All it needs is for him to see his wife's dog out and about and we'd be in exceedingly hot water with the RCVS. My feet wouldn't touch the ground!' Mr J added, in a tone of voice verging on the reproachful.

I nodded and smiled ruefully. 'It's not worth losing a licence over.'

'No,' he agreed. 'Why don't you return to your morning's consults and we'll pass Billy's collar through to you?'

'OK, thanks.' I looked up for the first time and saw Matt at the other side of the room. It occurred to me he'd probably end up having to do it. I smiled disconsolately at him and stroked at Billy's disproportionately large ears as I left. 'Sorry boy but the customer's always right, apparently.'

By the time Friday had arrived I'd packed my belongings in eager anticipation of our departure for Leahurst that evening. I had been willing the three nights, four days to draw to a close. It would be unfair to blame the charity and their sterling work for this. I was indebted to them for the chance to pit my wits against a whole morning's quota of consultations, and appreciative that they'd let me loose on some of their most trusted clients. Furthermore the cases themselves had been immensely challenging, both medically and emotionally.

'How did your last afternoon pan out in the end, Matty?' I asked, as we divided up our Indian takeaway.

'Yeah. It was enjoyable enough. Dragged on a bit, though. You?'

I grunted disparagingly. 'Fairly low key.'

'There comes a point when there's nothing to gain from simply watching certain procedures, I think,' he remarked. 'We need to be doing things like taking blood ourselves to get anything from the experience now.'

'Without question, mate. Also true to say that time passes a heck of a lot quicker when you're occupied with *something*.'

'I was the same earlier on; the morning couldn't end quickly enough!'

'I suppose the bottom line is that I'm just feeling jaded, Matt,' I confessed, peeling back the lid on my carton of chicken korma. 'You know, we're well into June now, fourth year began way back in September. I feel like I'm running on empty a bit. The sooner this whole rotation is over the better, it feels like a rotation too far after the exams *and* farm *and* equine *and* everything else.'

* * *

Another week, another subject. The SAH handbook referred to our next scheduled stop as Dermatology and Cardiology. The students who had most recently sampled its peculiar delights knew it simply as either *Dermaholiday* or *Dermacorridor*. Sadly the SAH's resident cardiologist had chosen our week to attend a conference in Denver, Colorado, exposing us to the full horrors of a week of undiluted alopecia, blackheads and coats lightly dusted with dandruff.

'Are we in for a busy week, Mike?'

Michael Nugent glanced down at a pair of shoes buffed to a standard only an ex-military man such as himself could ever aspire to, and considered his reply. When he finally spoke it appeared he was utilising as few facial muscles as humanly possible.

'Yes, we'll be kept fairly busy.'

I made a polite noise and pulled a face at Sophie while Mike kept staring at his shoes. In the stifling silence I loosened my tie and undid the top button of my shirt. The hospital had evolved into a radically different ecosystem since our last visit on the very cusp of winter. It had become a humid, suffocating cauldron. Fetid odours swelled in the windowless, claustrophobic miasma. Something seemed to occur to Mike and he silently left the tiny student lab.

Megan flinched. 'Am I the only one feeling the urge to scratch myself each time he mentions mites and lice? I'm sure they're all over me!'

'Hmm,' I stroked my chin pensively. 'Sounds to me like you've almost certainly got a dose of crabs, my lady.'

'Get lost!' she yanked lightheartedly at my tie, leaving an absurdly small knot.

'Right! That's criminal damage. Not been a good day for you has it, Em? Firstly I uncover your secret infestation with pubic lice and then you end up with a lawsuit on your hands!' I continued my diatribe, pretending to flounce out of the lab. 'I'll see *you* in court!' I turned and flounced straight into Mike, on his way back, nearly knocking a small tray of slides out of his hands.

'Problem, Steve?' he inquired, dryly.

I blushed deeply. 'No, between you and me I can't see it ever getting as far as the courtroom.'

'I have some skin scrapes for us to view under the microscope.' He was so adept at speaking without moving his lips I found myself wondering where he kept his ventriloquist's dummy. *Gottle of geer! Gottle of geer!* We pressed ourselves against the walls and each other to let Mike squeeze through to the hooded microscope. He lovingly placed the first of the slides on to the viewing platform

146

and announced, to no one in particular, 'Pruritic, alopecic dog; tell me what we think might be happening here?'

'Malassezia?' answered Georgia, perking up as the chance to create a good impression presented itself, her lisp emphasising the 's' in a way that made me want to snigger. I caught Natalie's eye, forcing the two of us to bite our tongues to suppress giggles of mirth.

'Anything else?' prompted Mike, bringing me back.

'Walking dandruff?'

'Yes, but more obvious than that,' he replied crossly. 'You really should know this.' The room fell silent once again except for the scratching sound of Mike's skilful knob-twirling as he scanned the slide. He gave up. 'Flea allergy!'

We all sucked our teeth and emitted a sound we hoped would convey recognition as well as acute disappointment. I leant forward, placing my sweating hands on my knees. I was finding the tedium almost unbearable as we perspired freely in the congested boxroom.

'No, nothing of note there.' Mike tossed the spent slide into the sharps' bin by his elbow. 'There's a case coming in at three thirty; a Westie with atopic dermatitis. Take a short break and I'll meet you all in reception at twenty-five past.'

We reconvened after spending ten minutes guzzling paper cups full of water and looking on sheepishly as students occupied with far more taxing weekly challenges than us buzzed by, juggling hefty presentation requirements with even heftier caseloads.

'Who's taking the history on this one, Matt?'

'Natalie's got hold of the client file.'

'Sounds good to me.'

'Are you and her...?'

'An item? No, we haven't really spoken since that TB testing night when you stayed in to wash your hair.'

'That's a shame.'

'What's a shame?' Natalie bustled into the room, her ears pricked at the hint of a tasty morsel of gossip.

'It's a bit...' I stammered, unsure of how to finish the sentence. Our eyes met and fire fizzed momentarily before flickering and going out.

Megan, Sophie and Georgia joined us in the small room. The six of us sat and fidgeted, unable to settle as we awaited the arrival of our itchy dog. I mopped my brow with the sleeve of my lab

147

coat as the air conditioning rattled and wheezed ineffectually on the wall above.

'Would you mind if I muzzled Trudy?'

Affronted, the owner leapt furiously to her dog's defence. 'She's never *ever* done *anything* like that before! She's normally good as gold.'

I looked across at Megan rubbing her recently nipped hand, and ploughed on, 'It's as much for your protection as anything else. I'd hate for you to get bitten as well; apart from anything else we'd be the ones technically to blame.' I dropped the muzzle over the Westie's snarling snout and clipped it together at the back as Megan restrained her with the lead. She then picked up where she'd left off with the clinical examination. Natalie, sitting on a stool at the table, chewed on her pen and worked through the specially formulated dermatology check-list in front of her.

'Any recent trips abroad?'

'God, yeah! Me and me mates just got back from Ayia Napa. It was wild!'

'Sorry, no, I meant your dog.'

'Oh, God! Sorry! No, she stayed behind with me mam.'

'Very wise.'

'Sorry Steve, what's that?' Natalie turned to me, deeply perturbed at the intrusion.

'Just saying *that's very wise*; Ayia Napa's no place for a Westie.'

Ignoring me, Natalie returned to her check-list. 'Any allergies that you are aware of?'

'Yeah, fake suntan!'

I had to turn away and pretend to search for something on the computer, my eyes streaming, as Natalie's wafer-thin patience took another hit.

'Does *your dog* have any dietary allergies?' she persisted, cleverly allowing the client to believe it was a fresh question.

'She's on that *wotsit* diet?'

'*No wonder its skin's fucked, if she's feeding the poor mutt cheesy wotsits,*' I whispered to Sophie, under my breath.

'It's called *ookanoo* or something?'

'Eukanuba?'

'Yeah, that's it! Is that a good one?'

'Yes, I'd have no qualms giving it to my dog.'

Megan got up from kneeling on the floor, having finished her exam, and sketched in the afflicted areas on the diagrammatic dog on the front of Natalie's sheet.

'Thanks, Em.'

Just as she finished Mike entered and stood silently next to Natalie, scrutinising her handiwork for several minutes as we melted into the background. He then took to the floor and confounded the client with a befuddling potted history of atopic dermatitis and its cavalcade of treatment options. Forty-five minutes later both were shown to the door, the dog straining at her leash, the owner dumbstruck by the barrage of information. She'd agreed to a course of Chinese herbal therapy.

'Trudy's coming back in next Tuesday, it's a shame you'll miss it. What are you all on next week?'

I peeled myself off the wall like an Elastoplast. 'Orthopaedics.'

Mike thought for a minute and said nothing.

'So, how would joint disease manifest itself in a dog that was presented to you? Let's go round everyone one by one.' Patrick swivelled from side to side on his padded office chair, stroking and flexing the stifle of the Jack Russell terrier obediently sitting on his lap. His shaved head and squat frame meant this made him look like the first *northern* Bond villain. *Ey oop Mr Bond, we've been expecting you like!*

'Pain?'

'Yes, Georgia isn't it?' She nodded.

'Crepitus?'

'Yes Sophie.'

Shit, that's what I was going to say! Umm...

'Umm ... poor range of motion?

'Uh-huh.' He looked at me uncertainly.

'Steve.'

'Yes Steve. Next...' He switched his attention to Megan, standing beside me.

'Joint effusion.'

'Very good, Megan! Sorry, I don't know *your* name.'

'Matt. Swelling and inflammation?'

'Excellent. That just leaves you Natalie.'

'Muscle wastage?'

'Yup, very good! I think you're all going to be teaching *me* at this rate!'

He took us through the bones of an orthopaedics clinical exam, including testing our scant knowledge of spinal reflexes with the help of the malleable and slavishly cooperative Jack Russell. I found the manner of his delivery conducive to learning and the period until 11.30 and the bilateral Rottweiller arthroscopy held over from Friday sailed past very quickly.

The six of us donned our scrubs, hats and masks and filed into theatre at the same moment as Nora, the student elected to monitor the anaesthesia, took up her position at the head of the table. I immediately picked up on her anxiety. She kept plugging her stethoscope into her ears with blind terror emblazoned across her features and was frantically fumbling through her patient's thick hair to locate a pulse.

Sophie had also noticed her panicky demeanour and dug me in the ribs. 'Nora's looking a bit on edge, isn't she?'

'Like a rabbit caught in the headlights; maybe she'll settle down once the procedure gets under way.'

We stood in a line with our backs against the chill of the wall and watched the large television monitor propped up on a trolley at the bottom corner of the table. Had it been *actual* television I'd have been reaching for the remote control and a bout of channel hopping. The initial novelty of viewing the canine stifle joint from the inside had worn as thin as the brittle, diseased cartilage Patrick was shaving off from his control point on the exterior of the joint capsule. He thoughtfully provided an insightful commentary but the combination of him having his back to us, his heavy brogue and the whirring of the arthroscopic flushing kept drowning him out.

Two hours into the procedure I began gazing longingly at the floor and wondering whether I'd still be able to see the monitor from down on the ground. I was shaken from my ponderings by Nora scrambling off her stool.

'The isofluorane gas is getting a bit low!'

'Top it up, then!' Patrick barely even registered that she'd spoken, partly because surgeons tend to view anaesthetists in much the same way as diners view the waiters in expensive restaurants, and partly because he was thoroughly engrossed in his cartilage chiselling. The sight-glass clearly showed that the gas was down to a bare

150

minimum. Nora leant forward, turning off the vaporiser and cutting the anaesthetic gas to the inert patient. This was the only way to top the gas up and, providing she moved moderately quickly, Nora had ample time to replenish the anaesthetic and reunite dog with gas. She pulled out the keyed filler and slotted the bottle's nozzle into the tray. The welcome sound of liquid glugging into the vaporiser was followed by the sight-glass registering full. Nora removed the bottle, screwed the lid back on and tried to slot the key back in place.

I could see from my vantage point across the table that the key was upside-down. I opened my mouth to begin to explain this but never got as far as forming any words. Nora forcibly tried to thrust this square peg into the round hole three or four times, each time with greater force. Frenetic with worry that the dog would wake up she then, inexplicably, turned the vaporiser back on to full. It hadn't been properly closed, though, and she only succeeded in spraying a cloud of isofluorane into the air with a sound like a high-pressure tyre pump.

Our eyes widened in amazement at what she did next. Mortified, she fled the theatre like a scalded cat. Her supervisor, Catherine, chose that very second to poke her head into theatre to check on the progress of her student. Seeing the gas spraying everywhere, polluting theatre, she made an instant bee-line for the hissing anaesthetic machine just as Nora was desperately seeking to vacate the premises. It was difficult not to laugh as both of them fought to pass each other. After what seemed like an eternity but was probably only a second or two, both jostled their way through the narrow aisle between table and wall. Nora scrambled her way into the corridor, a distraught sob following her out as Catherine switched off the vaporiser and re-inserted the filler key. Satisfied normality had been restored, she then went off in search of Nora and relative calm descended once again on theatre. The procedure drew to a close. The tranquillity of theatre was disturbed only by the sound of Catherine's squeaky tones, as she comforted a clearly inconsolable Nora in the corridor. Patrick speedily sutured up his incisions in the joint capsule and in the skin, and we were all dismissed for lunch.

Matt and I stepped across blazing paving stones on an utterly deserted precinct, blinking like moles in the sunlight. All the other courses at university had long since packed away their teaching manuals and all the chairs in the Students' Union had been placed on tables until the autumn. We sat on a low wall and ate lunch.

'D'you get your ticket for Saturday, Matt?'

'Yeah, last night. Hopefully it's a good one this year.'

'Who's at your table?'

'Jack put my name down. I'm guessing with all the guys on the corridor: Dave, John...'

'I'm at a table with some of the old fifth year, guys I used to be mates with when I was in that year.'

'That'll be good!'

'Hopefully. Might end up the last time I see some of them, so...' I shrugged at the sheer inevitability of this. Vet school had been normality for such a long time that it was hard to contemplate it ever coming to end or what might lie beyond its blue horizon.

'This time next year...'

'I know; don't say it, Matt!' I laughingly cut him off, only half joking.

'Best head back?'

'I guess so.'

'Hold still, stop squirming!'

'I *am* holding still, I *am* squirming!'

Brad was tying my bow-tie for me and the effort of concentrating was digging folds into his forehead. 'It's so much easier doing my own than someone else's.'

'I'd heard that about you, Brad!' I grinned, trying to remain starched and upright in my black tuxedo. He eyed me dubiously and pressed on with the task in hand.

'Conservative party ever get back in touch?' I burst out laughing and the knot disintegrated in his hands.

'No, that idiot never called back. Thank God; dreadful bore that he was!'

'He had *you* convinced!'

'I *seriously* need to get you back for that.'

'What have you been on this week, mate?' I inquired, in a thinly disguised ruse to change the subject.

'Equine,' he replied, focusing all his attention back on the tie.

'Hard or easy?' A distinction between equine's two separate rotations was often drawn. The one I'd toiled my way through

152

back in March was *hard* equine; the one that waited for me in October and consisted of practice, diagnostic imaging and anaesthesia was given the misleading prefix *easy*.

'Hard.' He tugged at the ends of the tie.

'Ooh, tough call! Glad it's done and dusted?'

I know I am!

He wavered, 'I'm sad it's over to be honest. I adored every minute of it.'

'Did you? I guess equine's your thing isn't it? A lot harder to track down those pesky foxes on foot isn't it? Little blighters!'

'So true,' he sighed with mock earnestness. 'How about you?'

'Last week? Small animal orthopaedics.'

'Good?'

'Yeah! I'd say it was the pick of that three. Scrubbed in on a cruciate op yesterday which was pretty good.'

'That's you,' he declared, pulling his hands away but leaving them suspended on either side of my tie for a few moments, as if he was a hairstylist checking his cut was symmetrical.

'Brilliant, Bradley, you're a consummate professional. I'll buy you a pint later.'

'Aye, a pint of McEwan's Export 'cos I'm fi Glasgie!'

'Scottish accent still needs a *lot* of work, though!' I grinned, unable to keep a straight face. 'Are you heading over?'

He looked at his watch. 'No, not just yet. I need to get my camera and ticket from my room.'

'Well, thanks again! I'll see you in there.' I then turned and headed over the small wooden bridge to the marquee and the deceptively tricky task of finding my table.

The shadows were shortening and the academic year was drawing to a close. I found myself tapping into the sense of euphoria and general end of an era sentiment percolating my table of departing vets. I sat next to Alex and finally felt in a position to enjoy his company free from the aching despair of being left behind. He was now departing for good and would begin work as a pathologist on Monday. That automatically shifted me up a rung to the final year and I was slowly becoming acquainted with the idea that the suit fitted. The stigma of failure had floated away on the breeze almost without me noticing.

'Final year goes by so fast, mate. I remember this time last year and it only seems like yesterday.'

I smiled at this and thought back to the previous year's summer ball and all that had happened since. I'd loved fourth year but was overjoyed it had now been consigned to the past.

'Onwards and upwards, mate!' He grinned, clinking my glass. This was dwarfed by a far louder clinking sound as Ron Jackson took to the stage rattling a teaspoon on his champagne flute at the microphone. His after dinner speech was a touchingly fond tribute to the outgoing final year, singling out individuals whose unintentionally humorous gaffes had been brought to his attention. The glassy-eyed audience offered rapturous applause to each and every recipient as if they were family. Ron then brought matters to a close by name-checking members of the newly installed fifth year who'd also done enough to warrant special mention. Thanks to Roddy I took my turn. I caught sight of his curly mop of hair, across the archipelago of tables, as he leant animatedly into Chloe.

'I would also like to suggest that Steve Weddell seeks extra help with his cow anatomy, in the hope he learns to distinguish one orifice from another!' A roar went up from my year and Alex slapped me heartily on the back.

The plates were cleared away, the lights dimmed and the ball lost all definition, morphing into a quintessential Leahurst gathering. Students diffused through the marquee like molecules through a semi-permeable membrane, clumping together in tight unions and then dispersing either to take on or shed fluid. My bow-tie, knotted with a budding equine surgeon's perfectionism, slipped off somewhere in the twilight of Leahurst lawn. I made a mental note to check on the grass when the sun started to come up. I knew I'd still be around when that happened; I was here for the duration.

154

18

Can I Have an 'H' Please, Bob?

The first thing I noticed on starting back at school was how pale and drawn people looked. I could only surmise that worry about finals was to blame. To take us up to that bowel-loosening week would be back-to-back rotations; in my case easy equine and the second instalment of farm. This would leave three weeks for knuckling down, alone with the books and losing all perception of reality.

It became harder and harder to relax as time wore on. The moment I let my guard down the ticking time-bomb of finals could be heard above the clink of snooker balls, the television or the crowd at Anfield. It became an impossibility to take pleasure from anything as the nagging gripes eventually increased in a babbling crescendo, drowning out all the other voices. *Got to work, don't know nearly enough! Still so much to cover. Haven't even looked at everything once yet! At this rate I shan't get a chance to even look at some things! Are people looking over ophthalmology? Everyone else knows much more than me and I'm in danger of being left behind here. Come on! Read! Stay focused!* The thought of finals coloured every waking moment and it reached a nadir with any extra curricular activity needing to be forcibly justified to oneself. I elected to keep my head down, construct a watertight study plan and chip away at my notes in as much of my spare time as I could stomach. It was under these heavy, doom-laden skies that we turned up for rotations, fearfully stealing ourselves for the storm we knew was brewing.

Our week of equine practice began with an invitation to choose a suitable subject for the obligatory 40-minute talk we would give at rounds on the Friday. We opted for dermatological diseases as we knew where we could readily lay our hands on the relevant information, plus it lent itself to being evenly split six ways. Our group was then split *two* ways and each threesome was assigned to a different practice vet. Matt, Sophie and I had barely blown on our coffees when a call came in and we were buckling up in Lauren's car, en route to a lame pony in Thornton Hough.

The work-up made for gruesome viewing. I'd seen enough lame horses to recognise that the misshapen, misaligned hooves splaying flat-footedly across the asphalt yard belonged to a pony with chronic laminitis. Lauren kept the examination to a mercifully bare minimum and then suggested to the owner that she gave orthopaedic shoes another try. She'd had a pair of heart bar shoes fitted after Christmas but given up on them after one had become detached. We packed up and got back in the car but not before Lauren had given the owner the number of a well-respected local farrier. 'He'll sort you out! Let me know how you get on.'

I rattled along in the back of the car disgruntled with my world, panicking wildly at the thought of finals. I was gripped by an unshakeable sense of urgency regarding the taking on of information. There'd been a total lack of any academic cachet back at the stables. Feeling profoundly insecure, I kept visualising all the other final year groups being hand-fed prime cuts of exam fodder while we squandered our time pootling around the countryside, learning nothing. I sat in silence and struggled to quell these irrational palpitations.

After lunch we had a session of pony rectalling with Dr Tom Dexter. We met under the veranda outside the equine hospital and trailed after him down the rutted track in twos like over-sized children on a school trip to the farm. He flicked the latch on the splintered wooden gate and we all entered the spacious field. It occurred to me that these ponies must have had to endure violation by a different set of arms every Monday afternoon for as many weeks as their equid brains could recall. They took one look at us and bounded off to the opposite side of the field.

'Hard to blame them, I suppose!'

'Especially with *you* around!'

'This is just going to run and run isn't it, Matt?'

He shrugged at me as if to say, 'and...?'

One by one we rounded up and caught all the ponies in the field, marching them back in a line to the equine yard. It became apparent there were only going to be five ponies to cover the six of us. We secured them in stocks and hooked up a platter of small bran mashes to keep our subjects as distracted as would be possible while undergoing such an intimate internal examination. We then stood in a line, rustling impatiently in our waterproofs and eyeing the swaying line of munching ponies.

'Have you chosen your pony yet, Steve?'

I screwed up my eyes and surveyed the row of swishing tails. 'I quite like the look of that dappled one at the end, Soph? Dunno if I'll get a go, though. Five into six doesn't go.'

She thought for a moment. 'Maybe Tom Dexter will blow a whistle and we'll have to race each other from the glove box to see who misses out?'

'They could make that a sport at the next Olympics. It'd be like a variation on Musical Chairs, except when the music stops some poor sod's left with nowhere to put their arm. I'd pay good money to watch that!'

In the end all six of us ended up rectalling every pony. Dr Dexter interspersed the session with a series of interactive mini-tutorials on equine anatomy as well as reproductive diseases and disorders. At each interlude one of us took a turn out and topped up the placatory bran mashes. By the time five o'clock arrived we were content that every anatomical structure theoretically within our grasp had been recognisably palpated. It dawned on me that to only ever appreciate those parts of the day that gave rise to potential exam pointers, did both the day and the rotation a huge disservice. Apart from the fact that becoming a vet has so much more to it than the repetitive acquisition of dry facts, it was an approach that squeezed the joy out of these days.

We spent the following three days discovering that the term *easy* equine was only applicable in a purely relative sense. We skimmed across the golden, early autumn countryside vaccinating and lameness checking; we sat ensconced in Dr Dexter's snug office, passing around the bourbon biscuits, listening avidly to him as he lectured to us on equine breeding; and we sifted through carousels of slides, searching for pertinent accompaniment to our burgeoning powerpoint presentation. I cursed and spell-checked my way through a drawn-out Wednesday night in the computer room, finishing my segment

157

of the presentation and emailing it to Natalie who'd selflessly agreed to assimilate the text and produce the hand-out.

On Friday morning we turned up shortly after eight and commandeered the seminar room until nine-fifteen for a dress rehearsal. Before we knew it our call arrived and we breezed through our talk without any glitches, over-running by around ten minutes. This never struck me as too big a problem as it cut into the time left at the end for questions. It would be a cold day in hell before any student audience member posed anything even remotely challenging, questions-wise. Everyone was too well aware of the undying enmity it would earn them from the group sweating under the podium spotlight. A few rogue members of staff had infiltrated the talk, though, and our group eyed them cagily as if they were a small cluster of wasps, hovering threateningly in the confined space of the seminar room. I saw Jill stir, pointlessly raising an arm.

Fuck.

'Who did the bit on sarcoids, sorry I've forgotten?'

Not me, phew!

Natalie diffidently owned up.

'Can I just ask what you said about their causes? I'm not sure if I missed what you mentioned on it.'

Natalie rifled obediently through her notes, the eyes of the room burning into the backs of her hands, making them quiver. 'I ... I just said there was a possible viral component ... with insect vector involvement ... we didn't feel we had the time to go *too deeply* into the causes of things.'

'Mmm-hmm.' Jill didn't look overly enamoured by this admission.

'But,' Natalie added, the strength and clarity returning to her voice. 'I think our notes mention that they're caused by a papillovirus?'

Get in!

'Well, that just happens to be one of several theories. The truth is no one really knows.'

Well, thanks for that pearl of wisdom! Next!

Edward, the vet in charge of practice with whom Natalie, Georgia and Megan had spent much of their week, got to his feet and ran a cursory glance around the room. 'Anyone else got any more questions? No? Well...' he began to clap, and the rest of the room quickly followed suit as they had on each of the previous three occasions I'd sat through rounds on a Friday. With each of those weeks I'd felt incremental pulses of dread as my own turn at the front of the class was brought that little bit closer. My stomach had churned queasily at the very thought of this talk and suddenly it was over. I leant back in my seat and gave a huge sigh of relief. I was at a loss to explain how I kept continually negotiating these vet school hurdles. I saw my compatriots take to the floor as if they owned it and it was an effort of mind to see myself in the same light. Eight weeks from sitting written finals and I was still having to expend energy to feel I belonged in such exalted company. I still felt like a gate-crashing fraud, only ever a matter of a few seconds away from being unmasked and turfed out.

We filed out of the now empty seminar room, the odd copy of the stapled hand-out we'd slaved over lying dog-eared and discarded on the slate-grey carpet tiles. The rest of the day was ours. I split from the group to return the slide carousel and followed the gravel path back to my room, lost in thought as the rain pattered all around me. The pleasure I'd taken from surviving to tick another rotation week off the list washed away as I felt for my key in the dripping doorway. I knew if I didn't devote the rest of the day to revision I'd quickly lose any sense of achievement and well-being.

To the untrained eye diagnostic imaging was one of the less taxing weeks of equine rotation. All it involved was taking pictures, after all! Unfortunately underpinning each and every X-ray snapshot was a need for anatomical expertise. Every view relied heavily on a deep awareness of skeletal geography. Without it, dorsoproximal-palmarodistal oblique and palmaroproximal-palmarodistal oblique navicular views (page one of the manual) were nothing more than alphabet soup. We spent Monday slowly familiarising ourselves with what was needed to ensure this vital link in the diagnostic chain held firm – learning the techniques for operating the clunky apparatus to line up shots accurately, sussing the requisite exposures for each of the views and becoming adept at developing radiographs in the darkroom. The hardest part, I found, relied on mastering all three, and that was the actual interpretation of the radiographs. It rankled with me how much I lagged behind and I skulked back to my room at lunchtime to photocopy an *In Practice* article which I would unashamedly dip into throughout the week. The equine practical exam in May always featured at least one radiograph; this meant guaranteed marks if you could nail the concept. This lit a fire beneath me, forcing me to get my head around a discipline I'd always laboured with.

The first time I set eyes on the equine anaesthesia drill I was immediately put in mind of a hectic pit-stop during a Formula One grand prix. I saw a team in matching overalls race against the clock, each member with their own personal remit, coalescing into a collective swarming over the grounded subject. Back then I'd been on soft tissue surgery, loitering in theatre under the pretext of helping to clear up but in reality delaying rejoining my group as I knew the ennui of another tutorial awaited. I ended up lingering with the anaesthesia students as the next patient pulled into the small padded box.

'So guys, tell me what we need to do first here?' A 'roaring' stallion was booked in for a Hobday operation later in the afternoon and our clinician, Catherine, had assembled us outside his stable to kick proceedings off.

'Take his shoes off!' pouted Georgia disdainfully, without even a hint of inflection in her voice. Her sulky body-language shouted from the rooftops that she found the question so elementary that answering it physically pained her. She'd been keen to project an image of an audaciously talented, equine aficionada; someone who rode to a very high standard every other weekend and was on first-name terms with all the senior members of staff. The previous week, on imaging, Matt and I had been admitting to a flimsy appreciation of equine limb anatomy when she'd butted in and confided patronisingly, 'Oh don't worry, it *comes*.' We were all, therefore, flabbergasted when Catherine curtly contradicted her.

'No! Pre-anaesthesia clinical exam; *very very* important!'

Sophie, standing in front of me in the stable doorway, kicked gently at my shin with the sole of her boot and I put my eyes down, fighting the urge to burst out laughing. I loved the way equine made absolutely no distinction between students who had an evangelical zeal for horses, who'd salivate openly at the mention of Burleigh and Badminton, and those like me who heard the word Badminton and thought shuttlecocks and tight white shorts.

'So, let's recap. We do our exam, yeah? Check there's no heart condition or anything else a general anaesthetic's likely to exacerbate.

160

Then, we take our horse in for its pre-med and *then* we take the shoes off *once* we're in the padded box.'

At the mention of 'shoes' Catherine nodded, slightly condescendingly, at a visibly irked Georgia who scowled back, her nominated first-choice action relegated to a rather poor third. Sophie kicked me again and I snorted with laughter and then tried to conceal it in a pretend coughing fit.

'Pre-med, then. What d'you want to use? Your shout.'

'Xylazine?' replied Sophie.

'As good a choice as any! Would we want to use ACP?'

'That's contra-indicated in stallions, so no.'

'Good, Megan.' Our group, Georgia exempted, slipped into a specific mode during these interactive sessions. Once one of us had answered a question we'd go quiet, allowing the others to respond to the open questioning. That way we *all* got to look good. If it was someone's appointed turn and it seemed like they didn't know the answer another person would bale them out, speaking up on their behalf.

'Right, so, our catheter's in, we've given our pre-med, we've taken the horse to the box he'll go down in, *we've taken his shoes off...*' Another knowing look at Georgia, another scowl, another kick on my shin and another poorly disguised choke of laughter, 'so, what next?'

'Induce him?'

'OK, Steve. You're the vet ... the pharmacy cupboard's at your disposal! Whatcha going to use?'

'Diazepam and ketamine?'

'Not too shabby. Sounds good to me! Let's go and start our clinical exam then.'

Forty minutes later we stood in the padded box supporting our heavily sedated stallion. 'Once you give the injection it's a case of ensuring he falls *smoothly* and onto his *side*; not on to *you*!'

Natalie squirted the contents of the syringe into the catheter, pumping the cocktail towards the horse's brain. I almost expected to hear someone bellow 'timber!' as the giant teetered, before crumpling in instalments like a mighty oak. With the stallion in lateral recumbency I fetched the winch from theatre, dragging it in at head height to our adjacent box. As I did this Matt, Natalie and Sophie covered the horse's feet with protective coverings and chained all four feet together with the horse swivelled on to its

161

back. While the three of them were occupied with this task, Catherine crouched with Megan and Georgia and showed them how to inveigle the endotracheal tube into the slumbering stallion's trachea. This would allow delivery of oxygen and anaesthetic gases to the horse's lungs throughout the surgical procedure. All seven of us then heaved the colossal beast into theatre, the winch chained to the horse's four tethered feet. With the horse suspended above the table I pressed the descend button on the winch, gradually lowering him, back first, on to the inflatable cushions covering the operating table. These would support his massive frame, limiting the damage caused to the animal by his own crushing weight. The horse was attached to the gas and wired up to a series of monitors to gauge blood gas levels, heart rate and respiratory parameters. We then stood back, suddenly flummoxed as to what we should do next. With the exception of Megan, who was hugging the clipboard, entrusted with the task of filling in the progress sheet every five minutes, we'd become redundant.

'It's a bit like flying a plane,' divulged Catherine, seeing our hesitation. 'Taking off and landing are the difficult bits; now we're just going to cruise along for a few hours.'

Around ninety minutes into our journey we were sprung back to life by a frenzy of activity from an irritated Prof as the stallion tweaked one of its hooves, beneath the blue drapes. An underperfusion of anaesthetic gas was shown to be the problem and, at Catherine's bidding, I began slowly compressing the giant bag to artificially inflate the horse's lungs. With the lungs now dispersing the anaesthetic once again, the stallion returned to his nonresponsive state and the surgery continued without further incident.

Prof emitted an indecipherable low-frequency rumble that signified he'd finished, plonked his forceps and needle-holders on to the trolley and left the room without a word. *Ladies and gentlemen, there will be no encores.*

'Right.' Catherine slid from her stool, 'Let's wake sleepyhead here.' It took a second or two for me to register that she meant the horse and not me; all six of us had been afflicted with droopy eyelid syndrome throughout the three-hour operation. The gas was switched to zero and disconnected from the tube and the stallion was winched back to the box. He gagged, wriggling momentarily. I removed the breathing tube under Catherine's surveillance and we left, sealing the disorientated stallion in the padded box. Catherine

162

flipped open the hatch and peered into the murky gloom. 'Could be a good while, yet! Best we just crack on with tidying this place up.' We flitted between scrubbing and mopping the blood-stained theatre and checking the progress of our patient as he rolled and slithered back to life.

The day was drawing to a close as Matt and I cajoled the slightly spaced-out stallion back to his stable. The yard was dotted with a spartan staff of students, the day's stragglers merging with those on duty, as we clip-clopped our way down the slope to block D. It was dark by the time we made our way back past the ever-dwindling crew. I was weary and had already decided I'd work on my presentation for Friday. I'd pulled the distinctly unsexy topic of *the irritational effects of injectable anaesthetic agents* out of the riding cap. If I *had* been feeling alert I'd only have persecuted myself for wasting the night on such a task.

Catherine had encouraged originality in our talks, keen as she was to avoid sitting through six fifteen-minute monotonous word-for-word recitals. I began to think that playing the originality card might not be such a bad idea when I discovered my meagre material would struggle to occupy fifteen *seconds*. I devised a plan to deliver my presentation in the style of *Blockbusters*; a recent and moderately popular tea-time quiz show. I drew up a board on the back of an old poster, sketched out the first letters of answers to questions loosely based on my subject and practised my best Bob Holness in the mirror.

Friday arrived, tinged with sadness. It was the very last day of the four rotations we'd all gone through together. I could not have imagined a nicer, funnier, more supportive bunch and I'd lost track of the number of times they'd come to my aid when the hour seemed at its bleakest. I fiddled with my rolled up poster and blob of Blu-tack as Megan took to the floor. I was the last one up, following her, and felt I was on to a sure-fire winner. That was until Megan began working her magic. Her talk was on local anaesthetic techniques in castration and the room exploded with uproarious laughter when she pulled from her pocket two clementines in a stocking as a prop, and demonstrated where, in the vicinity of the gonads, it was best to inject.

I can't compete with that! I thought, as Megan squeezed her balls one last time before returning to her seat. As it was, my talk went down well. Sophie volunteered to be my lovely assistant, colouring in the relevant squares on the board, and a team comprising Matt and Megan narrowly pipped Natalie and Georgia to victory. So we ended our time together on a high. We disappeared laughing into the night, seemingly without a care in the world.

19

The Final Countdown

We returned to farm for our sixth and final rotation and it felt like going back to what had once been a sizzling hotbed of fun and intrigue for a drab and depressing out-of-season return visit. We plodded into sopping smallholdings under sagging, heavily pregnant skies. Chilled waterproofs that never got the chance to dry, clung limply as they were pulled over indeterminate layers of clothing. Chloe and Roddy were now an established item, moving from edgy, flirtatious dilettantes to furtive life partners, oozing understated commitment. Air that used to hum as much with sexual tension as heavily laden bumble bees, now reeked of mildew and unavoidable reality. The vet school honeymoon was most certainly over.

The first week, clinical pathology, was a peculiar hybrid. At its best it helped to reinvigorate an ageing repertoire of culture and assay techniques and post mortem protocol, at its worst it just seemed like pointless busy time. We spent one dismal day undertaking a sixty-mile round trip to an abattoir on the outskirts of Crewe to swab a random and perfectly healthy piglet. Nice work if you can get it, *if* summer time beckons and you're dreamily running down the clock without a care in the world. One month from finals, though, it just felt like a kick in the teeth.

The second week, clinical skills, began with a smorgasbord of different activities as we skirted around all the other groups, feasting on the leftovers. As the week wore on staff, belatedly, twigged that finals were paramount in our minds, turning it and the following week into glorified revision sessions. Exams continued to inflate in stature in my mind, displacing, one by one, all the other contents. The rotation ground to a halt with a low-key departure at four-thirty on the last Friday. I walked back to my room like an automaton, programmed for one task and one task alone.

The final version of the timetable for our week of revision lectures was pinned up late on the Friday evening of the last rotation. These assumed a grave significance and we spent the week furiously combing the fabric of the talks for hidden clues like deranged Da Vinci code devotees on an outing to La Louvre. The week passed with us none the wiser, though, and the lecture timetable was promptly replaced with one giving our exam times: Monday 1st December at 2 pm was designated as equine, with farm and small animal scheduled for the same time on the Tuesday and Wednesday, respectively. Whilst the vast majority of the year was required to scoot en masse over to Liverpool to sit these, myself and the small number of other students entitled to extra time were granted special dispensation to sit the exams in a meeting room at Leahurst. I felt fortunate. It meant I'd be spared the nerve-jangling horrors of forty minutes on a coach reverberating with hyperventilating drama queens. Also, avoiding the grandiose exam hall and the clock tower that chimed every fifteen minutes, emphasising the marching of time, I'd be able to semi-delude myself that all I was doing was sitting a glorified class test. Lastly, I'd be back in my room, ill-advisedly rooting through my notes, checking answers, while the rest of the year were ensnared in traffic, helplessly undermining each other's confidence in true post-examination tradition.

Monday, Tuesday and Wednesday passed like Groundhog Day. I awoke with a start with invisible rain spraying against darkened glass and reached over for the sheaf of notes. Each morning I pored over wherever hearsay and conjecture had suggested the smart money lay. With midday bringing only a desultory brightening, I'd stroll around to the main building and stand on the saturated threshold watching most of the year clamber aboard the coach, anguished white faces pressed up against the glass. I'd shake hands with Jack as he briefly sheltered from the incessant downpour. I had an extra fifteen minutes for every hour of the exam (giving me a grand total of three and three-quarter hours). To allow for this, my kick-off time preceded the Liverpool contingent's by thirty

166

minutes and I'd drift tersely indoors as their coach pulled away. Ten minutes before we'd be due to start, Matt and Brad, also in my boat on account of the former's dyslexia and the latter's broken collar-bone, would sheepishly appear. All-in-all around ten of us stood in a tight circle and traded the accepted clichés as we waited to be ushered into our room.

'Here we are again.'

'I know; can't believe it was *only* yesterday...'

'I know *so* little.'

'*You* know your stuff.'

'I'm not sleeping...'

'No, I can't seem to switch my mind off!'

'Just want to get started now, get the damn thing over and done with.'

'Yeah, I'm almost beyond caring.'

'Me too! I wish it was Wednesday night and I was in the bar with a pint.'

'Well, that's *x* down, *x* to go.'

'God, I think I need to go to the toilet *again*, I'm *so* nervous.'

'You'll be fine, I'm *really* worried; seriously, I've neglected this one.'

'No, *you'll* be fine. But I *am* honestly a bit worried.'

'You'll *both* be OK; I haven't been able to look over *anything at all* since last...'

Once summoned in to take our seats I'd always look around the table and feel I was about to chair a rather fraught board meeting. I'd write my name on all my answer books, baulking at the prospect of having to write two decent essays *blind*, and marvelling at how much my nerves skewed my handwriting. Eyes danced around the table's periphery as some begged the reassurance of contact. Others snappily busied themselves, locked in their own, private, battened-down world.

'If everyone's ready you may as well just start, then?'

Shit!

I'd take a deep breath and turn over the essay question paper. My default position was always that I wouldn't have a clue what it was they wanted from me, therefore there'd be a searing pang of panic before it slowly dawned on me that I might be able to do something with one or other of the questions. Having tardily satisfied myself I could at least *have a go* at a couple of essays,

167

I'd turn my attention to the multiple-choice questions. By this juncture my nerves would always be at their most shredded; the exam had officially started, the stopwatch was going, people all around me were scribbling furiously as if their lives depended on it and I had yet to begin. I was still sitting on *nul pointes*. Battling this, I'd try to ease my nerves by finding an MCQ I categorically *knew* was correct. I'd sometimes have to go as far in as the mid-twenties before my nerves subsided sufficiently for the clouds to part, allowing me to tick my box with surety. I'd constantly lap the paper, returning for fifth, sixth, seventh and eighth passes at troublesome questions. A point would be reached, usually when around half to two-thirds of the MCQ paper was done, when I'd feel compelled to start my essays. I'd then spend the rest of the time switching between both of those and the MCQs. By the end I'd always have one essay I was relatively content with and one in which I'd resorted to demeaning waffle to pad out the holes in my knowledge. The MCQs seemed to start promisingly enough but always fell away when I quickly ran out of questions I was sure I could answer. I was left feeling I should have quit ten or twelve questions earlier than I actually had, thereby not diluting my previous good work. I was always bathed in a post-completion glow, the confidentiality box gummed down, by the time a largely tokenist, 'OK, pens down,' rang out. I always felt unspeakable elation at having finished and I could never button my jacket up properly for the short walk back to my room.

I was up and showered early on the Thursday morning, hardly able to credit that after an endless build-up, written exams had now been and gone. A mindset that was geared to filling every crack in the day had suddenly become obsolete and I had no idea how to fill the vacuum that remained. I left my room in Ritchie, cutting through Leahurst House, en route to the computer room. I stole a look at the wreckage of a party I'd barely dipped a toe in, and was struck by the sheer intensity of the release. Upturned tables and a splintered chair blocked my entry into the bar. Once inside you could have been mistaken for thinking a small nuclear device had just been detonated. *Such carnage*, I thought. My eyes rested on the bar, cluttered with unfinished pints of foaming lager and several ashtrays filled to the brim with a rank cocktail of beer, floating ash and disintegrating cigarette butts; in the background the juke box could be heard, still churning out random beats. *When did this party end?*

I picked up a fallen stool, allowing access behind the bar, and was surprised to find the seat wasn't warm. Once in there I killed the music with a satisfying clunk. I half expected to find a groaning reveller or two curled up beneath the empty crates. All I found was a vast stash of discarded beer bottles that clinked as I squeezed between packed black bins and two round puddles of vomit. I airlifted a can of coke and a Mars Bar from the disaster zone and continued on my merry way.

We were not to be left entirely to our own devices. The faculty had decreed that, as we'd spent x number of weeks with our heads lodged in the books, the Thursday and Friday post finals were probably an ideal time to slip in a mock practical and a mock oral. The student laboratory could accommodate thirty students at any given time (in two concurrent fifteen-person exams) and so four practical shifts had been timetabled to run throughout the morning and early afternoon. It was hoped these would prepare us for the sort of props and related questions we could expect come May. Although there was only *one* mock practical, it encompassed all three disciplines.

I turned up for my 11.30 slot and was almost knocked over by the odour of stale alcohol suffusing the lab. I felt that if I wasn't hungover myself, I soon would be. There were fifteen stations set out, in duplicate, on the rows of tables. I followed the crowd, making my way to an unattended stool. My first port of call happened to be a farm animal question and, with lecturers distracted pointing out the paper's various typing errors, I allowed myself a sly peek. It consisted of three petri dishes, each containing a bacterial culture that had to be identified. This would involve, among other things, lifting the lid and smelling the contents. As the stool I'd picked obscured me from the lecturers' line of vision, I sneakily prised the lid off Dish A and gingerly sniffed at it. I retched almost immediately, the pungent aroma making my stomach lurch. I quickly replaced the lid and tried to imagine how bad it would smell if I'd been hungover. I caught Jack's eye as he sat, limp and cue-ball white, across the lab. I waggled the dish and then held my nose, waving my hand as if to waft away an evil stench. He looked blankly back at me through watery eyes and,

169

seconds later, a bell sounded and the exam procession began. Every five minutes this alarm would shatter the pen-scratching silence and we'd all shuffle one place to the right. On a number of occasions students faced with the bacteria ID question reflexly slammed a hand over their mouth before dashing gagging for the door. On the last of these I happened to look up from my vain attempt to measure the heart rate on an ECG characterising atrial fibrillation, just as Jack was diving headlong into the corridor.

The test ended. I realised to my dismay I hadn't actually been able to complete *any* of the fifteen questions. The examiners were being ultra-generous, attributing the ineptitude of many performances to the previous night's drunken debauchery. I sat quietly and fretted. I hadn't touched a drop of alcohol and had slipped off to bed shortly after eleven with ear plugs and a splitting head ache. *What was my excuse?*

I knew I'd get extra time in the summer; it hadn't really been necessary for the mock exam. I'd be given an extra ten minutes above and beyond the norm which would work out at *one* extra minute per question. *Would that be enough?* I gulped and forced these worries to the back of my mind. I told myself that revising for orals and practicals entailed a completely different sort of revision and come the summer I'd make sure I was primed. I'd have studied radiographs, ECG traces, the properties of suture materials and the rest to such an extent that a stiff, swollen right hand wouldn't matter a jot.

Friday was the last day of term and, as I'd originally come from rotation group C, I was allotted a mock oral on the subject of small animal studies. I took my seat in a tiny meeting room upstairs in the SAH and Dr Baker tossed a bottle of Lopatol at me.

'Tell me what this is and what you'd use it for.'

Once it came back to me that I had a proton pump inhibitor in my hand I ended up negotiating the oral minefield satisfactorily. Dr Baker assuaged my fears about the time taken for me to identify the drug and I sped back to Leahurst in good spirits, to pack for Christmas.

We'd had it drummed into us that, generally speaking, students fared far better in these orals and practicals, making up any deficits incurred in the writtens. I hoped I'd have enough in my armoury to do myself justice when the time came. I knew from bitter experience that written exams often had me pegged at or around the 50% mark. I felt that if my performance had resorted to type I'd at least be in with a chance of scraping through at the first time of asking, precluding any need for the dreaded September re-sit. History also tended to dictate that five people *would* fail and, it was often said, if you could come up with five people in the year worse off than yourself, you could probably consider yourself safe. I wouldn't do anyone the disservice of predicting their downfall. Besides, in my eyes, that could only ever backfire. But, as I headed home to recharge my faltering batteries, I hoped I wouldn't end up as one of the infamous five.

20

I was Born a Snake-handler and I'll Die a Snake-handler

I spent an uneasy Christmas tormenting myself over my performance in writtens. An antiquated ruling, which our year would be the last to suffer, stated that our marks should be withheld until *after* orals and practicals. Unable either to comfort ourselves or focus attention on specific subjects in need of a touch-up, we were left to fumble anonymously in the dark.

On returning to Leahurst in early January I noted an immediate re-ignition of the slow-burning intensity I'd felt after the summer break; once again there'd be a period of acute stress waiting to ambush us at the end of term. But with written exams ebbing rapidly into the distance, there was less of a fear of the unknown, and a crystal-clear assertion that the end was very much in sight. To take us through to Easter and the unofficial end of the course (barring revision and exams!) were our electives. These let us indulge a particular interest in greater depth than lectures and/or rotations had permitted.

I had chosen an exotics elective based in Pembrokeshire, as this had remained my first love, and a pathology elective for an altogether different purpose. Since beginning the course, almost six years previously, the psoriatic arthritis in my hands had progressed more rapidly than I had anticipated. Rotations had revealed that, while I *could* perform surgery and virtually all the other assorted tasks presented to me, I was always left with a painful residue. Moreover, I was never totally free from the nail-biting concern that a task would crop up that was beyond my physical capabilities and there'd be nobody around to bale me out. In truth, this seldom seemed to happen but my anxiety was considerable, as was the

172

pain whenever I pushed myself too far. I didn't want a career I already knew to be taxing, placing me under even greater strain, especially if my worries pertained to the safety of animals in my care as much as they did to my own personal well-being. I decided I had to let the dream of becoming a vet go and concluded that a pathology elective might be just the ticket, allowing me to explore some of the other avenues open to me.

My first elective entailed spending four weeks with exotics expert Edgar Bryson, as he patrolled the south-west corner of Wales, servicing the needs of exotic pet owners and people with private collections. He'd limited the numbers to only two final year students per elective, creating the need to run it twice. Matt had also expressed an interest, tossing his name into the ring along with my own and those of two girls in the year, Nora and Claudia. I knew with a sense of grim stoicism that the draw would keep the two of us apart and so it proved. I was paired with Nora, a borderline reclusive Norwegian I'd last seen speedily departing from the scene of an orthopaedics theatre that was slowly filling up with anaesthetic gas. The plan was that after exotics surgery on Monday afternoons in the SAH we would relocate to Wales. Nora and I would spend that night as well as the following three at a guest house in Haverfordwest. We'd then return north once Friday's caseload had been addressed.

I was early, so I sat in my car listening to Radio 1 as 1.30 approached. At twenty past I locked my hold-all in the boot and walked around to the front of the SAH, skirting a couple of skinny prostitutes who had been alerted to my prolonged presence in the car park. One of them breezed nonchalantly after me, interpreting my earlier dawdling as a subtle indication of interest.

'Are you looking for business?'

'No, thanks.' Their presence barely registered any more and I skipped up the stairs without breaking stride, keen to see what exotics cases had been booked in. Edgar was late, he was driving up from Wales and been snagged by roadworks on the outskirts of Chester. He arrived, out of breath, shortly after two o'clock and the three of us leafed through the client file for the lone case, a six-month-old female ferret. Her owner, a spiky-haired female in her early twenties wearing a studded dog collar and a nose ring,

173

was sitting patiently in reception. Edgar paced rather shyly over to her to introduce himself. Then, with a sniff and a self-conscious push back of his drooping gold-rimmed glasses, he invited her into a consulting room. It transpired that Jenny the ferret was very poorly. She had come into season and was in dire need of either being mated or spayed. In the absence of a handy, sexually aroused male ferret, Edgar opted for plan B and spayed her.

'Aw thanks, Edgar, really. I was worried sick, like.'

Edgar blushed deeply and scratched his beak-like nose as the owner continued in her fulsome praise.

'I don't know what I'd have done if ... you know ... she hadn't woken up from the anaesthetic. Thanks, really!' She grasped his hand with both of hers and moved it up and down as if it were a water pump.

'That's fine. We'll keep Jenny in overnight; you can come by and get her tomorrow morning.' Edgar was fighting to maintain an air of quiet professionalism but couldn't help breaking into a smile as the owner leant forward and kissed Jenny's caramel-coloured head, as it poked out from beneath her blanket.

With Jenny coming round in recovery Edgar filled the interlude with a brief tutorial on the ubiquitous problem of rabbit dentition. One last check on the patient and it was time to depart for the valleys. For our inaugural excursion south Edgar had dutifully promised to lead a snaking three-car convoy down through deepest darkest mid Wales. There had been severe weather warnings all weekend and the whole zone was on high flood alert; warnings that would prove to have foundation. At one point we scrunched to a tyre-squealing halt on a pass high above Llandrindod Wells as a tree had keeled over, blocking the A483 in both directions. In the continued absence of the emergency services a small group us braved the teeming monsoon and dragged it to the roadside. I spent the remainder of the three-hour drive shaken by the near miss. Still fazed and trembling, I hung a healthy distance back from Edgar as I pursued his tail lights around winding hairpin bends and across undulating valley floors. Nora, by contrast, seemed hell bent on driving so close to me that I could have taken requests on which compilation tape to play next. *What d'you reckon, Nora, a bit of Crowded House?* Her panicky Nordic features repeatedly bobbed into view in my mirror as we motored south through the tumultuous downpour. We arrived at a spookily deserted Haverfordwest at ten-thirty and I felt like we'd come to the ends of the earth. I lugged my hold-all stiffly from my car, bellowing my thanks to Edgar for guiding us safely all the way down.

'Sure thing. I'll pick you up at ... ooh ... say, 9.30 in the morning?' he yelled back, blinking into the rain, as he returned to the sanctity of his car.

I'm going to enjoy this. I pulled off my squelching trainers and padded across the carpet to sign in; my toes waggling luxuriantly in the deep pile and my glasses steaming up from the delectable warmth.

Edgar devoted the Tuesday morning to showing us around the local practice to which he was affiliated and teaching us how to examine and tell the sex of snakes. For this he enlisted the assistance of the practice's resident Burmese python, Barry, coiled snugly in his herpetarium up in the converted attic. Edgar uncoiled the snoozing eight-foot python, dropping him into my arms while he hunted for his sexing probes. Fully awake, Barry transformed into a hyperactive, slithering mass of perpetual motion and I had both arms working at full tilt to keep him supported. He began looping around my neck and I could feel the coolness of his dry skin and his tight sinewy muscles brushing against the back of my neck. *Come on, Edgar! Find those probes will you!* I gagged, my Adam's apple compressing, and emitted a choking cough. *Edgar?* I felt sure Barry was only *pretending* to throttle me and I didn't want to appear a pansy, wimping out at the first squeeze from a slightly boisterous snake. *If he really meant business I'd probably be turning blue around about now*, I told myself as Edgar continued rooting through drawer after drawer. I pressed my fingers underneath the tight loop and prised him off my constricting throat. With the snake successfully unlooped I held him in loose ringlets as Edgar sorted through his probes.

'This medium-sized one should do the trick!'

Medium? You're having a laugh aren't you? I'd hate to see what you'd use the big one on. Nora, who'd been standing gormlessly beside me as I'd fought to disentangle myself from the unruly constrictor, held Barry's top half as I straightened out the body and flipped him on to his back. Edgar gently inserted the probe into the hemi-penis, a blind-ending cavity approximately four-fifths of the way down the snake's underside.

'If Barry was a female we'd struggle to get this even *this* far

175

in,' he purred, retracting the probe most of the way out. 'Don't put him back yet, hold on to him.' I stopped in my tracks. I'd been eager to reacquaint the increasingly fractious Barry with his warm tank.

'His loss of body condition's a bit troubling, isn't it? I want to stomach tube him some antibiotics.' Edgar took a black pencil and scored, at the top of tube, the distance roughly from Barry's stomach to his mouth, before feeding the tube down his gullet. Having stopped at the mark he'd made, he syringed a few millilitres of metronidazole into the tube before tugging it out and asking that I replace him.

'He's really not his usual self at all. He's quite subdued. Bit weak. Bit run down. Anyway, let's go back downstairs.' Edgar continued talking as he headed down towards reception with Nora scurrying in hot pursuit.

'Yeah, poor little mite.' I ventured unconvincingly, almost to myself, stroking at my tender neck. As I moved to follow them I caught a glimpse of my reflection in the mirror; there was a ring of red blotches circling my neck. I shivered as I headed out of the attic. What sort of mess would a fully fit Barry have made of my throat?

Before lunch Edgar broached the subject of our appraisals. We were both given a couple of exotics self-test books; I saw that my two volumes focused on reptiles and tropical birds and nodded my approval. *I like the sound of that*, I thought. We were also asked to prepare a presentation on a theme of our own choice for the final day. I casually leafed through one of the quiz books, noticing that the scribe was our very own Edgar. 'Nice book, Edgar!'

'Oh! Thanks very much, glad you like it.'

'Sure. I have to say I think it's really touching that you let your six-year-old son do a couple of the illustrations, too. That's a lovely touch!'

He frowned in consternation. 'No ... *I* pretty much did...' before catching my eye and laughing out loud. 'Get out! Go for lunch! Come back for two!'

'Sure thing,' I grinned, filing the books into my rucksack and slipping it over my shoulder. I found I couldn't wait to go through them. It was a novel experience; actually wanting to study in the evenings as opposed to feeling compelled to.

After lunch we set off for a miniature zoo/museum called 'The

Fragile Planet' which lay about 10 miles up the coast. Edgar was close friends with the owners and they'd asked him to take a look at one of their iguanas which had a suspected kidney infection. We arrived and got straight to work. I took a firm grip of the snappy lizard and held him at arms length as he tried in vain to whip at me with his muscular tail. With one hand I immobilised the front legs while using the other hand to do the same to the back ones. I then flipped him onto his back, allowing Edgar to take a blood sample from the tail vein. With the test tube safely stowed in the car, Edgar and the owners kindly gave us a guided tour of their menagerie. They possessed a wonderfully diverse collection that included leopard geckos, bearded dragons, red-eared terrapins, chameleons, African pythons, poison arrow frogs, tarantulas and a particularly fearsome-looking lizard I'd never heard of, known as a tegu. I was transfixed by the robust lizard's dazzling markings.

'I see you've spotted Monica, our tegu,' the husband commented, proudly.

'Yes. She's a beauty isn't she.'

'Hmm. Here, have a closer look.' He levered off the tank's heavy lid and invited me to peer in.

'Wow, Monica, you're a stunner!' I leant forward as the owner turned away, preoccupied with setting down the oversized lid on the scrubbed wooden floorboards with as little noise as possible. The tegu, without a hint of warning, suddenly dived at me and I threw my head backwards, feeling a blast of air as the lizard's powerful jaws clamped shut at the exact spot where, nanoseconds earlier, my nose had been. Missing me, the airborne tegu smacked headlong into the side of its tank, shifting it a few centimetres to the right and sending up a cloud of wood shavings which made the owner jump.

'Oh, someone wants more meal worms don't they! *Grumpy!*'

'Yes, *grumpy!*' I joined in, panting and fingering my nose to check it was still there.

Later I took the front passenger seat next to Edgar. I'd ridden shotgun on the way up and felt sure Nora would stake her claim for the return voyage. *Evidently not.*

'That'll teach you!'

'What?' Edgar shattered my reverie and I turned, quizzically, to face him.

'Making fun of my illustrations like that.'

177

I burst out laughing. 'So you saw my brush with Monica the irritable tegu, then? How close *was* she to nipping me on the nose?'

He said nothing but made a shape with his thumb and forefinger denoting half an inch.

'Ah well, close but no cigar.'

Nora and I sat across from each other over breakfast, exchanging the milk jug and coffee cafetière in a deep and lasting silence. It felt as though we were a stale and uncommunicative holidaying married couple who had run out of things to say to each other years ago and were only still together for the sake of the children. We finished up, wordlessly leaving the dining room and slipping out of the guest house to wait for Edgar outside. After a few minutes he turned up, politely switching off the radio as Nora and I got in the car. We made our way along the A40 to a practice on the outskirts of Swansea where Edgar held an exotics surgery every Wednesday and Friday morning.

'So, how are *you* this morning?' Edgar suddenly inquired, about ten minutes into the drive.

'Good, thanks!' I replied, looking over, mystified. 'Didn't you...'

'Much waiting for me at your end, then?' he went on, totally ignoring me. *Right. That'll be the hands-free earpiece, then.* I sunk embarrassed into my fleece, consoling myself with the fact that even if Nora *had* heard me make a clown of myself she'd be unlikely to ever tell anyone about it.

'Edgar, your first client booked in is Mr Baxter. He's got a *Testudo graeca* tortoise that's come out of hibernation too quickly, what with the warm weather and all, but do you mind if we let Mr Davies go first, he's turned up out of the blue and is in a bit of a tizzy!'

'Of course, Mandy,' he smiled, gently. 'Send him in.'

A man in his mid forties burst breathlessly into the consulting room. 'Edgar, I think my cockatiel's poisoned!'

Edgar was calmness personified. He fetched a tea towel and dug the fluttering bird from the cage, all the while maintaining eye contact with the owner.

'I let him wander around the house, Edgar. He loves it! Anyway, this morning I was feeding him sunflower seeds as a special treat, like; they're his favourite.'

I saw Edgar blink at this disclosure and could almost *hear* his oft-repeated remark, *sunflower seeds are the avian equivalent of McDonalds, of course he bloody likes them!*

'I noticed the inside of his mouth was all red and blistered and I found a piece of *this* in his beak!' Mr Davies held up a chewed piece of waxy leaf. 'D'you know what plant it is? If I'd known it was toxic I'd have kept him away from it. I thought a bit of greenery would do him the world of good!'

'First of all we need to ascertain whether or not the plant's poisonous. Ivor doesn't seem in any immediate danger so if you'll excuse me?'

'Of course, Edgar. Of course.'

He briskly left the room, the leaf pressed between a folded piece of tissue paper and I began to chat with the owner.

'Is the plant new?'

'No, son, the wife bought that old thing years ago!'

'Right. But he's never chewed the leaves 'til now?'

'No ... he's always at them.'

Something else has poisoned this bird!

'I see. OK.' I was quiet for a moment. 'Is there anything else that's changed, *more recently*, in Ivor's immediate environment?'

'Well, all he gets in his cage is his water and ... oh my God!' Mr Davies suddenly slapped his forehead with the palm of his hand. 'We're having the water supply flushed out and we were told not to use it as it had disinfectant in it. I filled Ivor's water up, didn't I?'

I put an arm out and patted Mr Davies on the shoulder. 'Don't worry! I'll just go and tell Edgar; I'll have him back here in a jiffy.'

'I've killed him haven't I?'

'I shouldn't have thought so, I can't see him taking in very much; it must've tasted absolutely foul. We'll see what the vet says, though.' I found Edgar in reception, trawling through a pile of plant taxonomy books, and quickly told him what I'd found out.

'Ah! That makes *much* more sense! Nice work.'

Ivor was discharged with a deliriously happy Mr Davies and some drops of baytril antibiotic, in the unlikely event of his blisters becoming infected.

'Morning' surgery dragged on until after four o'clock as we

179

were waylaid by an after-hours visit to a garden pond the size of a small boating lake, across the road from the practice, which contained a koi carp with a fungal disease. After being roundly drenched we finally netted the elusive, splashing beast and Edgar injected him with an anti-fungal agent. Still sodden, we stopped off at Starbucks on the way back where Edgar held an impromptu tutorial on the subject of water quality as it relates to fish husbandry. I sipped on my mocha as he spoke. *This is what I've missed from lectures all these years*, I mused. The tutorial ended and we chatted, finishing our drinks.

'You must both come up to my place for a meal on the Thursday night of your last week. My girlfriend cooks a mean curry and you'd both be most welcome.'

'Superb, Edgar, love to,' I replied.

'Brilliant, that's a date then,' he smiled, gathering up his coat and nodding at us both. 'Now, let's get you back.'

The days flew by and I happily flitted to and from south Wales, treasuring the time away from the hurlyburly of Leahurst. The elective was a joy and it shielded me from the daily chatter surrounding the topic of finals. The final week dawned and I found myself very reluctant to give up the tranquillity of this elective lifestyle.

Edgar had worn down the staff at The School of Tropical Medicine in Liverpool with a barrage of phone calls and emails, and they'd eventually given in, granting him and his elective students a grand tour of the venomous snakes section. Here, among other things, venom was harvested from live snakes to produce antisera and the poisons' toxic effects were studied in great detail. Edgar had little faith they'd ever grant him a *second* audience with the hallowed Professor of Toxicology and summoned the two other elective students to accompany us, if they could wangle out of their current electives, for a couple of hours. We arrived at 2.30 on the Monday of our final week to be met by a rather pallid, actively perspiring professor. As he led us through to his facility, Matt stopped to let me catch up.

'How many times d'you think *he's* been bitten?'

'He doesn't look too healthy does he?' I whispered, behind my hand. 'I'd probably guess at five or six?'

'And *this* is where we keep all our venomous snakes!' Matt and I immediately perked up at this, our eyes widening as we crossed the high-security threshold. 'What to show you ... what to show you...' The professor rocked on his heels as he stood in front of the bank of sealed compartments, lost in thought. 'Ah, this,' he explained, unlocking the clasp on a box with a large toxic skull sticker emblazoned across it, 'is the puff or death adder!'

I instinctively took a step back.

'It kills, on average, 30,000 people a year in central and west Africa.'

The statistic seemed to remain, suspended, in a speech bubble over his head. I took another step back and found I'd clunked my head on the wall behind me. I was still close enough to make out the distinctive camouflaged pattern, the half-inch-long fangs and the unreserved irritation of this deadly assassin. The professor immobilised the adder's head with a prong before reaching forward and picking the snake up by the head.

'She can't bite me now, despite the fact, as you've probably gathered, that she'd really, really like to.'

You're not kidding sunshine! The adder was writhing furiously, attempting to manoeuvre its lethal fangs within striking distance of the professor's pale flesh. He took us through to the next room, still carrying the limp form of the deadly snake. 'You'll get a better look at her in here.' He re-applied the prong, disengaging his hand and then stepping back, leaving the snake, unfettered, on a table in the corner of the room where we could truly feast our eyes on her sinister splendour. She repeatedly coiled and uncoiled, rising to appear more threatening and then sinking, all the while viewing us with a deep mistrust.

'She's getting wound up, let's put her back shall we?' The professor expertly immobilised the head again and the five of us parted to each wall to let him pass and return the snake to its pen. A couple of minutes later the professor returned with his fingers pinched around the head of another snake. This specimen was far larger, I estimated it had to be a good two metres, about double the length of the adder and we heard it before we saw it.

'This is an Eastern Diamondback rattlesnake; the largest and most deadly snake in North America.' He set the rattler down on the table and stood over him with the prong poised. I assumed this was because the rattler appeared very twitchy, repeatedly buzzing

181

its rattle and licking the air, tasting our smell. He had an overt restlessness and seemed far less intimidated by our presence than the adder had been. The adder had seemed to view us as a potential threat; the rattler, on the other hand, was very clearly sizing us up. He suddenly made a resolute break for it and began slithering off the table in our direction.

'Oh no you don't!' The professor read the rattler's intentions perfectly and trapped it, pinning its head to the table. 'Back you go!' He picked up the rattler and dropped him back in the box before turning to face us with a smile. 'I hope it's been of use to you?'

I realised I'd been holding my breath. We all thanked him and quickly left the building, breathing easily once more.

I spent the whole of the four-hour drive south unable to stop myself ghoulishly raking over some of the snippets of toxic trauma caused by snake venom; acute haemorrhage, cellular damage, neurotoxicity... I kept recalling a night I'd spent camping in the Australian outback at Yulara near Ayer's Rock. It had been well after midnight when I'd been on the point of turning in. A ranger had raced over to where a group of us were drinking.

'Guys, I've just spotted two Tiger snakes in the compound; when you get to your sleeping bag *shake it out thoroughly* before you get in! It's a bitterly cold night and there's nothing those little bleeders would like more than to snuggle up in there with you!'

I'd fumbled my way back to my tent in pitch blackness and fearfully shaken out my sleeping bag before noticing, to my sheer panic, that the zip was broken on my hired tent. The memory of that sleepless night, as I huddled, petrified in the darkness, my tent continually flapping open and rustling in the breeze, haunted me all the way down to Haverfordwest.

'So, this guy we're going to see is a snake dealer then?'

'He is. Specifically Burmese pythons.'

'And he sounded really worried on the phone?'

'Well, yes, he's found one of his prize males dead this morning and if it ends up that something contagious killed him, it could wipe out his entire collection.'

'So we'll post mortem him?'

'Yes, although it may not reveal that much. We'll almost certainly have to send off some of his organs for analysis.'

Nora and I were now over halfway through our last week and I realised with a jolt that I wouldn't be around when the results came back. It was a thought that made me sad.

'In you come Edgar, old boy!'

'Hi Jim, these are a couple of my elective students; Nora and Steve.' We all shook hands and then followed him up the plush carpeted staircase. At the top Jim held out a bin liner bulging with the unmistakable shape of a dead snake.

'That him?' enquired Edgar, rhetorically.

'Can you let me know as soon as you find out anything?' pleaded Jim, nodding in response to Edgar's query. I saw his face was bitten with concern.

'You know I will, Jim.'

'Want the tour, then?' Not waiting for a reply Jim led us into a converted bedroom in which one whole wall was stacked from floor to ceiling with countless small, latched wooden drawers. He randomly pulled one open and removed the snake that was curled up inside. It was a relatively young specimen which possessed a slightly unusual but nonetheless striking violet hue. 'Got a buyer for *her*. She'll go for £15,000,' he stated, matter-of-factly.

My jaw hung open. Before I could think of anything to say he yanked at the drawer above and whipped out another colour morph; a python with a tangerine tint. *'She'll* go for upwards of twenty grand. I was wanting to mate her with that chocolate male that died,' he went on wistfully. 'Their offspring might have gone for anything up to a hundred grand. I'd have mated them with other morphs, too ... if you get my drift!' He tailed off, regretfully.

Oh I do, Jim. No wonder you were so upset your pet died.

He leafed through several more drawers displaying pink, bronze, cream and lilac versions of the same basic Burmese stereotype. The longer he went on, the more they just became mere trinkets – brightly coloured fashion accessories, adornments that people wished to own because they liked what they thought their prized possession said about them. *Wow, you truly are exotic aren't you?*

'We'll PM your snake this afternoon but it's Thursday today isn't it? Probably going to be into next week before we hear anything.'

'No problem, Edgar.'

I shook Jim's hand as I stepped back out into the street. 'Thanks for the tour.'

'Pleasure.' I got the impression he meant it.

After a quick bite on the hoof we returned to the Haverfordwest practice and Edgar was met by a surgery list that read: two rabbit castrations, a ferret spaying and a chinchilla dental. 'Damn, I'd forgotten they were all booked in for this afternoon!' He scratched his head and then thrust the bin-liner at me. 'Here, you guys do the PM. Give us a shout when you've opened him up, yeah? Gloves and instruments are in that cupboard.'

'No problem, Edgar!'

I'd done a couple of snake post mortems during a two-week stint of practice at Chester Zoo the previous summer and couldn't wait to get started. I stretched and pulled on my gloves with gusto. Nora held the snake for me, ensuring it remained flat and stationary. I made a mid-line incision with the scalpel blade before snipping through the snake's tough exterior with scissors, unzipping it straight down the middle. Edgar appeared at my shoulder, supporting a heavily sedated chinchilla in the palm of one gloved hand.

'Nice handiwork,' he smiled appreciatively. 'Now, can you take out the liver and lungs ... in fact you may as well send them the kidney, heart and brain, too. They're all fresh! Pop 'em into a formalin tube and write the name and date on it, please!' He made to go and then stopped and turned. 'Oh. I meant to ask,' he nodded at the small, furry mammal in his hand, 'how d'you like your chinchilla again?'

'Medium to medium rare, Edgar.' I grinned, taking the joke as a subtle reminder that Nora and I had a dinner date that night.

'I'm happy to drive. I don't really drink, you see.'

'Oh, OK Nora, but neither do ... yeah, fine, that'd be grand!'

Nora parked just outside Edgar's picturesque cottage and we were met warmly at the door by him and his girlfriend, Christine, who immediately dived back through to the kitchen. 'Vital stage of the proceedings,' he explained.

'Chinchilla still a bit too rare?'

'Something like that. Here, come and have a look at my seahorse collection.' We followed him into his cosy, dimly lit living room and I spent what seemed like an age staring awestruck at the graceful yet somehow bumbling creatures, before Edgar broke the spell, handing me an ice-cold bottle of beer.

As we all savoured Christine's superb curry, the conversation progressed and we all began to try and entice Nora out of her shell, encouraging her to voice her opinion on a variety of subjects.

'So, Edgar, you've got your collection of seahorses, but if you could have any animal in the world as a pet, what would you take?'

'It'd have to be a Bengal tiger!'

'Totally impractical, mate! Think of the mess it'd make of your sofa with its claws.'

'Probably right. What about you?'

'A manatee,' I said, po-faced.

'Because they're just *so* practical aren't they?' giggled Christine.

'All it'd take would be for Sainsbury's to start selling sea grasses, I'd be sorted then!' I pretended to protest, smiling at them both.

'How about you, Nora?' prompted Christine, flipping the top off another bottle of Stella and sliding it over the checked tablecloth to me. I mouthed my thanks as we waited to hear Nora's answer.

'Oh I couldn't possibly say.'

'Aw come on!' I prodded. 'For the purposes of a joke.'

'Well...' she smiled, 'I really like tapirs.' Her Norwegian accent made her pronounce it '*tay-pirsch*' and I found this incredibly funny.

'Really? Can you do that standing up?'

I realised I was drunk, and in the ensuing awkward silence pledged only to speak when spoken to and, even then, to keep my output down to the bare minimum.

On the Friday morning all that remained of the elective was for Nora and me to give our talks; Edgar had said we'd be free to head back north as soon as we'd done them. We found ourselves back upstairs in the attic of the Haverfordwest practice and I couldn't help but steal a swift glance at Barry, lurking coiled at the back of his tank. I was glad Edgar hadn't seen fit to rouse him again for any more sexing and/or stomach tubing. Edgar stepped up into the attic with a tray bearing three mugs of tea. 'Well Steve, are you still wanting to go first?'

185

'Yeah, may as well get it over and done with, Edgar!' I sighed, pulling a chair out from beneath the small round table we'd sit around. I'd chosen viral diseases in psittacine birds as my topic, as I'd found an excellent recent article to shamelessly plagiarise. I delivered my twenty-minute presentation with only the odd, cursory glance at the hand-written notes lying out in front of me. My talk ended to a ripple of applause and I shuffled my notes together like a newsreader, blushing self-consciously. Edgar popped out to put the kettle on again, prior to us hearing what Nora had to offer. He returned with more hot beverages and she began her talk.

Wouldn't you know it, once she started talking it was well nigh impossible to get her to stop? Her presentation, on avian nutrition, clocked in at a very thorough one hour and ten minutes. Once she'd released us Edgar and I both clapped, the sparse applause echoing around the cluttered attic. We all shook hands, the elective already in the past, and I hit the road; the time had come to re-enter the storm.

21

It's up for Grabs Now

I returned to Leahurst and stepped straight into an elective in pathology. The Liverpool staff, inexplicably, took the option not to set us any mini project/presentation to do. Whatever their motives I certainly wasn't going to hang around to question this pronouncement and it's fair to say that, all in all, the elective asked very little of us.

A typical day would begin with us spending the morning helping out on the post mortem of a cat or dog which had expired overnight in the SAH with an inconclusive cause of death. The period immediately before or after lunch would be filled with us sorting through a rack of tubes containing tissue biopsies. These had been hacked off potentially cancerous pets by worried vets and we'd chop them into thin slivers to study the nature of the cells on histological slides. We'd then spend the rest of the afternoon hooked up to a group microscope, assessing the previous day's tissue slides. I was fairly happy with the relaxed regime, as it left me fresh and sprightly for an evening of revision.

After a few weeks, though, the monotonous nature of these days began to wear thin and I managed to wangle a final week based at Leahurst, on zoo animal post mortem duty. It meant I was at the mercy of whatever animals happened to die at Chester Zoo that week, but enough of them did to make the time captivating. I was able to help PM a Humboldt's penguin, a flamingo, an axolotl, a puff adder, a green iguana and a still-born elephant. All in all I felt the elective had spared me the rigours of physical exertion and the stresses of a hefty extra-curricular workload and for that I was deeply grateful.

As the days slowly drew in I found I couldn't bear to revise

187

alone in my room. I *had* to escape those clammy breeze-blocked walls, and yearned for comforting human contact. I began spending my study days with Jack and, occasionally, Hannah in a meeting room, hidden away in the back corridors of the main building. The room became a secluded haven; we'd take breaks from our work to light-heartedly quiz one another, reassuring ourselves that we'd sussed the essentials. As time pressed relentlessly on I couldn't face being alone with my books at all; studying together in the meeting room was the vet student equivalent of a child wanting to sleep with the light left on.

The days ceased to have any form or distinguishing features, merging into each other. I discovered which students I needed to give a wide berth, during the desperately agitated run-in. Jack and Hannah were both of a similar disposition, content to plug away quietly and supportively. Others regularly unsettled me. Any conversation that began with, 'So how much have *you* done?' would always end with 'Oh my God, that's *so* much more than me!' regardless of how much or how little I'd owned up to having done. I knew exactly what was happening here. Students were preparing themselves for the worst case scenario, getting their excuses in first, while simultaneously scaring themselves rigid; making them work *all the harder*. A self-perpetuating cycle fuelled by an unhealthy mixture of fear, self-loathing and occasional anti-depressants. I hated what the pressure did to people. I returned home to my parents to get my own spinning, head together, before returning for the big push.

The timetable we faced matched to the letter the one Danny and Sam had taken me through, ashen-faced, exactly a year ago. They'd long since flown the nest and now it would be *my* ugly reality. The practicals came first: farm animal on Friday, equine on Monday and small animal on Tuesday. Wednesday, Thursday and Friday were set aside for the three orals and the order differed, student by student. For me, the order conveniently remained the same as it had been for the practicals.

Traditionally the farm animal practical had earned a reputation for being fiendish. The previous year's exam had students up in arms. So bitter had been the recriminations that the percentage the practical counted for was whittled down to a meaningless nubbin.

188

I entered the muted lab riddled with self-doubt and praying that the repercussions from last year would result in the faculty over-compensating this year, offering us up a cow-cake walk. Sadly this was not to be the case.

I took my seat next to a window that had the blinds taped down at the sill, and felt paralysed by fear. I forced myself to take deep breaths and waited for the bell to go. My first station was a collection of seeds and grains. I felt like blowing a kiss to the heavens; I'd been suitably moved, with my mate Jamie, to spend one evening meticulously analysing all the seed types and constituents, and nailed the question at a canter. *Oatso simple, indeed, Jamie!* I moved on, breathing more easily. I became flustered on the next question, a colour blow-up of a bovine ovary and when I began my answer I found I couldn't get my hand moving quickly enough before the bell went. I shook the worry from my head, moving on to the next station. *Go back to that one at the end, no bother, Stevie. No bother, son. Keep it together.*

The pattern was repeated at the next station and the next and the next. I found the stress of the situation had taken my arthritis up and off the scale. At question ten I leafed, frantic with worry, through my paper. With the exception of the seed question, every other one was littered with blanks and scribbled out, semi-formulated answers. The extra time came and went in a breathless blur. I spent it flapping non-productively between stations; filling boxes with words, just to fill them with words. 'Right pens down!' I hadn't done half the paper! I looked around me. Only a tiny number of students had lingered to the bitter end, dotted throughout the airless lab.

'Helen! My hand! I... ' I held out my red, swollen hand with its fat painful digits. 'I need more time!'

I fought back the tears. I saw her look at me and my hand and then, after the tiniest of delays, she smiled placidly at me.

'Well, you'd better take what time you need, Steve.'

I nodded my thanks and took my seat once again, as the other extra-time students filed out, exhaling and grabbing at one another in relief. I began frantically hoovering up the questions I'd only touched on, as Dr Bennett burst into the lab, totally unaware of my presence. He was whistling, hopelessly out of tune, and began tipping exam props I'd yet to look at into a huge bin-liner.

'Colin! Can you leave them … Steven's not done yet; he needs a little bit of help with his writing.'

'Does he? Why's that then?' He gawped at me, nonplussed and I remember, even then in the heat of the exam battle, wondering how on earth that could possibly be. *They all knew, didn't they? He* certainly should; he'd taken me out on countless farm visits where he'd been responsible for my well-being. I returned to picking the carcase of the exam with a slight shake of my head. I hadn't completed the paper but it bothered me that I was getting this preferential treatment, and I wasn't sure I actually deserved it any more than anyone else did. I finished the answer I was on and moved towards the door.

'Thanks *very* much Helen! I'm probably done.'

'Well, we're nice people who want to help, you know!'

'I know that,' I replied, flushed and feeling tearful as I handed her my scribbled answer sheet. 'I appreciate it *so* much.'

The equine practical, as with farm animal before it and small animal after it, gave me a slot in the final 4 pm exam sitting, as a direct result of the extra time I was entitled to. A system had to be in place that stopped students marching straight from the lab to their mates and trotting out a list of specifics to look over. So to guard against this potential risk our group, along with the second half of the year, arrived en masse at one o'clock and were sequestered in a secure lecture theatre until it was time; even innocent visits to the toilet necessitated a chaperone. Every hour on the hour, a group of twelve students would receive their summons and trudge gravely down the stairs to the exit. Hushed words of heartfelt support, from the ever-depleted ranks left behind, would echo in the tense air. Four o'clock came and our group was escorted to the lab. I caught sight of students from earlier sessions checking their email as I passed the computer room and wished I could be like them; sitting on the other side of this practical. Helen took me aside as I entered the lab. She informed me she'd spoken with the equine and small animal people, and I'd get any extra time I needed. I smiled in gratitude but rebuffed her with a swagger born more out of blind optimism than any sense of realism.

'I'm really not expecting to need it but thanks, Helen.'

As if to rubber-stamp this stance my equine practical passed without a hitch. The questions sought shorter, snappier responses and I only took a very small bite out of the additional time Dr Douglas had also kindly assured me I could have.

I was getting used to this routine. I had the whole morning to potter around and check my notes. Even the three-hour internment in the maximum security lecture theatre didn't seem quite such an ordeal any more. It left more time to compare notes with Matt and put off the moments we were all dreading. I'd decided the farm animal practical was nothing more than a blip, a temporary aberration. I remembered back to Danny and Sam the previous year and surmised I'd been subjected to a similarly brutal exam experience. *Just a one off*, I repeated to myself over and over as I took my seat in the lab for the third and, hopefully, last time.

Like the farm practical I got off to an absolute flier. My first station was a selection of suture materials and I sped through the one- and two-word answers in record time. I kicked my heels for a few unreal minutes, flicking coolly through the rest of the paper. It felt like sitting in the eye of a hurricane, waiting for chaos to descend once more. The bell moved me along to the next question and my heart sank when I saw the size of the box I was supposed to fill. I fumbled anxiously with my pen as I read the question quickly. It required a long calculation and all workings had to be shown.

I began scribbling the start of the calculation and my already stiff hand began to ache. Determined there would be no repeat of the farm debacle I pressed resolutely on and continued with my answer despite the fact it was difficult to make out what I'd written. I screwed my eyes up, trying to convince myself my workings were legible. I could feel my heart pounding and looked up to see a labful of students writing furiously as if the hounds of hell were after them. My pen squirted out of my hand, landing beneath my stool. I bent down to pick it up and began again, switching the manner in which I held it to write. I began to see a possible solution to the problem in front of me just as the bell sounded, making me jump. I dropped my pen again and took five or six attempts to pick it up, holding up the person following on behind. I whispered a faint apology without even looking up to see who it happened to be.

My hand was now throbbing and even just holding the pen hurt. I read the next question but found it impossible to truly immerse myself in what it was asking; the pain from my hand kept bursting in to interrupt my thoughts. I began penning the answer with my left hand but it was an unintelligible scrawl and I switched back, scoring out what I'd written and almost tearing through the paper in a pique of frustrated rage. The bell went and I'd written nothing.

I lurched forward, on and on, from station to station. I found myself picking up marks on questions where I could begin writing straight away. It wasn't always possible to hit the ground running, though. The worries set in when I was forced to read the longer questions over and over. I knew, for these, I wouldn't have time to finish an answer in the ever-dwindling time and it plagued me, obstructing my thoughts all the more. I knew I had to fight to stay positive and towards the end I went on a prolific run of four semi-decent answers.

Suddenly I was back at the start again. I could not comprehend where the time had gone. I ploughed on as all the others left, briefly checking with Michael Nugent that I had his authorisation. Ten minutes, fifteen minutes passed, the pen was a bar of soap in my bulbous hand. There were boxes I'd just crammed with nonsense. Going back to them later was all well and good but there was nowhere left to write my proper answer now I had the time. What I needed was this extra time divided more evenly among the questions; that way I might have put it to more effective use. I scribbled more answers down but kept looking at my watch, distracted, unable to settle or truly focus.

I handed Michael my paper with a tight smile. I had left a few boxes unanswered but the pain in my hand clouded my thoughts and I couldn't escape the lab quickly enough. I hoped the Christmas written exam and the oral that lay in wait would cover what might have been a disaster.

I strolled back to my room beneath leafy glades, soothed by the evening sunshine and buoyant that practicals were now all over. Next on the assessment conveyor belt would be an oral in each subject. We'd been coached on these by staff acutely aware of how nervous and tongue-tied they made us. They all preached the same sermon. *Remember* ...

'*We* want you to pass.'

'No one's looking to trip you up.'

'They'll begin very easily, with basics, getting harder for more points.'

'At some point you won't know an answer to a question we ask you; expect this.'

'Ask an examiner to rephrase a question if you don't understand it; they'll then have to simplify it.'

'A common starting out point is, "So, what have you been seeing while out on practice?" Have a few things up your sleeve that you can talk at length about.'

Despite the undoubted wisdom expressed in the above sentiments, my first oral, farm, was an undoubted worry and I just wanted it out of the way. Although the discipline was considered by many to be the easiest of the three to pass, it was the one I felt the least comfortable with. It was the basics I lived in fear of. I'd never really shed the sense that I was just an ignorant city boy when it came to farming practices.

My viva was to be held in a small cottage on the equine yard and I turned up shortly after 10.30 for my 10.40 KO. They were running the obligatory fifteen to twenty minutes late and so I paced around nervously. I was banking on being asked to discuss something I'd seen on practice. I felt my best (only?) chance lay in such a request. If I could keep the examiner on that subject I could eat up lots of valuable time and reduce the risk of being cruelly exposed. Downer cows and milk fever swirled through my head as my name was called.

The external examiner began by asking me a few general questions on beef cattle which I bluffed my way, unconvincingly, through. I began to get more and more nervous as the oral progressed; I couldn't shake the gravity of the situation from my mind. My throat went dry and I feared I was floundering. I looked pleadingly at my two examiners as they quizzed me and had a strong feeling that they just wanted to reach out and physically pull me over the finishing line. At long last I was asked, by Colin Bennett, the question I'd longed for, and replied, 'An *awful* lot of milk fevers...' praying he'd take the bait. He did, and spent the last fifteen minutes squeezing out every last ounce of knowledge I'd absorbed on the subject.

My brain felt like a wrung sponge as I stood up to leave. I felt I might have done enough overall and before I could rein myself in, shamelessly enquired, 'Was that OK?' Their reticence made me

193

immediately regret my stupidity and I guiltily pulled my jacket off the back of the seat without a word. I walked back to my room in stifling heat with my jacket slung over my shoulder, and played back chunks of the dialogue in my mind. I heard a car's tyres grip the tarmac behind me and turned to see Sophie behind the wheel of her VW Golf. She leant out of the open window as I approached.

'Hey you! What have you just had?'

'Farm,' I replied, leaning with my hand on the roof of the baking hot car.

'How'd it go?'

'Not *too* bad. Bit of an iffy start. The external examiner asked me about beef cattle...' I rolled my eyes at this and Sophie laughed, her elbow poking out of the window. 'But then Colin Bennett just let me waffle on about milk fever for absolutely ages. You?'

'Just had equine!'

'Fuck! How was it? Who did you have?'

'Prof and Andrew, Prof was lovely, Andrew was ... well, Andrew.'

'Oh, OK. How d'you think you got on?'

'Honestly, I don't know. I wouldn't like to say. Just want to wait and see.'

'I know what you mean, Soph.' I smiled, 'So what joys have you got tomorrow?'

She pulled a face. 'Small animal.'

'You always *really* knew your stuff on rotation.'

'Hmm, I don't know about that. I just get so nervous with these, Steve ... anyway, enough of that! What have you got tomorrow?'

'What you've just had, equine!' I snorted a derisory laugh.

'Aw you'll be grand. Talk yourself out of anything you!'

'Thanks very much!' I grinned, turning and screwing up my face in the bright sunlight. 'Anyway...' I patted my hand twice on the roof of her car, 'best of luck for tomorrow.'

'And you!' she replied, slipping her sunglasses back on and accelerating off down the leafy slip-road. I smiled to myself. It felt as if we were all in this together and the sense of solidarity moved me beyond words.

Back in my room I had a distracted play-around with my equine notes, deliberately leaving the earlier farm notes in an untouched pile on the desk. My equine viva wouldn't be until the middle of the following morning. I didn't want to wait. I still had my shirt and tie on and if it had been up to me I'd have just marched back around the corner and got the blasted thing over and done with. What I didn't want was the onerous task of having to use my time responsibly. I decided I'd run through the basics: vaccination, respiratory disease, causes of lameness and colic.

I sat on a chair in the corridor of the equine hospital; it'd been weeks since I'd smelt the building's distinctive aroma. It conjured up images of late nights and early starts, of bandage changes and lameness work-ups. Despite the undeniable hardship, I thought back to those days and had a wry smile. My good spirits suddenly dissipated as the door was flung open and Catrina, timetabled before me, emerged blubbing uncontrollably into the corridor, shattering the ambience. I didn't want even to look at her, let alone engage her in any way, shape or form. I stared intently at the ground and fought to compose myself, all the while racking my brains to work out what on earth they could possibly have asked her to elicit such a reaction. *Not nerve blocks, surely?*

The door opened again and I was invited to enter. I saw Antonia Dennis, the head of anaesthesia, and a heap of breathing circuits, and cursed silently. Thrusting this to the back of my mind I concentrated on looking Andrew in the eyes as he was first to engage me. He showed me a series of photographs on his laptop; emaciated horses, a field with ragwort in it and a horse with a nasal discharge. He probed me on each of them and the information dropped, seamlessly, into my head. I knew I was flying and didn't want his portion of the exam to stop. I could see Antonia and the anaesthetic machine out of the corner of my eye as Andrew wound up, and I hoped I wouldn't now go and undo all that good work. I felt that as long I didn't clam up completely or dream up some idiotic, half-baked anaesthetic protocol that would *kill* the hypothetical horse, I'd be safe. Hardly daring to breathe, I swallowed hard. *Focus, boy! So close.* I managed to identify all the circuits and mentally gave a massive sigh of relief. Time was passing and I still hadn't really messed anything up. Antonia moved on to flow rates and I stalled for a moment; the information wasn't there. A combination of guessing, of acting like I knew the answer all along when told it and of confessing I knew the answer but that my mind had gone a complete blank, took me to the very brink. I knew I was clear; there was no time left to seriously mess up.

'We'll have to leave it there, well done Steve!' I couldn't help smiling broadly at them both. I was as certain as I could be that I'd passed equine.

I drove into Neston and treated myself to a full English breakfast in Wetherspoons, my first meal of any sort in days. *One more push, Steve! One more push. Come on, boy!* I went to bed that night feeling that equine and farm might be in the bag and that small animal would go right down to the wire. This time tomorrow I'd know the result; one way or another my fate would be revealed.

22

The Day after Tomorrow

28th May 2004. It finally came, the day of reckoning. After six years of fearfully sticking it to the back of my mind and refusing to peek, suddenly it had arrived. I stretched out an arm, swiftly cutting my alarm clock off as it drew breath, ready to state the obvious. I knew, regardless of the outcome, that things would never be the same again. I had, as the final part of my examination, the small animal oral. This, out of all three, was not only the most extensive but also the most daunting. There was a bamboozling array of topics to sort through. My room now resembled a bomb site, superstition staying my tidying hand. To have filed away notes, folders and articles would have been too much of a statement, a staunch declaration that the whole process of assessment was over and done with. To me that smacked of complacency and invited mishap. I couldn't bear the thought of jinxing myself at this late stage.

Unlike the two previous orals, this exam required a jaunt over to Liverpool and the small animal hospital. The previous afternoon I'd heard from someone with a viva time close to mine that they had an inkling of who their examiners might be. By a process of extrapolation I deduced I could very well be facing an oral with the vet in charge of the first opinion clinic. As I had no other leads to follow I gladly seized upon this possibility. At such a late hour the implications of what to spend the precious final minutes looking over were excruciating to consider. I constructed a generous pile of notes next to me in bed. It addressed many of the elements of first opinion medicine: vaccination, flea treatment, worming, spaying, castration and parturition. And then for absolutely no reason whatsoever I took a two-hour trawl through cardiorespiratory disease. Everything stuck. Not for the first time in my life I ruefully wished I could somehow bottle this pre-exam alertness and attention to detail. I then had to leap out of bed and sprint for the toilets, recalling that such prolific absorbing of information came at a price.

Shortly afterwards, I showered, the cascading heat breathing new life into joints cemented in the night. I manfully fought the tide of worry swilling through my churning guts. All night long I'd been battling as wave after wave of self-doubt rocked and threatened to sink me where I lay. Just as one foe would be wrestled and vanquished, leaving me breathless in the night, another would strike and the pattern would be repeated endlessly. I padded back to my room and, gulping back the fears, climbed back into the same shirt and tie I'd worn for an hour on each of the two previous days. It felt as if I was getting suited and booted for a date with destiny. Elated when sufficient time had elapsed for me to dump the books and finally relinquish the burden of being able to influence proceedings by acquiring new information, I leapt into my car and headed out over the water. I turned up my music, desperate to have it mask the inescapable sense of dread.

I took my seat in reception with the two other students sharing my 1.20 pm time slot and tried valiantly to make light of the situation. Our agony was prolonged by the fifteen- to twenty-minute delay. The three of us spoke tenderly and, despite being fraught with panic, quietly reassured each other. I trusted I wasn't extinguishing my chances of passing by not reading notes or silently sifting through the meagre and completely arbitrary set of facts my brain had perplexingly found memorable. I hoped that my personal brain library was still present in my head and hadn't floated off somewhere like an unmoored dingy. It was like the fear I'd had as a child at bedtime. When the light was switched off, was everything still in place in my room despite the fact I now couldn't lay eyes on anything?

Once in the seminar room I saw, as predicted, the head of first opinion. I sighed quietly, comforted that I should, barring tragedy or act of dog, at least be familiar with some component of the exam. I took a seat. The nerves made me feel detached from my body. My hands were shaking uncontrollably as I fumbled uselessly and took three attempts to hook my jacket over the chair. After the briefest of putting-at-ease conversations I found myself being probed on possible differentials in a collapsed dog. The freshness of my last-minute cardiorespiratory revision eased me into my answer. It provided a foundation and gave me the confidence to open my mind further, broadening the horizons of my repertoire. After ten to twelve minutes of rambling discourse I knew I'd covered most of the main points. Sadly I'd been a jittery bag of nerves throughout and knew my disordered scattergun approach would count against me. The second half of my viva consisted of parturition in the dog. I'd covered the whole birthing process at length in the morning and couldn't believe my luck. I deliberately fought to remain calm and ordered. I dug the Ferguson reflex from the remotest recess of my brain, a fact I hadn't even realised lived there. All in all I delivered what my gut told me was an above average oral exam. I shuddered when I considered the ghastly questions I might have been asked had the oral strayed from this path. *Heaven forbid being asked something I hadn't just looked over.* I breathed a massive sigh of relief and skipped down the stairs, back to my car.

I felt there or thereabouts. If I were to fail small animal it would have to have been on account of Tuesday's practical. Written exams and the recently completed oral felt more than satisfactory. I phoned home, transmitting a mood of cautious optimism, before driving back to Leahurst. I had been one of the final few to be viva'd and the whole year was now left hanging on trembling tenterhooks, counting down the remaining nail-biting hours until six o'clock. There was a distinctly eerie atmosphere around the campus as I parked my car and walked back to my room. Leahurst was like a graveyard. It felt as if everyone on site had taken a sharp intake of breath in anticipation of what was about to unfold. I thought of all the thousands of students down through the last hundred years who had reached this very point before departing to live out the rest of their lives. When I shut my eyes I fancied I could make out voices on the wind; it was as if all the suited graduates in the black-and-white photographs decorating the walls of the main building had come to life and were reminiscing about their own hopes and dreams.

I unlocked my door, ripping off my shirt and tie and relishing freedom from the compulsion to cram my remaining waking hours with unrelenting and productive study. I still couldn't bring myself to tidy any books away and hopped around removing my shoes on a carpet made from paper. Jack, Jamie and I took the football out on to the lawn and knocked it around, partly to relieve the tension of weeks of secularity and partly to kill time away from the oppressive angst of fretting students. I didn't want anyone else's psychoses tapping into my own personal malaise.

At around 5 pm we decided to hit the showers. I turned the corner and noticed that a marquee was hastily being constructed on the lawn adjacent to Leahurst House. The sight of it chilled me to my very essence. Sure, the marquee would be up and everything booked and paid for: the band for tonight, the graduation holiday, the graduation gown, the graduation ball and hotel rooms for family and close friends. But weren't we all forgetting something here? Hadn't there been a gross oversight before we unfurled the bunting and plugged in the fairy lights? What about the most important element of all? Had the student who's just sat a week's worth of exams, written the cheques and borne the brunt of expectation passed the course?

A splinter group of us sat on the lawn a short distance from the throng as it bustled impatiently outside Leahurst House. I found I was shivering despite the late May sunshine. Without any warning someone gave a cry and the crowds began to filter indoors. I stood up, feeling sick to my very stomach. *This was it.* In spite of having so many friends around me I suddenly felt completely alone. At a time like this having friends seemed to count for so very little. Our whole raison d'être was to appear on that list. If you were on it, you'd been verified, you were free to scream at the heavens, joyously unshackled at long last. But if you weren't? What then? I *had* to be on that list. Everything else in life was merely a footnote.

The crowd ebbed like a single, giant, multi-lobed organism. All at once: screaming, fainting, yelping, hugging, crying, dancing, falling. It was swarming, unmitigated madness. Peals of laughter and screams of delight ripped at the air's underbelly. This was happening all around me as I stared intently at the list, my face flushed and etched with worry. I ceased to be. I couldn't join them. I couldn't join in. It wasn't there. Suddenly I was invisible to the hysterical masses. *It wasn't there.*

I desperately scoured the list all around where my name ought to have been. It wasn't there. Was it on the next piece of paper by accident? Please God let it be there, let there be an explanation. Release me from this agony. I turned, blinking away tears as the

200

enormity of this horror rampaged through me. I'd seen Danny shell-shocked and distraught a year ago and realised with a jolt that I was to re-live every scrap of his personal nightmare. Results night party? Where could I go to avoid the humiliation and disappointment?

I trudged up the stairs to Prof's office. All that still remained was to have the full extent of the damage communicated to me and for me to pick myself up and slink off to lick my wounds. I felt as if I never wanted to see any of my year mates ever again. As I neared the top of the stairs all I could think of was disappearing off home. Facing them would mean facing up to myself as a failure. I'd see myself through their eyes; I felt repulsed by the stigma of being the only one in my circle of friends (in the whole year?) not to have done enough to warrant a place on that list.
The corridor outside Prof's office was bathed in semi-darkness. I took several seconds to locate two more forlorn figures almost indistinguishable from the shadow. Jonathon was crushed and weeping uncontrollably. Imogen stood in silent contemplation at the first-floor window. *So, three of us; three outcasts.* From below, snatches of delirious celebrating diffused up and into the world we now inhabited. I wished with all my heart I could be down there.

It was well after six-thirty and the insistent vibrating of my phone had been increasing with each passing minute. I left it burning a hole in my pocket. When I eventually dug it out I uttered my first word in what seemed like an age. 'Failed,' was all I could manage and that one syllable seemed to sap every last iota of strength I had left. I answered 'no' to everything else and hung up when I couldn't bear any more of elsewhere's disappointment.

My turn came and I took my place in Prof's salubrious office, sitting opposite him bowed and beaten. He peered at me over the top of his horn-rimmed glasses, hairy hands clasped together on the giant teak desk. 'You have gained only a partial pass in your course,' he enunciated gutturally. 'You've failed small animal studies.'

'How much did I fail it by?' There would be no solace in his response but I *had* to know.

'Forty-eight. But you didn't pass the other two by *that* much, so it may well be an issue of your exam technique.'

201

What? Why quibble for God's sake!

'But I did pass the other two?' I stated with rhetorical defensiveness.

'Were you booked to go on this holiday that's been planned?' He blinked back at me, neatly changing tack. The very notion left me cold. To contemplate flying out to Rhodes a week on Wednesday with eighty-five members of my year meant glimpsing life being perceived as a failure. I'd be *the one who failed*.

'Well, I'm not so sure...'

'Go on it!' He rumbled emphatically. 'You'll find people will be good with you.'

These were the only crumbs of comfort I scavenged from his panelled table. I stood up uncertainly. The conversation had dribbled wearily to a halt. 'Thanks for your time,' I heard myself say, the words sounding pitifully hollow.

I wasn't sure what to do or where to go. I passed through echoing, after-hours corridors, until I reached reception where a number of people had gathered. I became aware of a minor commotion. Sophie was speaking in heated, urgent terms to Michael Nugent, her pleading eyes streaked with mascara. She was wringing her hands over and over, deeply distressed.

Not her!

I hung back discreetly. Michael was the head of small animal studies and it therefore made sense that I heard what he had to say to me. After appearing to reach an uneasy compromise, Sophie shakily got to her feet and teetered unsteadily towards the exit, supported by her boyfriend. Her unfocused eyes took an age to catch mine and when they did she put her hand over her mouth.

'Oh ... Steve...'

I met her gaze with sad eyes and just slowly shook my head. No words would come.

'It broke our collective hearts you know,' Michael said.

'Oh ... I never knew. Are you OK now?'

'It's not *that* bad,' he deferred, furiously back-pedalling. 'It just appears you weren't really supposed to sit the practical in that fashion.'

'Right. I don't get you.'

'It seems you should've had a scribe to do your writing for you or 50% extra time or...' he coughed embarrassedly and looked away, 'both.'

'I ... um.'

'The university had somehow forgotten you had your condition, I'm afraid and there's no record of you ever being sent out any of the appropriate documents.'

I sat silently fuming.

'You never *said* anything, though did you? Never chased it up.' The slight tone of accusation in his voice did nothing to improve my mood.

'No. I hate making a fuss and besides when I went to see Ron Jackson at the start of fourth year to express my fears and ask for my condition to be taken into account, I *assumed* people would be looking out for me.' I fought in vain not to raise my voice in the echoing corridor.

'Yes, well, welfare dropped the ball on you, I'm afraid.'

'Was it the practical I failed on?'

'Hmm. You did get quite a low mark for it, yes.'

'But if I'd known my options, if my options had been *communicated* to me I'd have passed, right?'

'So it would seem. I mean, you and I could quite easily have gone around together at the end with me writing your answers for you.'

'Fine.' I saw a narrow chink of sunlight and scrabbled desperately to prise the coffin lid back open. 'Now that we've established my *options*! Put together another practical; I'll go around with you tomorrow...'

'That won't be possible. But don't worry, we'll definitely ensure you get all you are entitled to when you come back in September.'

'September! What about *now*? You *know* this is totally unfair. I didn't make a fuss because I can't stomach whinging, self-obsessed hypochondriacs. Instead of that earning me respect all it's done is make you forget I had the condition in the first place!'

Michael said nothing.

'Why wasn't this addressed at the examiners' meeting?'

For the sake of two measly per cent.

'The faculty felt, unanimously, they'd done all they could for you. They couldn't justify bumping you up! It's a whole two per cent.'

'Does that strike you as fair?' I implored shrilly, gesticulating wildly.

'I believe we've taken this as far as we can,' Michael said impassively.

'Come on!' I flailed frantically. 'I can't be alone in thinking this is grossly unfair can I?' I knew I was veering dangerously close to Kevin the teenager territory but all my pent-up frustrations bubbled to the surface. 'Can I?'

'It's gone as far as it can!'

I slunk back to my room, not wanting to ever reach my destination but having nowhere else to go.

Leahurst had gone quiet. I assumed it was because everyone was either sobbing tearfully into mobile phones or holed up somewhere excitedly discussing what to wear to the party or how amazing grad holiday would be now that people knew they'd definitely passed. There was a knock on my door. Jack and Matt entered solemnly. I was lying on the same pile of first opinion hand-outs from the morning. The nerves I'd felt back then, and my post-exam euphoria, all seemed so meaningless now. After my practical I had always been destined to fail, I just hadn't known it. My room remained a tip. I hadn't earned the right to tidy my notes away and besides I'd need to be digging them out for the re-sit in no time at all.

I couldn't bring myself even to look up as they entered. Matt sat awkwardly on the end of my bed while Jack wordlessly walked over to me and gently ruffled my hair. I eventually forced myself to acknowledge them and caught Matt's eye. We'd been through all 18 weeks of rotations together and an unspoken acknowledgement of what we'd shared passed between us. I sighed deeply. It felt so deflating and demoralising that we wouldn't be going on to graduate together, re-telling our rotation yarns at grad ball in July. He pulled a dejected face and seemed genuinely troubled I hadn't made it. His misery was compounded when I revealed that Sophie, another member of our treasured small animal/equine team, had also failed to come through unscathed. It meant so much to me that they were upset, that they'd just come in and sorrowfully expressed shock and disbelief. Matt and Jack were my friends; I was glad they were the first people I saw and that they acted the way they did. I felt relieved I hadn't shot off home.

Matt and Jack left, promising to look in on me on their way out to the party. Before long the DJ arrived and a tub-thumping beat began to shake Ritchie House to its foundations. A half-empty glass of water on my desk began rippling like the puddles in *Jurassic Park* that telegraph a visit from *T. rex*. I felt sullied and tousled, still caked in the day's manifold stresses. I peered through a narrow gap in my curtains, from the vantage point on my bed, and made out discrete bands of party-goers. They were polished clean, parted from the day's grime. I watched them pale into the distance, excited voices light and lingering in the rarefied atmosphere. *Not a care in the world.*

At the last minute I decided I *would* make an appearance. This was my reality. The sooner I became acquainted with it, the sooner it would stop hurting me so much. I didn't want to keep mentally retracing my steps, replaying those moments seconds before I stepped up to the list, before I found out. To twist the knife that bit deeper I was unable to stop wondering just how amazing it would have been had my name actually been up there. No, the sooner I met this head-on, the better. Besides there were a whole set of conversations that were totally unavoidable; it was merely a question of *when*. If I could stomach this party I'd be able to get most of those conversations out of the way once and for all.

It ended up being totally different from how I had imagined it would be. It was pitch black and the party was in full swing by the time I finally ventured outside. I'd envisaged undergoing a series of self-justifying interrogations. I thought I'd be the down-trodden pity case vying for credibility in a gently nodding crowd of condescension. I shuffled self-consciously across the lawn. I could feel the heat of everyone's gaze on me and felt like withering in shame. Jack brought me a beer and I gratefully took a deep draught from it, glad to have a prop to occupy myself with. Brad sidled over and I gave him a lop-sided grin.

'Aw, mate,' he said and hugged me tightly.

'I know,' I replied, overwhelmed, my eyes remaining clamped firmly shut.

'You know we're all here for you, don't you?'

'I do.'

It was a message that was reiterated over and over in a night that managed to be uplifting, reassuring and brimming with heartfelt emotion, as well as horribly upsetting.

23

The Heat is On

In the aftermath I had a brief deluded dalliance with the university appeals process. Prof had initially been ultra-sympathetic to my predicament, confiding in Antonia Dennis, the new head of welfare, that I had a very strong case. Unfortunately his mood hardened overnight, when the news reached him that two of the other four students to fail were considering legal action against the university for reasons too tiresome to go into. I finally managed to track him down, fully one week on from the events of black Friday, for a conversation that would slam the door well and truly shut.

'Hi Prof. Any chance of a quick word?'

He grunted in affirmation and I launched into a well-rehearsed spiel. 'Really just wanted to start by saying I realise most of this is my own fault and of my own doing...' I began, before being derailed by a look of puzzlement. 'Sorry ... the university's negligence? Yeah, umm, I made such a good job of hiding my arthritis, you see. It was easy for everyone to forget I had it. Also, my buddies on rotation were amazing; they'd just step in and shield me from certain tasks I might have struggled with, but the fact still remains I *was* entitled to a scribe and if I'd...'

He scythed through me with a low growl, 'So, what you're basically telling me is that you achieved your rotation marks fraudulently, then.'

I blinked at this, taken aback, and we both regarded each other for a few moments. I became aware of the sounds of the equine yard filtering in through the open window; a horse whinnying, the bustle and babble of raised voices.

'Thanks for your time, Prof.'

I stood up to go, wondering if there was anything else left to

206

say. I suppose I always knew, at some level, that once my name didn't appear on the list, I'd need to go through the rigmarole of the re-sit but it was only when I stepped back out on to the yard, that the full realisation hit me. My fall from grace had been cushioned by the faint hope of an appeal. 'Well, you were right about one thing, Prof...' I murmured to myself as I slipped back through the black equine gates, 'I *definitely* need a holiday.'

Once I'd got over the shock of seeing, in essence, our whole year transplanted to a hotel and apartment complex in Rhodes, grad holiday became an utter delight. I shared a ground floor apartment with Jamie as well as Sophie and her mate, Jenni. Exam results were a million miles away as the four of us flip-flopped down the winding path for daily visits pool-side; our skin already starting to burn. The days oozed, dreamily by. When we weren't lounging lazily, reading cheap airport fodder, we chatted in the blazing sun and took countless dips, irking German holidaymakers by annexing the swimming pool. I'd decided I'd get much more out of the holiday if I drank, and each morning would be spent nursing a hangover under a gently billowing parasol.

'Are you coming in, Steve?'

'Still a bit woozy, Jamie!'

'Come on, a dip'll do you the world of good.'

'Oh go on then.' I deposited my lotion-encrusted copy of *The Wasp Factory* on my towel and joined Jamie and Jack in the tempting waters. 'How's *your* hangover, Jacko?' He made a *so-so* gesture with his hand. I kicked up my feet, reclining on my back as they tossed a ball to and fro across the pool.

I wished I could freeze time. I didn't want to go back; the holiday was shooting by and I knew what was waiting for me at the other end. As I floated, the silky waters soothed and caressed me and I could feel the fears and doubts slowly ebb away. I knew they wouldn't stray *too* far, though.

One night, near the end of the holiday, around fifty of us commandeered a fleet of taxis and headed up the road to Rhodes Town for one last night out. We dispersed into discrete clusters, rendezvousing at a prearranged cocktail bar. It took seven or eight bars before the flurry of free shots eventually seemed to register in the demeanour of the party-hardened vets but, by pub number

207

nine, the scene was one of alcoholic chaos. I'd felt compelled to limit my intake of alcohol. My lack of resistance had made me a very cheap date indeed. I caught up, timing my late run to perfection. We swarmed all over the dance floor as the drink continued to flow into the wee small hours. A live band took to the stage and we began bouncing up and down and punching at the air. During interludes in the music everyone was drunkenly and sweatily hugging each other, promising with an earnest sincerity to stay in touch. Not one person made the slightest mention of my re-sit, they all seemed to assume I'd pass, and it made me love them all the more.

I was back at Leahurst and in many ways it was as if I'd never been away. The only difference was that we were now into the start of August and, as I moved through the main building, I was like the last man on earth. It had been the same in Ritchie House. I'd hear a door slam, ponder whose room it had emanated from and then have to correct myself, painfully. The previous inhabitant of that room was long gone, having vacated it to start their life; I was probably hearing a bespectacled foreign-exchange student blundering around upstairs in the futile search for an exit hatch to the equine yard. I found the re-sit timetable on the board and stared, lost in thought: 31st August, written and practical, 1st September, oral. *And, if I fail, 2nd September, call the Samaritans!* I grinned to myself at the bleakness of the hour.

'I spoke up on your behalf, you know.'

I nearly jumped out of my skin and turned to see Colin Bennett standing behind me.

'Sorry?'

'At the exam board meeting? Results night? I held up your farm practical and said *Look, the poor bugger couldn't even hold his pen! Let alone write! Look!*'

'And?'

He shrugged. 'Those buggers wouldn't listen to me would they? Made no difference at all, Steve, but I tried.'

'Well, thanks Colin.' I squeezed him on the shoulder. 'I really appreciate you doing that for me.'

'Well, I know you and I haven't always seen eye to eye but I worked with you on the clinical skills week and didn't have the slightest problem with you. Besides I'd always stick up for someone if I felt they'd been wronged.'

'Sure, that means a lot; it really does!' I remembered back to my first farm rotation and what he was referring to. Colin had lodged an official complaint with my tutor after our group presentation on TB testing. I'd been chewing gum throughout my talk and he'd labelled my antics *disgusting* and *unprofessional*. 'I know, it's all forgotten, now. Seems light years ago, to be honest.'

'I really didn't know what you were going through.'

'I realise that.' I shrugged as if to say *what are you going to do?*

'Well, what kind of shape are you in for the re-sit?'

'Not too bad. I'll load up on steroids and I've got a scribe and much more time.'

'You'll be fine. OK, then...' He turned and left and I watched him go, bitterly regretting that I'd been so scathing about him in my staff appraisal. The chewing-gum incident had really got to me. I'd wanted to create a good impression on the rotation and was worried my reluctance to do certain tasks might be construed as a bad attitude. I'd ended up hurting myself in the pursuit of a decent appraisal. To cope, admirably, with the rotation's physical component but be pulled up for chewing gum struck me as nothing more than petty spitefulness. And in the end it was Colin, out of all of them, who spoke up for me. *What a crazy world.*

All I'd been told about my scribe was that her name was Annette, she worked upstairs in the main building and that she'd be taking on all my writing duties for the day. In addition to the services of a writing slave I'd also been afforded an extra fifty per cent exam time. The written portion was timetabled to begin at 9.30 and I had until a staggering 2 pm to finish up. I couldn't help feeling that, with *that* much extra time, I could probably have written both essays with the pen in my mouth but after all that had happened I wasn't about to stop and quibble. Besides, anything that spared me another practical horror show got my vote. All five re-sitting students were doing the exam in the equine cottage and as I passed through the gates I saw Sophie disappear up the stairs to her room. As I'd need to be telling my scribe what to write I was scheduled to take the exam in a room of my own. I turned up at twenty past nine, figuring it made sense to meet my scribe beforehand. I wondered if she'd slyly tip me the wink on some of the tougher MCQs. She *was* supposed to be a vet after all. *Tap once for A, twice for B.* No, probably not.

At 9.25 Michael Nugent came into my room, the re-sit paper clasped protectively in his right hand and a harassed look on his face.

'Isn't she here yet?'

I shook my head, eyeing the exam paper and trying to catch a glimpse of a key word or two. We stared at one another, unsure of whether or not it was worth our while beginning a conversation. The cottage had paper-thin walls and we sat in complete silence; the generalised scuffling from upstairs along with an occasional door banging shut was punctuated only by Michael tutting and shaking his head in disbelief. Half past nine came and went. I stared at the clock on the wall above Michael's head and sighed as a veil of silence descended on the cottage. I knew that the other four had turned their papers over and now knew what lay beneath. They were aware of what they needed to overcome to pass and whether their revision strategies had paid off or not.

I shifted in my seat, disgruntled and sweating as the clock ticked on. It seemed ludicrous; filling in the computer-marked MCQ sheet required nothing more than scoring a dash with a pencil, like filling in a lottery ticket. At 9.50 I could bear the suspense no longer and blurted out, 'Can I not just start, Michael? The MCQ isn't going to hurt my hand; it was just the practical I needed help with.'

'No, we'd best wait for her. Just in case. I'll see if I can phone her, track her down.'

Ten minutes elapsed with Michael whispering uselessly into his mobile. I felt close to snapping. It was now ten o'clock; the exam was supposedly half an hour old and I hadn't even been allowed to look at the paper. I just sat and stewed, the agony piling on with each passing minute. At five past ten Annette finally turned up and the tension eased slightly. She seemed totally unaware of what was at stake and sauntered, in a dreamy almost trance-like state, into the room.

'Hiya guys!'

'Can we *please* just get started.' Michael snapped icily, eyeing her with total contempt. She stifled a yawn before agreeing and taking her seat next to me. I looked queryingly at Michael, incredulous that this pantomime was my *finals*. *Where did they find her?*

In an unreal atmosphere I began flicking through the MCQ paper, begging for a stonewall answer to help quell the desperate unease I was feeling.

'OK, umm ... twenty-three, C?' I turned to the next page. As I did I looked up and spied Michael leafing through his copy and checking my answer with a tiny, inscrutable nod of his head. He spent the next twenty minutes stalking my every unsteady exam footstep, frowning quizzically at each of my declarations. I'd completed a decent segment of the paper when, seeming to tire of the game, he rose and tiptoed out the room.

I stopped talking after answering thirty-six of the forty-five questions. I didn't want to take any chances with blind guesses this time and, after a little arithmetic based on the answers I felt *sure* I'd nailed, I worked out that I'd got between fifty-seven and sixty per cent. Fortified by this and the time surplus still on my hands, I unveiled the essay questions. I felt a further upturn in my fortunes when I saw a question on cruciate disease. It was a topic I'd lavished extra attention on and seized upon it vigorously. My head was fit to burst on the subject and I just wanted to pour it all out while it was still fresh.

'Right, part A, question two please...' I sat back, poised to spill forth. 'Part one; I'm going to give you a list of things here, just write them down one after the other, please...' *I could get used to this*. I was required to offer a list of conditions that may be mistakenly diagnosed as cruciate disease and was keen to deliver them in order of prevalence. 'Osteoarthritis ... patellar subluxation ... septic...'

'Sorry, what was that last one again?'

'Patellar. Sub. Luxation ... septic arth...'

'Sub what?'

'Luxation?'

'Oh!' I watched her write the word, distracted from my train of thought. The word she put down wasn't 'luxate'. It had a 'g' in it.

'Sorry, must be my accent,' I flannelled, taking the pen off her, scoring out her *Countdown* conundrum and writing it myself. 'Don't tell Metal Mickey,' I whispered urgently.

'Right.' she looked at me doubtfully as I began again. I knew

211

the full benefit of having a scribe would come into play during the practical where writing against the clock was beyond me. This charade was a small price to pay for that peace of mind. I moved on to the next section; a detailed outline of the anatomical layout of the canine stifle. Annette constantly interrupted, reining me in and pegging me back. Time after time she'd ask me to repeat what I'd just said. I'd forget, in the process, what it was I was on the verge of saying or, in fact, what I had just said. It was thoroughly off-putting, compounded by my need to stop and spell out any word greater than three syllables.

We took our ham-fisted double-act on to section B. I elected to do a question about an itchy Westie that required a putative diagnosis on the strength of clinical signs and signalment. I knew the Westie had a condition known as atopic dermatitis (they always do at vet school) and realised that, if I could re-tell what I undoubtedly knew, I'd almost certainly have passed the written paper. I drove on, keen to press home my advantage. The answer I 'wrote' was far less technically orientated than my previous dictation and we got through it with fewer mishaps.

I finished off the paper, leaning back in my chair and feeling I was the head of national conglomerate, dictating a letter to my dizzy secretary. *Read that last part back to me, would you and what's a guy got to do to get a cup of coffee around here?*

'OK, Annette, thanks for that! I think that's me probably done now unless you can think of anything I might've missed?' She stared blankly at me. *No, thought not.*

'My practical begins at four on the nose. Might be an idea to try and get there about five or so minutes *beforehand*, just so we can sort out any logistical problems?'

As opposed to over half an hour late!

She waltzed off for lunch and I returned to my room, possessed by an unbridled sense of relief. The first third of the re-sit was in the bag and I felt it had left me in the credit column. The atmosphere surrounding the re-sit was strangely paradoxical. As far as I could make out, no one had ever failed the finals re-sit and had to repeat their fifth year. Far from this realisation soothing my fears, it actually made me worry more. The pressure was intensified because everyone, up until now, had passed. *What would it say about me if I failed?*

Back at my desk I spent a productive lunch and early afternoon looking over my ECG notes. I felt their presence was the one and only banker of the practical and the interpretation of the trace was a task I always toiled over. The information never seemed to make the transition from short- to long-term memory, needing constant replenishment.

Happy I might be able to take a decent stab at an answer, I headed over to the main building. As I walked I fought to keep a tight hold of this 'fresh' intake of information. I entered the cool, shady interior and sat down with Sophie's mother, brother and boyfriend. She was sitting the practical from three o'clock to four with a couple of the other students and when they'd all vacated the lab, it'd be my turn. Her family quietly fretted on her behalf and tried to engage me in polite conversation. I didn't have much to contribute. My insides were turning somersaults, I felt breathless and was sure I was going to throw up. I was on the point of making my way to the toilets when the lab door creaked open. Sophie was the first to emerge. The worries had vanished and she was now bathed in a glow of relief. She joyfully hugged her family as I crept around them and into the lab. 'It'll be OK, Steve,' I heard from the corridor. I kept walking, too nervous to acknowledge her properly.

'Right, you have a choice Steve.' I hadn't even noticed Michael, squatting like a garden gnome at the far end of the lab. 'Either you can have nine minutes per question, or seven minutes per question and twenty minutes at the end to go around anything you feel you missed.'

'Can I take the seven-minute option, please?'

Michael nodded once, immediately adjusting his stopwatch accordingly. My scribe turned up with seconds to spare and we had a brief wrestling match over the hand-out.

'Sorry, but I need to *read* it, please?'

The exam started and I found vocalising my answers made me extremely self-conscious, even more so with Michael sitting eavesdropping in the corner. A positive aspect, though, was that I felt far less inclined to fill boxes with gibberish when I wasn't certain of the answer. *Writing* nonsense came far easier to me than dictating it word-for-word and I chose my words very carefully, eking out conclusions I wouldn't otherwise have reached. Time wasn't a deciding factor this time and I only needed to return to one station; to change my ECG trace to say it was third-degree

213

AV block instead of atrial fibrillation. I busily dictated my changes and when I'd finished a wave of euphoria swept through me; I felt the way Sophie had ninety minutes previously.

It was all so tantalisingly close now. I knew all I needed to do was keep it together for one final hurdle and I'd be free of this nightmare. I could join my friends in the Promised Land and re-start my life.

Sophie came out of the cottage beaming from ear to ear. I cursed the alphabet for constantly making me go second. 'Happy?'

'Steve, they were *fine*; the external examiner was lovely! Really, absolutely nothing to worry to about! Go on!'

'What?' I turned and saw Michael beckoning me from the doorway. 'Oh, sorry ... there's usually a delay...' I prattled on, to no one in particular and followed him obediently indoors.

'Give me a call when you're done.'

'Yeah, well, we'll see how this pans out.' I half-turned, smiling hesitantly.

'It'll be *grand*.'

The external examiner shook me warmly by the hand as Michael introduced us. The first question he asked related to an answer I'd given in the practical, concerning the interpretation of a radiograph of the canine shoulder. I knew my practical answer had been correct, and beginning on such a sure footing calmed my nerves. He used it as a springboard to interrogate me on the subject of canine orthopaedics. It was a topic I'd studied in great detail and I kept my cool, answering everything that was asked of me and elaborating where appropriate. His ten minutes raced by and before I knew it he was winding up.

'Here's a really tough one to finish on. I tell you, get this and you've definitely earned a biscuit!' We both looked down at the plate of chocolate chip cookies and, although I wasn't even remotely hungry, I replied, 'Mmm cookies, even *more* incentive!'

'Can you tell me a condition, you touched very briefly on it before, that occasionally afflicts the spine of German shepherds?'

I knew it. It was OCD. I felt my heart lurch. I *had* to be there. *That went too well to mean anything else.* Hardly daring to believe I was on the cusp of emerging from the darkness, I put my eyes down and gathered my thoughts for the final onslaught.

'Very good! Well done! Go on, then, take one...'

'Thank you.' I grinned. 'I might save my prize until after? I don't want to be all *biscuity* for Michael!' I laughed in an attempt to lighten the mood. I'd had a couple of practice vivas with Michael and he'd always succeeded in making me feel worse than I had when I'd started. I never coped particularly well with his brand of po-faced inscrutability. I hated the fact that when I answered his questions he'd neither encourage nor discourage. He'd remain totally impassive, leaving the student unsure of whether they were on firm ground or not.

'Right,' he began, the mood of the viva altering already. 'Tell me if you think the skin on this dog looks pruritic.' He swivelled his lap-top around to show me a close-up image of the flank of a Doberman. The air was now distinctly cold and unforgiving.

'I can't see it too well, Michael.' Sunlight was strafing in through the window at my back, glazing across his screen and obscuring the image. The whole question hinged on my answer and I reiterated, 'It's *very* difficult to make out.'

He peered at me, treading a fine line between cool reserve and utter indifference. *Right. Yes. Good point, my problem. In practice this might be something I'd have to deal with.* I got up, turned his screen back around to face him and ended up virtually sitting in his lap to make out the image properly. *Weren't expecting that one were you, Micky boy?* It was a microcosm of the viva in general. There were no easy points up for grabs and absolutely no quarter given. Every single ounce of the advantage I'd built up from the first part was dismantled, brick by brick, as I crawled in slow motion to the end of my oral exam.

'So it's a...' Michael prompted.

'Colour dilution alopecia,' I responded wearily, suddenly feeling drained by the whole episode. My performance in Michael's half was so poor that the doubts about my pass/fail status re-emerged. I got up and in a thinly coded plea for reassurance asked if it was still OK to take a biscuit. When they both agreed, Michael albeit reluctantly, I took it as a positive sign.

I stepped outside into the blazing sunshine, munching on my biscuit. Sophie was still on the yard with her family. 'God, it's all right for some ... they never offered *me* a biscuit.'

'S'all right,' I replied, my mouth full. 'There's a whole plateful in there; I'll nip in and get you one if you want.'

215

'That isn't the point and you know it.'

'No ... I know,' I grinned impishly.

'How d'you get on, then?'

'Aw Soph, great first half, absolutely diabolical second. Honestly, totally dire! Maybe it evened itself-up.' I shrugged. 'God, how I hope so.'

'Yeah, it's got to be OK! Hey listen, we've got two and a half hours to kill before the list goes up and I've no intention sticking around here to wait.' We both recoiled at the memory of the last time we'd tried that. 'I dunno about you but I haven't eaten in days; we're all going into Chester for a spot of lunch. You've got to come along.'

'I'd love to.' I didn't want to be alone as the minutes ticked down.

Sophie's mother leant forward across the sleek black table of the trendy bistro we'd chosen to dine in. 'So *when* does this list go up?'

Sophie and I looked at each other, reluctant to give a time, to give the moment substance. 'About two,' we replied in unison.

'Shouldn't we be heading back then?'

'NO!'

A few more minutes elapsed and we couldn't put it off any longer. Ten minutes from Leahurst we were hurtling along the Chester High Road when I felt my phone vibrate in my pocket and dug it out. 'Sophie, Imogen's ringing. She's never rung me in her life. That *must* mean the list's gone up.'

'Please...' she implored, 'don't answer it. I couldn't bear it! I need to see it for myself.' She looked over, gratefully, as I let it ring out.

'I'm guessing you also don't want me to read this text she's just sent either?'

A few minutes later we sped up the slip road, the juddering cattle grid matching, beat for beat, my pounding heart rate. We slammed the car doors shut just as one of the other re-sitting students approached from around the side of the main building. I saw her put her hand over her mouth when she saw us. It could have been for any reason, but it made me think the worst. 'Sophie, why is she...?'

'I don't know! Come on! Don't wait for her.'

I felt like being sick. *I can't deal with this, I can't.* We entered the main building and Janine Weller, on reception, leapt out from behind her desk, extending her arms. 'Well done!' she beamed expansively. '*Both* of you,' she added, in an attempt to quell the anguish and doubt I knew I was exuding. I smiled and put my head down, determined I wouldn't allow myself the minutest glimmer of belief until I'd seen my name on that list with my own eyes. There was too much at stake and it hurt too much to contemplate my hopes and expectations being dashed a second time.

We'd expected a list to be up in the main building but it was nowhere to be seen.

'I can do without this,' I bitched, feeling worn down by the tension.

'Leahurst House?' panted Sophie, staring straight ahead.

'Must be,' I concurred and we both quickened our pace, breaking into a light jog and accelerating away from Sophie's entourage. We pushed open the back door of Leahurst House, shoulder to shoulder, and I could see the list as we approached. It was far easier to check if I'd been successful this time; if five names were on the list, I'd passed. For some reason my eyes played a cruel trick on me, showing me only four names and I gasped in distress. I marched straight up to the board and devoured the list with my fearful eyes. I stared, intently at my name, convincing myself it was true. Sophie and I stood together, six inches from the board, for what seemed like an age. The memory of three months ago, the heartache and misery of that horrific night, came flooding back. I found I was sobbing. I turned to see Sophie quietly weeping and we linked arms.

'Well done, you deserve it,' she said quietly.

'And you.' I couldn't get any more words out and stepped backwards as Sophie was engulfed by her ecstatic family.

I walked through the doors and out of the building, emerging into the sunlight, blinking my tear-stained eyes. I was shaking with so much excitement I couldn't work my phone. I shivered with delight as it eventually started to ring.